Intelligence and Metadrama
in the Early Modern Theatre

Intelligence and Metadrama in the Early Modern Theatre

Bill Angus

EDINBURGH
University Press

Edinburgh University Press is one of the leading university presses in the UK. We publish academic books and journals in our selected subject areas across the humanities and social sciences, combining cutting-edge scholarship with high editorial and production values to produce academic works of lasting importance. For more information visit our website: edinburghuniversitypress.com

© Bill Angus, 2019, 2020

Edinburgh University Press Ltd
The Tun – Holyrood Road
12(2f) Jackson's Entry
Edinburgh EH8 8PJ

First published in hardback by Edinburgh University Press 2019

Typeset in 11/14 Adobe Sabon by
IDSUK (DataConnection) Ltd

A CIP record for this book is available from the British Library

ISBN 978 1 4744 3291 7 (hardback)
ISBN 978 1 4744 3292 4 (paperback)
ISBN 978 1 4744 3293 1 (webready PDF)
ISBN 978 1 4744 3294 8 (epub)

The right of Bill Angus to be identified as the author of this work has been asserted in accordance with the Copyright, Designs and Patents Act 1988, and the Copyright and Related Rights Regulations 2003 (SI No. 2498).

Contents

Acknowledgements	vi
Introduction: Errant Intelligence – The Devil's Own	1
1 'Subtle sleights': Amity and the Informer in *Damon and Pithias*	39
2 The Parasites of Machiavel	67
3 *The Knight of the Burning Pestle* and the Menace of the Audience	92
4 The Reluctant Informer: Humanising the Beast	110
5 Metadrama and the Murderous Nature of Authority	132
6 The Burning Issue: Metadrama and Contested Authority in Chettle's *Hoffman*	154
Conclusion: No One Is There – Ubiquity and Invisibility	175
Index	182

Acknowledgements

Michelle Houston and all at Edinburgh University Press for their acumen and efficiency, Massey University for precious leave to put pixels to screen and Ethan Neville for invaluable and indefatigable Research Assistance. I also thank the deeply inspirational people Amy, Joseph, Stephen, Sonny, Georgie, Aidan, Dan, Amelia, Jacob, Elin and Ciara for their continuing humour, patience and good will, and mostly Sarah, who is properly loved.

Introduction: Errant Intelligence – The Devil's Own

It is the argument of this book that the perception of the intelligencer permeates both early modern dramatic production and its reception, and generates the self-conscious metadrama which is often found in the plays of the period. This connection between intelligencing and metadrama expresses a shift in the conceptual and moral landscape of the time, instancing an 'articulation . . . of changes in consciousness', as Raymond Williams might say, operating at the boundaries of social structures and perceptions.[1] The social arrangements and physical situations that intelligencers might exploit in order to get their hands on useful information are replicated in the metadramatic structures of plays which use multiple hidden eavesdroppers and overlookers to advance their plots and storylines. In narrative or dramatic form this may well give a frisson of pleasure to an audience, but it also carries an alarming reminder in an early modern context that the intelligencer's often unseen presence portends mischief of some kind. It may be no surprise in this context that popular cultural metaphors for the intelligencer revolve around imagery of the demonic or the devilish. Besides its various dramatic functions, early modern metadrama registers an increased perception of the debasement of intelligence systems upon which the authorities of the time are so dependent. The fact that intelligencers are not only perceived as inherently mercenary but also that their testimony is typically regarded as tainted with sulphurous associations inevitably calls into question the moral legitimacy of those that rely on these insidious agents. The problematic perceptions of the intelligencing community in early modern England are rooted in questions of both systemic moral ideology and individual probity; their appearance in the metadramatic forms of the theatre shows just how public these issues had become.

In the history of theatrical interpretation, metadramatic modes and structures have been understood in various ways, but a dominant perspective has been that the primary impetus for the use of metadramatic forms is artistic experimentation. Sometimes this facility for dramatic experiment has been offered as evidence of the superiority of one artist over another. Another recurring suggestion is that authors are using metadrama to explore the relationship of drama with 'truth' or 'illusion', perhaps with reference to the workings of what are described as 'levels of illusion'. Some of these are robust studies of dramatic structure while others tend toward the speculative. My own methodology aims to establish a historical basis for the authorly imperative to create drama of this kind, and to read metadramatic strata according to both their aesthetic qualities and their material contexts. To this end, my subject is how metadramatic constructs are informed by particular social pressures, including ideas related to corrupt authorities, the emerging perceptions of authorship and the potential for misapprehension by empowered audiences, all of which are informed in turn by public perceptions of the work of intelligencers.

My ongoing study of metadrama has followed the logic of Williams's argument that early modern dramatic form registered 'altered social relationships' and that revolutionary undercurrents of some kind could be found in the 'deep formal qualities of the dramatic mode'.[2] I have previously outlined uneasy correlations between authors, informers and audiences, and some of the social experiences that drove or facilitated much metadramatic practice.[3] One of the themes arising from this was the tendency for the onstage informer to operate as a distorted mirror image of the author, a circumstance that causes authors to want to dissociate themselves from such embarrassing and dangerous doppelgängers. In this, a simple Freudian 'narcissism of small differences' was discovered in operation, in which one group attempts to distinguish itself from another by exaggerating the slight differences between them.[4] The irony of this process is that it also flags up the very likeness which is the source of the need to establish such difference in the first place. Furthermore, having established that authors' perceptions of the threat posed by informers were not histrionically exaggerated, the intelligencer and informer were found to stand out as significant figures in the metadrama of the period.

Metadrama often emerges as what Gerhard Fischer and Bernhard Greiner have called an 'agency of action and reflection in the context of cultural conflict', and the experience of the author and the intelligencer is certainly to clash and converge in their cultural moment, as the metadrama often reflects.[5] My argument here is that the particular forms of theatrical self-reflexivity generated by onstage intelligencers and informers reveals the perception that authority is tainted by the association with such figures. As they explore the nature of authority's compromise with the corrupt and the deceitful, however, a kind of resistance is to be found in the deep structures of metadrama. In some respects, the figure of the dishonest intelligencer works in early modern metadramatic forms both as a function of corrupt authority and a means of its destruction. If the metadrama does not quite attempt its own explicit deconstruction of this area of cultural conflict, its capacity as an agent of reflection nevertheless allows for a visceral anatomisation of the contradictions inherent within the underlying structures of early modern authority.

In the present twenty-first-century cultural context, the word 'intelligencer' might be said to resound with interesting and excitingly positive connotations around 'intelligence', which could perhaps even be abbreviated to the much sexier 'intel', suggesting a secretive and protective network or 'community' on which our personal safety and national security rest.[6] Similarly, the late sixteenth-century sense of 'intelligence' also carried associations of higher-level thinking and sagacity, and included nuances of collected information. The common core understanding of the nature of the intelligencer, however, was distinct from ours in many ways. When Thomas Nashe's character Master Bodley, despite apparently being content to be known as a spy, objects to being referred to with the 'hellish detested *Judas* name of an Intelligencer', we may assume he is expressing a popular distinction.[7] It is one which often gets biblical in its condemnation of the latter. The canonical Judas is of course the archetypal evil schemer of western culture, the principal betrayer of Jesus Christ, who infamously informs against him for money and treacherously identifies him to the authorities with a kiss: a gesture whose very superfluity registers a refinement of evil intent.[8] In early modern texts, the terms 'informer' and 'intelligencer' are almost always interchangeable, and the present study follows this usage. Speaking of Bodley and his acquaintance Thorius, Nashe elaborates that to be suspected for an intelligencer 'is to make eyther of them worse pointed and wondered at than a cuckold or wittall, and set them up as common marks for everie jackanapes Prentise to kicke, spit, or throw durt at'.[9] He likens the intelligencer to the usurious popular caricature of the Jew, 'that but for the spoile loves no man', and goes on to list the other characteristics of the intelligencer, claiming that he is a metaphorical 'curre, that flatters & fawns upon everie one . . . till he may spie an advantage, and pluck oute his throate', or an 'ingratefull slave' that habitually 'spendeth the bitterest of his venome, where hee hath received most benefites'; he is a 'hang-man, that dispatcheth all that come under his hands' and a 'drunken serjeant or sumner, that could not live if (like the divell) hee did not from time to time enquire after the sinnes of the people'.[10] Unpredictable and volatile dog, poisonous slave, merciless hangman, drunken policeman: the intelligencer's reputation reverberates with insulting accusations and is assaulted with disparaging imagery from many angles. But it is perhaps the religious aspect of this characterisation that is the most revealing of the social impact of the figure. Simply put, the informing intelligencer is not only a scheming Judas figure, but actively a promoter of evil on the most fundamental level, 'like the divell'. Through to at least the late seventeenth century, this religious figurative language is used to disparage and curse the person and the actions of the intelligencer. When his own community is feeling the pressure of plotters and intelligencers, the leading Quaker dissenter George Fox angrily takes up this cudgel to complain that an informer 'is a Persecutor, and Spoiler, and a Destroyer; and the DEVIL is the Head of all Informers.'[11] In this emphatic, doubly capital, satanic accusation one may hear the resentment of the victim, and indeed Fox was himself informed against on a number of occasions.[12] Another Quaker writer of the time, George Whitehead, also weighs in with religious metaphor, inveighing against informers as 'betraying Judases, Devils Incarnate . . . Dogs [and] Wolves . . . of the Synagogue of Satan'.[13] This narrative is continued in the late seventeenth-century tract, 'The Informers answer to the late character vindicating themselves from the scandalous truths of that unlucky pamphlet', that ventriloquises the arrogance of the informer, boasting that 'if ever we should be called to account, will march to *Tyburn* with most Heroick Gallantry, and have it engraven . . . on our Tombs that we dyed the Laws *Scandal* Religious *Scourge*; and the Devils *Martyrs*.'[14] To pause to consider the implications of these terms, the functions of the spy and the intelligencer may be seen to reveal complex interactions of loyalty and betrayal, with the spy nuanced towards the former in our cognition and the intelligencer tending to evoke the latter. For the non-religious mind this may seem a fine distinction, but if we were to imagine the Devil as God's 'spy' or 'secret agent' this would of course reflect significantly on the character of the Almighty. An informer lacks the spy's cosy licence and seems to offer a self-serving facility that contaminates what it touches. If, as György Lukács has suggested, 'the principal spectator of tragedy is God', to some extent this is at the crux of the issue in the perception of the relationship between intelligencers and the authorities they work for in the early modern period.[15] Whether or not a surveillance device itself is reliable, as Georges Banu has said of a more modern era, 'it denounces, in a roundabout way, the motivations and identities of those who are putting it in place'.[16] John Stephens's depiction of an intelligencer in *Essays and Characters* (1615) as a 'protected Cheater, *or* a Knave in authoritie, licenced by authoritie', resounds with such resentment at the concession to dishonesty that association with such figures demands.[17] Only a truly Machiavellian perspective could suggest that the character of authority might be untainted by its reliance upon the devices, assertions and testimonies of society's most Judas-like and devilish characters.

Although in his *Characters* the seventeenth-century writer Francis Lenton echoes the common early modern view in describing informers as 'hated of all . . . the scum of Rascality', with his contemporary Joseph Hall agreeing in *Cases of Conscience* that 'every man is loath to be an Informer . . . out of the conscience of his owne obnoxiousnesse', some complexity must be allowed for in the nature of the choice to occupy oneself in performing such a role.[18] To a significant extent, of course, this social phenomenon is driven by economics. In his *Kind-hart's Dreame* (*c.*1607), Henry Chettle, taking the ironic comedic voice of Richard Tarleton, outlines the necessity that drives petty informing, cony-catching and such on low pay and high rents in saying of his landlord, that 'he knows by honest courses I cannot pay the rent . . . indeed sometimes I have my Landlordes countenance before a Justice, to cast a cloake over ill rule', justifying himself with the rhetorical question 'why not I as well as my neighbors, since theres no remedy'.[19] Besides this hint at legal recourse, and possibly even at informing against his landlord, Chettle bemoans contemporary city life in general as a cause of predation, crying, 'I would the hart of the Cittie were whole, for both within and without, extreame crueltie causeth much beggerie'; this is a time, he says, when the weak are sorely oppressed, where 'the Lyon hunteth the Wolfe, the Wolfe devoureth the Goate, and the Goate feedeth on mountain hearbs: so among men, the great oppresse the meaner, they againe the meanest.'[20] This offers a social and economic context which may be heard to resound in Thomas Overbury's description of one who is 'Informer-like-dangerous in taking aduantage of any thing done or sayde'.[21] It is apparently at least partly an understanding of the necessity that drives the predatory informer which makes people 'as carefull of their speeches and actions as the sight of a known Cutpurse ... makes them watchfull ouer their purses and pockets'.[22]

Nevertheless, despite the depredations of such a harsh social environment, the choice to become an intelligencer is still perceived as a primarily moral decision that takes one into the moral territory of the Judas, and into the theoretical and theological hinterland of the Devil himself. The apparent correlation of intelligencers and devils in contemporary society may be confirmed by a reading of texts such as Thomas Dekker's *Lantern and Candlelight or The Bellman's Second Walk* (1608). Here, it is term-time in the court of Hell when the fiendish proceedings are halted for the entry of 'a certain spirit in the likeness of a post', which Dekker calls 'an intelligencer sent by Beelzebub ... into some countries of Christendom, to lie there as a spy', carrying with him 'a packet of letters from several lieges that lay in those countries'.[23] In Chettle's dream, he is visited by 'a knight of the post, whome in times past I have seen as highly promoted as the pillory'.[24] The 'knight of the post' is a messenger who is also a professional perjurer or informer, and may perform the role of 'an ingrosser, an intelligencer, a constable, or a usurer', as Sandra Clark says.[25] The designation of 'post' also carries a pun on the whipping post to which an intelligencer might send his hapless victims.[26] Elizabethan and later pamphleteers see this as an appropriate disguise of the Devil, as Clark notes.[27] Chettle's demonic postman turns out to be the Devil's own informer who, weary from dealing with Pierce Penniless's message to Lucifer, is now 'returning to contaminate the ayre, with his pestilent perjuries, and abhominable false witnesse bearing.'[28] Meanwhile, Dekker's similarly Satanic postman's packet contains a warning to be delivered to the Devil of the eponymous Bellman's informing work in exposing what he calls the 'secrets of the best trades that are taught in Hell, laying them open to the broad eye of the world, making them infamous, odious, and ridiculous.'[29] This is an instance of a writer writing of an intelligencer who is informing on a writer that is in turn playing the informer to society. Not only is this last informing entirely justified, since it is on the nefarious activities of Hell, but it is also performed in the most public manner. As the demons moan with what must be the utmost irony, the Bellman 'very spitefully hath . . . set them out in print'.[30]

In response to the Bellman's intelligencing against them, Dekker's Devil advises his 'hell-hounds' that they 'never had more cause . . . to grow politicians', to use another term of contemporary disparagement often applied to intelligencers and ambitious, morally compromised courtiers.[31] It is with more deep irony that such a figure laments that the Bellman should be willing to 'pry into the infernal mysteries . . . and, having sucked what knowledge he can from them . . . turn it all into poison, and to spit it in the very faces of the professors, with a malicious intent to make them appear ugly and so to grow hateful and out of favour with the world'.[32] Seeing this, the Devil orders his demons to punish what he calls 'that saucy intelligencer, the Bellman of London', to various suggestions from the demonic crew.[33] One foolish devil suggests that another intelligencer, whom he calls 'the Black Dog of Newgate', should 'be let loose, and afar off follow the bawling Bellman, to watch into what places he went, and what deeds of darkness every night he did'.[34] The fact that this raises only laughter may be ominous. In Luke Hutton's *The Black Dog of Newgate* (c.1596), the cony-catching deceiver Black Dog is both Machiavellian accuser and employer of informers, as may be seen in his use of common bestial and financial imagery to say of one informer, 'man's life and soul this dog seeks to subdue. / His mouth to stop, angels I gave him two'.[35] When the Black Dog next attacks, the speaker uses the typical dog metaphor, saying that 'like a subtle cur in speeches halts he / With thousand sleighty wiles, old shifts compacted, / Charging me oft with that I never did', the very image of the informer, adding further implications of the canine with 'in his smooth'st looks are cruel bitings hid'.[36] As a 'madding cur who doth from kind regress', this description concludes, 'of mothers' sons this dog has spoiled a hundred'.[37]

Although Hutton perceives this particular social malaise in the familiar garb of the cony-catcher, again this world overlaps with that of the intelligencer, to the degree that cony-catchers also often depend on one or another species of false accusation for the operation of their devices.[38] Hutton describes them as being 'sure to have intelligence . . . [from] some odd fellows which are inquisitors of purpose, who always what they hear rumoured, they presently come and certify their good masters cony-catchers, of all.'[39] This is intelligence-gathering for nefarious purposes as much as any other. Hutton's dedication to Sir John Popham, Elizabeth's Lord Chief Justice, offers a species of informing of his own, which aims to 'certify you of the notable abuses daily committed by a great number of very bad fellows, who under the colour of office and service, do mightily abuse both justice and Justices'.[40] To further matters of intrigue along these lines, he asserts that he is issuing the book despite the 'malice of the threatening cony-catcher who hath sworn, if I publish this book, they will do me what mischief they can.'[41] The author thus becomes informer and suffers under the threat of the mischief-makers he publicises.

Meanwhile, Dekker's Bellman notes the network of demonic intelligencers that one young gull is to be predated by: 'first are scouts sent out to discover his lodging; that known, some lie in ambush to note what apothecary's shop he resorts to every morning, or in what tobacco-shop in Fleet Street he takes a pipe of smoke in the afternoon.'[42] The Devil's intelligencer then takes this information and seals up 'a letter full of it' to send to the Devil.[43] As a result of this, Dekker's Devil sends a minor devil as intelligencer with the instruction to 'wind thyself into all shapes; be a dog to fawn, a dragon to confound; be a dove, seem innocent . . . creep into bosoms . . . and there spread the wings of thine affection.'[44] As Pamersiel, the Devil's intelligencer or 'infernal promoter', rides around surveilling the sinning public, Dekker imagines the scene theatrically, exclaiming that 'a thousand of these comedies were acted in dumb show, and only in the private houses', and describing how the Devil's messenger hastens home 'having filled his table-books with sufficient notes of intelligence.'[45] He alludes further to the universality of informing and intelligencing of various kinds when he describes how his intelligencer 'laughed so loud that Hell heard him . . . because so many watchmen were continually called and charged to have an eye to [the night's] doings'.[46]

All of this speaks of a contemporary awareness of the function of the intelligencer and the informer that bears resemblance to the invisible world of devils and demons with which Christians have historically populated the dark edges of their imaginations. This draws on a highly Pauline fantasy of ruling 'principalities and powers', an insidious demonic pantheon which popular opinion seems to see made manifest in recognisable form in early modern England. Biblically speaking, St Paul's letters shift their ground fairly unintelligibly on the concept of the power and influence of devils such that conflation and confusion can be the only outcome for the thinking believer. In his letter to the Ephesians, St Paul claims that 'we wrestle not against flesh and blood, but against principalities, against powers, against the rulers of the darkness of this world, against spiritual wickedness in high places' and thus clearly identifies the hidden powers with devils and demons.[47] In Colossians, he claims firstly that God created 'all things . . . that are in heaven, and that are in earth, visible and invisible, whether they be thrones, or dominions, or principalities, or powers', thus including the devils and demons; then secondly that in the act of crucifixion, he 'spoiled' principalities and powers, 'he made a shew of them openly, triumphing over them' on behalf of the believers.[48] Further, in his letter to Titus, he reminds believers to 'be subject to principalities and powers, to obey magistrates', which conflates the concept of demonic jurisdiction jarringly with specifically worldly authorities. With this background it may not be surprising that contemporaries versed in this kind of teaching might also tend to conflate the demonic and the worldly powers in their own religious imaginations or worldviews.[49]

In a move which connects the author and the informer explicitly, Dekker refers to his Bellman as 'our spy that came lately out of the lower countries', which is not only a cute reference to Hell, the ultimate 'low country' (containing a bawdy pun), but also a self-conscious association with his own Dutchness which casts himself as both the satirical conscience of the society and the informer sent to collect information for the correction of the 'abuses' he attempts to rectify.[50] When the intelligencer and the Bellman meet, 'the mariner of Hell opened his chart' and from this book of abuses, 'the Bellman drawing forth a perfect map, they parted; which map he hath set out in such colours as you see.'[51] Thus the whole invective testimony of this Second walk of the Bellman is supposed to mirror the intelligencer's report to the Devil, and though it functions as high satire, this proposes the essential oneness of author and intelligencer.

The multi-layered and reciprocal nature of the worlds of spying, informing, intelligencing and cony-catching are abundantly evident in these extracts, as is the general perception of the demonic nature of these forms of surveillance and social control. It is perhaps unsurprising, in the ubiquitous atmosphere of informing and intelligencing which pervades his society, that Dekker also finds some of this reflecting back upon his own writing person. In his *Martin Markall, Beadle of Bridewell* (1610), Samuel Rid accuses Dekker, in the person of the Bellman, of being 'a most injurious and satirical libeller' for attacking only the weakest sinners and beggars and leaving the fat-cats alone, or what he calls 'those fox-furred gentlemen, that harbour more deceit under their damask cassocks, than is in all the poor rogues in a country', reproving Dekker for doing this because, as he says, 'they be your good masters and benefactors.'[52] Dekker is thus imagined as complicit with the corrupt authorities, as is typical of the libellous informer, but in a sense he has already admitted something of the same order himself and so the accusation falls flat.

Throughout all of this discourse we find a general consciousness that is very much in keeping with the dangerous proliferation of loathed and venally motivated informers and intelligencers across all ranks of society, and an atmosphere in which there seems to be no escape from the 'back-biting tongue of an impure mouth' as John Harington's 1591 preface to *Orlando Furioso* puts it.[53] This 'shifting legion of freelancers', as Charles Nicholl calls them, plied the authorities with information on every salient sphere of life, from the moral to the political and from the theatrical to the ecclesiastical.[54] Their employment increased throughout this period, as I have described extensively elsewhere.[55] On 26 August 1594, an information was passed from the intelligencer Richard Topcliffe to his superior Robert Cecil of the ample confession of a mariner called William Randall, who claimed a part in this proliferation, maintaining that he 'hath conveyed a greater number of traitors of all sorts into England ... Jesuits, priests, practisers and Intelligencers, than any other of English birth.'[56] Intelligencers are certainly found in all parts of the country, and records note that in the seventeenth century the Corporation of the northern town of York 'paid a fee to an "intelligencer" for sending weekly reports to the Lord Mayor', as P. M. Tillott notes.[57] The practice was ubiquitous geographically and hierarchically, and even Queen Elizabeth herself had cause to beware what Cecil called 'slanderers or false intelligencers who are apt to calumniate her proceedings', as his letter to James VI of March 1594 shows.[58] The perception of this carries abroad too, and although it is obviously primarily the propaganda of the age there seems to be a core of truth in the account of *The Copy of a Letter, Lately Written by a Spanishe Gentleman, to His Friend in England* (1589), which describes an 'intolerable feare ... more manifested in your Englishe Gouernment, then in any state els in the whole world'.[59] It is, the writer claims, 'a laborinthe to looke into'.[60] The impression given is of

> spyings abroade, and inquisitions at home: searchings of houses more at midnighte then at noone dayes, apprehensions, examinations, and such daily exercise, and practise of the racke, as neuer the like was hard of ... extreme tyranny, and deepe dissimulation ... being the grounde and substance of their gouernment, and conteyning ... infynite nombers of deceatfull practises, false fictions, and slaunderous lies.[61]

An international reputation for extensive intelligencing and informing is clearly behind this disparaging if propagandist vision of the English state. The Italian verb *toplifizare* was invented as a synonym for 'to torture' to express the particular characteristic input of the above-mentioned Topcliffe to the intelligencing system, which may serve as another indication of international infamy on this score.[62]

Although the focus of this book is the kinds of correspondence we may find between structures of intelligencing and the typical structures of metadrama, and it therefore usually focuses on the kinds of oversight and overhearing common to both, some historical examples of how intelligence was actually reported might also help to develop a fuller picture of this correlation. Showing the internal workings of the network and its problematic politic nature may help elucidate the nature of the pressures which might be brought to bear on those, including writers, who fall foul of its systems.

On 20 May 1593, the intelligencer Robert Bowes sent a note to William Cecil, Lord Burghley, which in turn describes a further note that has been sent to him by his own intelligencer:

> I received this day a little ticket written in these words, viz., 'My lord, ther was a band sought to have bene granted and subscribit be ane nobleman of thir feildis to have conjoyned with ... [Lennox], Huntlay,

Angusse, Erroll and others . . . The comissioner suter is a courtier; his name wilbe knowne at metinge, with some farder particulers. This was done not lange syne.' The intelligencer is of very good credit, yet not void of some dry affection against . . . [Lennox].[63]

The layered nature of this transaction, as information passes from intelligencer to intelligencer to intelligencer, speaks about the potential for ambiguity and misinformation to creep in as any written information undergoes such passage, potentially right to the top as we shall see. This report includes an assessment of the possible motivation, and thus trustworthiness, of the original informer, a claim which is clearly worth making. Passing this information upwards then was not without its own hazards, as is amply evidenced in Cecil's letter from the Court at Royston, 3 December 1610, to an intelligencer in the field. This recalls a recent conversation of his with King James about 'a private intelligence' that was given of 'some seditious spirits' who had purposed to ask Parliament to petition the king 'to remove or to send home those Scots that so much consumed their supplies.'[64] At first, as Cecil recounts it, this reported conversation seems straightforward enough, with the king taking the matter 'very merrily and laughingly'. However, on further reflection, the king becomes troubled and wants to know the source of the intelligence, as Cecil elaborates, with the king asking him 'whether it were spoken of Scots only or of others; also whether of all Scots or of some.'[65] Cecil responds, 'I prayed his Majesty to excuse me, for I did not take it as a speech I had any charge to report to him, and did not attend to the particularities of it. It might be I had mistaken it in the telling, and that it was not only of Scots.'[66] However, the king's commandment was 'to know the truth and the party' and Cecil's attempt to weasel out of the situation is unsuccessful.[67] Cecil is then forced to try to protect not only his sources, and his sources' sources, but also the system itself from the king it is designed to preserve:

> I answered it might be that he that gave you the intelligence had never named the party but spoke in generality. Then said he; My Lord may name me the party from whom he had it. To that I replied that if his Majesty would press Councillors to discover those by whom they received intelligence, they should be able to do him no more service in that kind.[68]

The king's reaction was somewhat hot-headed it seems, and somewhat ominously he 'discoursed long to show in what degree of treason they were that would seek to remove servants from a Prince'; as Cecil laments, 'all would not serve but he would know the author or the intelligencer.'[69] Passing the buck, Cecil attempts to fob the king off on his intelligencing addressee, telling 'I prayed his Majesty to forbear till your Lordship and he met, for I did not doubt but that you had many secret informations and many observations of the disposition of the House, which you reserved till you might have speech with him.'[70] However, even this arrangement was still not quite satisfactory to the ultimate authority in the kingdom: 'the conclusion still was that he would not bide so long'.[71] The fact that the ostensible head of intelligence matters in the nation can find himself wriggling uncomfortably to protect his sources from the king himself evidences the compromising ambiguity with which the apparent unreliability of its bases infect the power structure here.

The naive impatience of the king in these matters notwithstanding, Parliament was intimately involved in the processes and practices around intelligencers and informers, both from the legislative perspective and on a more personal level. Not only were the larger issues of informing debated in the House, but informers were sometimes examined there too. The *Journal of the House of Commons* entry for 28 April 1621 describes an intelligencer named Chambers being 'called in to the Bar, kneeling', and confessing 'he is the King's Servant, a Messenger, and is also an Informer.'[72] In this case, the informer was there to give information upon Sir Edward Francis, 'for his Wife's Recusancy'; this was a fairly high level of information, it would seem, and about a not inconsiderable matter. An example of successful intelligencing to Parliament appears also in 1621, in this case against 'abuses in Fleete Prison'.[73] The intelligencer is one 'Kenny', who accuses the 'Warden of the Fleete' of 'Locking Men up; keeping their Children from them, and Meat; making many of them lie in One little Room, more like Dogs than Men', including the 'strange barbarous Usage' of Kenny himself, in which, 'after he had paid his Debts, and ... Lodging', he was allegedly kept for '22 Months imprisoned, oft close Prisoner'.[74] After examining the case, the Warden of the Fleete was 'brought to the Bar, and charged by Mr. Speaker' that his treatment of prisoners was 'worse than the Inquisition of Spayne, or Gallies among the Turkes'.[75] This is how an informing system is supposed to work, with reliable information being given to competent authorities and resulting in a grievance solved.

Despite operating up to the level of government, the prevailing opinion, however, seems to be that informers and intelligencers are fundamentally untrustworthy and not to be relied upon. As Leicester writes to Burghley on 6 April 1586: 'I pray you, as you are wise, so beware of our common intelligencers hence; you shall find here be shrewd "pick-thinks", and hardly worth the harkening unto.'[76] An example of the instability of the use of 'information' from intelligencers may be seen in one Mr Weston who, in contributing to the debate in Parliament around the issue of 'Examining Members on Oath by Lords', pleaded that 'he informed, not upon his own Knowlege, but by Information; so as he can swear but he was told so.'[77] This tactic, besides offering the comfort of deniability, is highly suggestive of an understanding that 'information' sourced thus is inherently dubious. This may be partly, or significantly, because intelligencers were widely thought to be creative in framing their incriminating evidence in ways that would maximise the potential for them to get money. On 20 December 1580, a letter was sent from Cobham to Walsingham enclosing copies of two French letters, and 'beseeching you to let me know your opinion of them, whether they seem to be true copies, or framed as these intelligencers will devise to procure money.'[78] Cobham asserts, 'In my judgement they are to be suspected.'[79] This potential for the intelligencer's point of view to combine the negative construction of events with the generation of income suggests that there is every incentive for them 'to *create* information, to see conspiracy where none exists', as Nicholl says.[80] The late seventeenth-century tract, 'The Informers answer', asserts in this respect that these figures 'know no Religion but getting of Money, nor Law, but power.'[81] Walsingham himself was well aware that intelligencers might furnish him with 'toyes and matters of their owne invencon.'[82] In Ben Jonson's *Poetaster* (1601), Envy promises to interpret the play with 'wrestings . . . applications, / Spy-like suggestions, privy whisperings, / And thousand such promoting sleights' (Ind. 23–6).[83] In another context, the clergyman Faithful Teate uses the term to describe the intelligencer's wish to 'wrest what he hears to the Preacher's destruction.'[84] The 'wrestings' Jonson's Envy is concerned about are self-interested misinterpretations that aim to apply the play's plot to aspects of 'the present state' (Ind. 34) in order to denounce the play to the authorities, to the informer's advantage. Jonson of course was troubled by real wresting detractors and spy-like 'promoters'.[85] Since construing and relating things in an augmentative manner is common to both author and informer, the fact that the informer is perceived as notoriously untrustworthy offers some incentive for authors to attempt to distance themselves from these other 'plotters'. Given the relatively precarious position of writers in the period, this propensity accounts to some degree for a preoccupation with misinterpretative overhearers in the drama, and therefore for the metadrama this produces.

Cecil's own trouble with one of his intelligencers, who appears to have been spending his money unwisely and generally failing to keep his mouth shut, was expressed in a letter of 17 January 1601/2 to one Mr Nicholson, which complains that Cecil has been 'often bitten with the discontented humour of intelligencers when they have spent my money a good while . . . and so play me some slippery trick'.[86] He accuses this particular informer of 'trifl[ing] away my money for his intelligence to little purpose', further protesting 'I had rewarded him as well after he went into Ireland, whence he brought me but idle intelligences . . . sometime he wrote me truth, but often very many lies', asserting that he would wish himself 'buried when I . . . hear them whom I must employ for the service of the State to babble or prattle', and concluding 'I think never poor man hath been oftener belied than I have been in such cases.'[87] If the system is so deeply dysfunctional at this high level then we have reason to think that the ordinary citizen's experience may have been much worse.

In fact, the state of the situation in the nation throughout the period was such that a series of acts of legislation were thought necessary against abusive and dishonest intelligencing at all levels. Elizabeth's 'Act to redress Disorders in common Informers' (1576) shows a concern to limit the ability of informers to act without going to law, and to limit the time and place of accusations which did so.[88] Henceforth, informers could be punished at the pillory for suing 'out of process', and this might be accompanied with the sizeable fine of £10.[89] This act also responds to informers who were in the habit of delaying their suits in order to profit from extortion, often of those desperate victims who might want to circumvent a risky court appearance.[90] Chettle describes those intelligencers who serve false writs and then get others to pay them to delay going to court, and speaks of good lawyers in contrast with these 'pettifoggers'.[91] It was said of one 'crafty Informer' that he would first 'pick some feeling of money' from his victims, and then bring them 'to composition' in what seems to be the same manner, to be rid of the torment with which he would visit them.[92] The act also provides for some potential financial redress if their intelligence is, after all, found to be flawed.[93] Judging by the predominance of its appearance in the drama of the time, this provision seems to address a chief paranoia of the age.

The fact that these things are brought to the point of legislation implies their necessitation by emerging unruly circumstances, but that the legislation was not immediately effective may also be adduced from the 'Act concerning Informers' which followed thirteen years later in 1589. Its stated purpose was because 'divers of the queen's majesty's subjects be daily vexed and disquieted by divers common informers upon penal statutes, notwithstanding any former statute that hath been heretofore made against their disorders'.[94] This seems suggestive of the failure of the first act to have any real impact on informing malpractice. This act adds to the first of 1576 by additionally restricting acceptable actions to those brought within twenty days and within the same county in which the offence was alleged to have taken place.

A further clue to the ubiquitous extent of informing practice at the time may be gleaned from the large amount of exclusions and exemptions from the restrictions mentioned for which the act provides. The freelance intelligencer is released from such temporal and geographical limitations if the information given concerns any of the following:

> champerty [where an unassociated person finances a lawsuit with a view to sharing the proceeds] . . . buying of titles or extortion . . . Land Merchandize from beyond the Seas . . . sweet Wines . . . defrauding the queen's majesty . . . of any custom, tonnage, poundage, subsidy, impost or prizage . . . corrupt usury . . . engrossing, regrating or forestalling.[95]

The fact that this exemption pertains also to any offence where a possible penalty might exceed £20 makes it potentially very broadly applicable.[96] The further necessity for a set of legislation in James's tellingly entitled 'Act for the Ease of the Subject, concerning Informations upon Penal Statutes' (1623) shows that, despite Elizabeth's best efforts in her acts, this problem seems to have again proliferated in the intervening years. James's act complains again that 'the poor commons of this realm are grievously charged, troubled, vexed, molested and disturbed by ... relators, informers, and promoters by prosecuting and inforcing them to appear at his majesty's courts' in a refrain which is becoming very familiar.[97] Again, the Act aims to restrict the informer's business to certain courts, jurisdictions and timeframes, and again certain offences are exempted from this legislation, adding the following to Elizabeth's list of offences that are subject to unrestricted intelligencing: 'popish recusancy ... those that shall not frequent the church and hear divine service ... transporting of gold, silver, ordnance, powder, shot, munition of all sorts, wool, wool fells or leather'.[98] It is careful to say of any one of these misdemeanours that 'such offence may be laid or alleged to be in any county at the pleasure of any informer, anything in this act to the contrary notwithstanding.'[99] This expansion of exemptions on many significant activities again shows amply how widespread the practice of intelligencing and informing was, but it also seems hardly calculated to work to the greater 'Ease of the Subject', as its title seems to promise. Perhaps these many exemptions and caveats provide some basis for the fact that the courts and lawmakers were perceived to be very much in cahoots with the informers they legislated for. In 1592, Robert Greene describes a 'M. Informer' as looking like 'some handsome pettie fogger of the law', either despite having 'as much slie knauerie in [his] side pouch ... as woulde breede the confusion of forty honest men' or because of this.[100] Honesty and all that the law means in terms of legitimacy and authority are at issue here.

Some suggested amendments and comments made in debating the 1623 Act may go some way to explicate further concerns over contemporary intelligencing. In the discussion on this in Parliament, Sir Edward Coke conceded that the bill was indeed 'more easeful for the Subject' and stated that this was 'an excellent Bill', yet asserted it was 'defective, and to be helped by Addition', and advocated some extra provisions. These included the suggestion that the informer should be required to 'bring with him a known Man to the Judge, to testify the Sufficiency of the Informer', which speaks to the perception of the informer's character as typically doubtful. He also proposes that if the informer offers a 'Trick ... to exhibit an Information, to put off all others by Covyn', a conspiratorial agreement, then he should never 'be admitted to inform afterwards, and to be bound to his good Behaviour'.[101] Rather than simply offering a new perspective, these seem to be aimed at preventing known abuses.

As Cecil's struggles with his errant intelligencer above suggest, intelligencers could make a very comfortable living from a successful career in the field. Walsingham's guiding principle in an age which ran on this kind of surveillance was that 'knowledge is never too dear' and his personal subvention from the Crown for paying informers went from £750 in 1582 to £2,000 in 1585 (c.£200,000–£500,000 in 2018), and continued in this manner for some time afterwards.[102] In a letter of 24 March 1598/9, Cecil's agent Dudley Norton talks of 'the 4,000*l*. I brought from Dublin' for this purpose and enquires how best to employ the money 'for the special furthering of her Majesty's service' in what he openly calls 'gifts to spies and intelligencers and rewards for services (by which means no doubt good things may be effected)'.[103] If the figure he gives is accurate, the most conservative equivalent for this amount of money in 2018 terms would be just over £1 million. This would be intended to cover travel and living expenses, and was no doubt supposed to filter further down the pecking order of informers and intelligencers to widen any given net as required, but it still indicates an appreciably augmented level of commitment to the business of intelligencing through the period. In a singular case, when Thomas Kyd was arrested over the 'Dutch Church libel' in 1593, the reward offered for information on him alone was a substantial 100 crowns.[104] In another which is referred to in a Parliamentary debate of 1621, one Mr Alford complained of 40 shillings that was 'demanded by an Informer, for a Pike-staff', presumably the metonymy for a beadle.[105] Although this was one twentieth of Kyd's bounty, it still represented a significant amount of money when a close contemporary of 1629 might earn seven shillings for a week's work in a lead mine.[106] But besides these kinds of payments, informers were typically entitled to up to half of whatever fine was imposed or the value of the commodities involved in their informing.[107] Since this might involve, for instance, a ship's whole cargo, then one can see the earning potential of such activities, and thus the material incentives involved in the production of information for intelligence purposes.[108] This was of course potentially problematic, as Walsingham's wariness of intelligencers' tendency to produce imaginary 'toyes' suggests.[109]

Drawing these issues closer to the environs of the theatre, the legal foundation for the threat of intelligence against an author or actor is made sufficiently obvious in Elizabeth's royal commission of 1581 to Edmund Tilney, the Master of the Revels. In this, Elizabeth authorises Tilney to have any offending player arrested, and to 'remaine without bayle or mayneprise untill such tyme as . . . [he] shall thinke . . . theire imprisonment to be punnishement sufficient for [their] offences', which is presumably as long as Tilney sees fit. Elizabeth adds threateningly that those found not 'aydinge supportinge and assistinge' Tilney in this 'will answer to the contrarie at [their] uttermost perills.'[110] Tilney was further authorised to ban authors and players from writing or acting 'forever hereafter' and thus depriving them of their living indefinitely for a breach of the established rules of propriety.[111]

Scholars have long argued for the understanding of these material contexts as producing a culture of repression and harassment that has a substantial effect on the drama of the day.[112] It is clear that, once suitably motivated, authorities could act with 'almost paranoid ferocity, threatening death, mutilation or prolonged imprisonment' as Richard Dutton says.[113] However, circumstances certainly did not always go the informer's way. This may be seen from the Commons debate over the type of punishment most appropriate for an alleged libeller and suspected intelligencer Richard Floyde who was charged with 'speaking against the Bible [and] against the noble King and Queen of Bohemia'. In this indictment, besides a nominally agreed and presumably ruinous £1,000 fine, increasingly inventive punishments are suggested by enthusiastic MPs eager for the application of the lash with varying severity. Sir Thomas Row expresses a desire to have Floyde 'whipped through London' and Sir Francis Seymor elaborates that he should be whipped 'from Westmynster at a Cart's Tail, with his Doublet off, to the Tower, the Beads about his Neck, and as many Lashes by the Way as Beads'.[114] Sir Edward Gyles calls for the use of the public pillory where he should be confined 'with a Paper of his Head [sic], containing his vile Words', then a whipping 'at the Court Gate; and so at the Temple, and Cheapesyde' with, since he is a Catholic, 'his Beads and Crucifixes, and especially his Friars Girdle, about him'.[115] Sir Francis Darcy helpfully adds to this that he should be disabled by 'boring through his Tongue'.[116] Sir Edward Cecill agrees, and puts in that he should also be branded with 'a B. on his Forehead', while Mr Angell requests the nicety of a 'gag in his Mouth, to keep him from crying, and procuring Pity'.[117] Sir J. Horsey specifically agrees with the suspicion that he is 'an Intelligencer; which may be discovered by his Papers', and takes things a little further in wanting him to 'have his Tongue cut out, or slit at least'.[118] Sir Thomas Weyneman, meanwhile raises the stakes to a terminal level by suggesting a 'search of his Papers, to find Matters to hang him'.[119] It must be pointed out, however, that these punishments are also theoretically open to any unwary author who might be denounced in such a way and accused of slander or libel. Christopher Marlowe may well have gone further in 'speaking against the Bible' at least, although his terminus was of a different kind.

Throughout the period, examples abound of authors and actors caught up in the paranoia of authorities and their desire to control the creative output of artists using their established networks of intelligencers and informers. In 1579, both John Stubbs and his publisher were mutilated for addressing Elizabeth's marriage in *The Discovery of a Gaping Gulf whereinto England is like to be Swallowed*.[120] In 1593, Thomas Kyd was ferociously tortured over alleged writings and died the following year. In 1597, Ben Jonson was imprisoned with fellow players Gabriel Spenser and Robert Shaa, and feared defacement after being informed upon for his part in *The Isle of Dogs*.[121] In 1599, John Hayward was almost executed over his *The Life and Reign of King Henry IV* and was imprisoned for the remainder of Elizabeth's reign.[122] In 1605, George Chapman was informed upon and imprisoned with Jonson for *Eastward Ho* and later in 1608, with his actors, for his *Byron* plays through one who 'plaied the bitter Informer before the french Ambassador'.[123] In 1610, Sir Edward Dymock was fined £1,000 and imprisoned for staging a derogatory play, while three of his actors were each fined £300 and whipped and pilloried in both Westminster and Lincolnshire.[124] In 1633, William Prynne had his ears cropped and served seven years imprisonment for his royal-bashing in *Histriomastix*.[125] It should not be too much of a challenge to see how such prospectively brutal pressure exerted by contemporary authorities might generate the dread of misinterpretation that emerges in the drama of the time, articulated both overtly in personae and plots and more covertly in its metadramatic forms.

This book will of course deal with many generic dramatic and metadramatic representations of intelligencers and informers, but somewhat unusually there is one play that refers directly to a named, real-life informer. In the sub-plot for John Webster and William Rowley's *Cure for a Cuckold* (1624–5), the lawyer Pettifog tells a story about 'an Informer' who is 'a precious knave'. Pettifog's companion Compass declares 'I cannot away with an Informer' and asks him 'will not the Ballad of Flood that was prest, make them leave their knavery?' (4.1).[126] Compass is referring here to the notorious informer Griffin Flood whose anonymous biographical tract, *The life and death of Griffin Flood informer Whose cunning courses, churlish manners, and troublesome informations, molested a number of plaine dealing people in this city of London* (1623), sports one of those self-explanatory early modern titles which seems to require little extra comment.[127] Flood was thought so dangerous on the streets of London that even this small dramatical reference seems to be licensed by his demise in 1623, when he was 'pressed' or crushed slowly to death for murder.

In the world so far described, it is small wonder that the figures of the intelligencer and the informer are significant elements in how the audience is imagined by early modern dramatists. The poet Edward Ward gives us an interesting glimpse of the early modern informer in the context of an audience at the Saddlers Wells Theatre as he 'began to look down, and examine the Pit':

> Where Butchers and Bayliffs, and such sort of Fellows,
> Were mix'd with a Vermin train'd up to the Gallows.
> As Buttocks and Files, House-breakers and Padders,
> With Prize-Fighters, Sweetners, and such sort of Traders;
> Informers, Theef-Takers, Deer-Stealers, and Bullies,
> Old Straw-hatted Whores with their Twelve-penny Cullies,
> Some Dancing and Skiping, some Ranting and Tearing,
> Some Drinking and Smoking, some Lying and Swearing.[128]

The sheer vocal activity of this ranting, lying and swearing audience is striking and perhaps this is what makes the presence of the informer at the heart of it all seem so menacing. At the other end of the seventeenth century, John Day's *Isle of Guls* (1606) seems to catch at the same mood and also makes allusion to the presence of the informer in the audience when its Prologue complains of 'the boundlesse hate / Of a confused audience', lamenting that if the satirist would 'strike at abuse, or ope the vaine of sinne / He is straight informed against for libelling'.[129] This would be a dangerous outcome, as we have seen, and it justifies Day's concern here.

Further, within the satirical tradition and the dramatic practice of social commentary, parody and critique, there has long been an obvious potential for crossover with the business of the intelligencer.[130] This intersection generates an area of some ambiguity around the role of satire and the legitimacy of a critical viewpoint. Witness in this respect *Kind-hart's Dreame* where Chettle is using the sardonic, histriomastical voice of Tarleton to rail against the theatres, declaiming 'fie uppon following plaies, the expence is wondrous; upon players speeches, their wordes are full of wyles'.[131] This is exactly the accusation that is often levelled against intelligencers, and sometimes by their employers, as Cecil's concerns over his informer in Ireland may show. Chettle's Tarleton continues in this vein, asking 'is it not lamentable, that a man should spende his two pence on them in an after-noone ... and in lively gesture see treacherie set out, with which every man now adaies useth to intrap his brother'; the ironic critique concludes, 'if these be the fruites of playing, tis time the practiser were expeld.'[132] Here Chettle mockingly ventriloquises anti-theatrical preachers in casting players as untrustworthy sources, and simultaneously describes the critical environment which invites the intelligencing against authors and actors we have been describing. In 1615, the writer known as T. G. claims a similar connection, as he says, 'players, Poets, and Parasites doe now in a manner ioyne hands', and cites players' propensity for producing 'artificiall lyes, discoueries of cousenage [and] scurrilous words'.[133] This echoes many descriptions of the deceitful creative practices of informers. Chettle then develops this in the ironic voice of the deceiving cony-catcher or informer, claiming that advertising their 'devices' in plays then spreads both knowledge and practice of these to wider society: 'no sooner have we a tricke of deceipt, but [plays] make it common'.[134] This works as either a critique of, or apology for, theatre, but either way it evidences connections between the devices of the dishonest practisers in the real world and the theatrical devices of plot and metadrama, and thus between intelligencers and authors.

The murky territory wherein the perspectives of the author and the intelligencer meet is reflected in some interestingly theatrical narrative devices found in Dekker's expository tracts, which suggest similar associations. Wandering in the woods away from the 'peopled city' with its 'unruly multitude' and the 'stings of envy . . . bullets of treason . . . [and] clamorous suits' of the world that we have been discussing, Dekker's speaker in *The Bellman of London* (1608) finds a kind of arena, a 'grove set thick with trees, which grew in such order that they made a perfect circle; insomuch that I stood in fear it was kept by fairies'.[135] In this *Midsummer Night's Dream*-like location he decides to 'divide the day into Acts, as if the ground had been a stage and that the life which there I meant to lead should have been but as a play.'[136] In this theatrical frame of mind, the speaker, seeing smoke nearby, discovers an open cottage and a kitchen busy with preparation for some mysterious guests. Bribing the cook, he is 'conveyed into an upper loft' where, as he says, 'unseen I might, through a wooden lattice that had the prospect of the dining-room, both see and hear all that was to be done or spoken.'[137] There, like a menacingly concealed intelligencer he forms a hidden audience to the arrival of what he calls the '*Ragged Regiment*'.[138] These he describes as 'knaves by profession, beggars by statute, and rogues by Act of Parliament . . . the idle drones of a country, the catterpillars of a commonwealth, and the Egyptian lice of a kingdom.'[139] Dekker uses this narrative form in a sense to literalise the vision of his first-person narration, but it is significant that this replicates both the oversight of the hidden intelligencer and the unseen audience of much metadramatic structure. It may also be a natural form for a dramatist to use to inform us of this array of what seem to be beggars and petty criminals, but perhaps more so since they might just as easily be itinerant players who were also 'rogues by Act of Parliament'. This seemingly natural connection between the work of the intelligencer and that of the observing author is precisely what authors often feel most compelled to distance themselves from at this time. Ben Jonson's *Poetaster* exemplifies this desire as a play which forcefully describes his rivals not only as wannabe poets, but also specifically as informers who are complicit in the corruption of authority.[140] In his *Covent-Garden* (1638), Thomas Nabbs clearly conflates the author and the intelligencer in the observing and writing character of Littleword who seems to operate on the 'troubled threshold of commonplace collecting and intelligence-gathering' which Lorna Hutson identifies.[141] Characters are reassured that Littleword's writing in his table-book in a corner is merely 'his practise of observation' and that he is only 'taking a humour for a Play' (4.3.60). The response is telling: 'that silent Gentleman is an intelligencer; . . . Hee'l informe against you.' (4.3.73–4).[142] Dekker's devilish messenger mentioned above similarly 'fill[s] his table-books with . . . notes of intelligence.'[143] Furthermore, as I have elsewhere noted, the roles of intelligencer and author have overlapped in historically verifiable ways.[144] On the most obvious side of the equation, contemporary examples of authors who were also very possibly intelligencers include Christopher Marlowe, George Gascoigne, Thomas Watson, Michel de Montaigne, Anthony Munday, John Lyly, Anthony and Francis Bacon and Ben Jonson.[145] On the less obvious side, Nicholl cites one informer named Thomas Drury who, he argues, is primarily motivated in his creative intelligencing by frustrated ambitions as an author.[146]

It is the contention of this present study then that the structures of early modern metadrama are fashioned under the social pressures of a culture suffused with the fear of the empowered and corrupt witness of the intelligencer and the informer. Metadrama is a dramatic mode which either implicitly or explicitly comments or reflects upon its own dramatic ontology in its form or content.[147] This may be plainly defined as drama about drama, where theatrical codes are themselves a part of the dramatic discourse.[148] Early modern metadramatic structures take many forms. They are typically flexible or fleeting, potentially shifting from one metadramatic mode to another in an instant; they are also often overlaid one upon another. They include a mode of simple self-reference, where the dramatic processes are alluded to or openly expressed in some way. They may involve open or closed frame narratives, operating on any scale from role-playing within a role to the play within the play and often entail some form of overt or covert oversight and overhearing between characters.[149] Especially where there is a play set within the primary play narrative, this often results in offstage audiences watching onstage audiences and sometimes vice versa. In the first case, the onstage audience may work as a representation of the offstage audience. Otherwise, the offstage audience may be constructed as itself, seen through the eyes of the actors onstage, or be represented as some other gathering of people – a crowd at a fair, a senate, a jury, or even in one case as a tapestry.[150] Metadrama always implicates the audience in some manner more explicitly interactive than non-metadramatic forms allow.

Metadramatic self-reference can be as straightforward as a mention of the play's title and as historically intricate as a nuanced reference to an understood social context of the theatre, perhaps to an anti-theatrical tract or the characteristics of a popular actor. The *theatrum mundi* aspect of such self-reference leads one towards a view of reciprocal performativity. This is a metadramatic mode that reveals social roles as essentially theatrical but, at the same time, demonstrates the inherent ambiguity of a dramatic representation which claims to have purchase on the social fabric. This is perhaps a defining factor also in the self-reflexive business of satire which poses such troubling similarities with the intelligencer.

With both open and closed frame narratives, the offstage audience is often offered the position of the intelligencer, that is one in which a particular hidden watcher or overhearer gets to know more than the other characters about the plot as it unfolds. Drawing attention thus to the dramatic structures in which they exist, and by which characters are defined, suggests a potentially active role for the offstage audience in the outworking of the metadrama. It also produces a sense of dramatic irony which is empowering to them since it emphasises the dependence of the drama upon their interpretation. Despite this apparent empowerment, however, frame narratives may employ dynamic structures which act upon an audience in order to suggest the appropriateness of certain responses. The perspectives of onstage audiences of frame narratives can have a dramatic effect, either negative or positive, on those of offstage audiences. This effect can be dependent on the extent to which the inner frame narrative provides its own closure and thus either perpetuates the integrity of the dramatic structure or disrupts a sense of theatrical 'reality'. It can also be inflected by the dramatic status of an onstage audience, in terms of whether the primary diegetic focus is on the inner play or whether it is on the onstage audience, a mode in which the matter proposed for interpretation is the interpretative authority of the audience itself. Since this mode places an audience under the guns of their own critique it may also serve a certain defensive function for the author. Another defensive mechanism is where the offstage audience is explicitly referred to as themselves, and perhaps offered either a respectable interpretative position or one which mimics the actions of the intelligencer. This mode may be used to draw attention to the latent menace of an audience's misconception, or worse the active dangers of deliberate misconstrual, the prospective material results of which for authors are by now familiar to us.

Some technical terms may be useful in thinking about how audiences are engaged with drama through visual and narrative mechanisms that can be employed to shape either perception or interpretative legitimacy. The narrative term 'diegetic gravity' describes the effect of experiencing a frame narrative inside a frame narrative and so on, and designates the force which pulls the attention inwards through each concentric device to the inmost narrative. As the spectator's perspective is drawn through each successive frame, the outer frames may becomes less noticeable. I describe this 'frame-blindness' as an effect in which an audience may experience the inner play as if it were the outer play. This often tends to place them in close relation to an onstage audience in a process which may suggest confraternity or collusion with those spectators, whether they form a full audience or a single hidden observer. In that a failure to recognise one's dependence on the symbolic systems by which one is interpellated by culture may compromise one's autonomy, Jacques Lacan's concept of *méconnaissance* may be useful in understanding this form.[151] Complicating this are the ways in which various metadramatic strata in a play relate with a type of hypotaxis in causally, spatially or temporally subordinate modes. Also, wherever an offstage audience shares the perspective of an onstage one, they may experience 'metalepsis', in which a fleetingly shared narrative level allows them to perceive the interaction of two levels and to be able to interpret them in terms of each other.[152] The term 'scopic pulsion' relates to this but designates a specifically visual mechanism in which a centripetal impetus directs us towards the inmost point of the drama.[153] As with diegetic gravity, metadrama may both encourage or discourage such motion, depending on how it configures each inner narrative level.

By expressing the very material power relations of the era, the structures and mechanisms of early modern metadrama offer exemplary models for theories of subjectivity. Lacan describes how the subject is constructed through a network of relations in the scopic fields of others.[154] His term 'the gaze' was based on Jean-Paul Sartre's reciprocal 'look', a mechanism of mutually constitutive association referring to the 'permanent possibility of *being seen* by the Other'.[155] In this model of mutual watching, the seer and the seen mould each other's subjectivities. Lacan, however, refuses the 'fundamental connection' with the Other that this implies, and instead 'conceives of an antinomic relation between the gaze and the eye: the eye which looks is that of the subject, while the gaze is on the side of the object and there is no coincidence between the two'.[156] It is my contention that metadrama allows the author to exercise a form of structural authority over meaning-making dramatic form by foregrounding the ideological elements of its 'network of relations' and thus potentially subverting them. This not only allows the author some form of entry into the symbolic order, but also allows a kind of resistance to malicious construction by 'psycho-social positions' offered by the proxy authority of the intelligencer. Since the subjectivities of both author and intelligencer are mutually informed, even to the point of similarities felt to be in need of repudiation, a Sartrean understanding of these mechanisms will be the most applicable to the present study.

In the texts chosen for this book, metadrama is employed in a variety of ways and the intelligencer figures differently in each. In *Damon and Pithias*, metadramatic self-consciousness is a vehicle for an authorial and social ideal of a kind. The metadrama in this case acts as a register for an abuse of power which perhaps reflects its own conditions of writing while challenging these with an equalising ideal of classical amity. In turn this produces an idyllic kind of authority and proposes a friendly society in which both the author and the audience are freed from predatory self-promotion and even afforded a kind of redemptive transformation.

Considering the metadrama of the stage Machiavel of the era, Marlowe's *The Jew of Malta*, Middleton/Tourner's *The Revenger's Tragedy* and Marston's *The Malcontent* all serve to suggest that the use of intelligencers weakens the moral authority of the hierarchy they help to sustain. Perhaps even discrediting God on the way, intelligencer personae work as cautionary dysfunctionals, of a kind with Marlowe's Barabas, who plays the scapegoat for a society consumed with the ties of finance. Framed within metadrama, these demonic provocateurs serve as both inheritors of the role of the medieval Vice figure and metaphors for discrepancies in the authority structures of their societies, allowing the exploration of ambiguous connections between the Vice depicted as an anti-authoritarian devil and as a tyrannous authority.

As parasitic outsiders operating inside the political establishment, they stand for a society which is dysfunctional in its control mechanisms, and as metadramatic actors they satirise the decadence or corruption of social forms. With or without finding their own redemptive agency, their own fates are bound up with those of the intelligencing structures they inhabit.

In Francis Beaumont's *The Knight of the Burning Pestle*, the metadramatic structure offers us untrustworthy onstage spectators whose wild-card antics imply an authorship endangered by an audience empowered by the threat of intelligencing. Beaumont's disruptive onstage citizens may be humorous but their intimidation has some foundation in the real world of contemporary playwriting. Their negative onstage audience model suggests a general interpretative disquiet and stages a crisis of legitimate interpretation and authority. Such metadrama aims to define the parameters of an audience's interpretation, both giving a sense of negotiation in the creation of meaning and dramatising an implicit correlation between author and interpreter. This desire for control suggests a defensive fixation on the mechanisms of power and thus the play's metadramatic structures reproduce the critical atmosphere of the drama and of the material context of its production. This tells us something about the pressures under which contemporary authors must write and in presenting this Beaumont reveals the precarious nature of his own authority.

John Webster's Bosola is an exemplary combination of actor and intelligencer, traversing metadramatic structures in a self-consciously Machiavellian manner. He is, however, unusually complex in a moral sense, and as the Duchess's tragedy unfolds he is finally able to offer some resistance to the expectations of the role. His perception of the Duchess's conduct in the travails he imposes upon her is a factor in this but the revelation of the nature of his own role in the oppressive mechanisms of the state is also a key determinant in his conversion. Playing the reluctant informer, Bosola's belated transformation under the dictates of his conscience suggests a humanising possibility: that the intelligencer, and therefore the morally bankrupt structures of authority themselves, are redeemable.

The metadrama of Philip Massinger's *The Roman Actor* combines some of these issues with the suggestion of theatre's own potential for complicity in the mechanisms of social control. It was the source of the author's authority which informed much early modern debate around the legitimacy of theatre and the precise nature of this authority is what is at play here. Considering the notoriously theatrical court of Charles I, a contemporary audience might well pause to contemplate whom the play's title might reference. Meanwhile, the defensively self-deprecating metadrama it contains allows Massinger the comforting position of the satirist who remains relatively untroubled by the potential for misinterpretation by intelligencers and informers.

In Chettle's *Hoffman* the metadramatic form proposes an authority which is a performative construct deeply troubled by its own mechanisms of control and whose own machinery of power questions its legitimacy. The metadramatic devices in this play have alternately undermining and recuperative functions in the service of an authority which is inherently destabilised, being in various ways displaced, usurped or the object of frustrated ambition. *Hoffman* in this respect, like many metadramatic plays, forms something of an exploration of the nature of authority.

Complemented by the readings of Shakespeare and Jonson that I have given elsewhere, these perspectives are offered not as the final key to understanding the predominance of metadrama in the early modern period, but as describing one fundamental element in the historical understanding of authors' imperatives in creating drama which related to their world in materially intelligible forms. The metadramatists have many reasons to create drama as they do, some of which will be a matter of conscious deliberation and some merely conventional within the artistic process, but all of these serve to reproduce the social forms which define authors in material ways, both as artists and as functioning social beings.

Notes

1. Raymond Williams, *Culture* (Glasgow: Collins, 1981), p. 142.
2. Williams, pp. 142, 158.
3. See Bill Angus, *Metadrama and the Informer in Shakespeare and Jonson* (Edinburgh: Edinburgh University Press, 2016).
4. Sigmund Freud, *Civilization and Its Discontents*, trans. J. Riviere (London: Hogarth Press, 1930), p. 90.
5. This is in relation to the German *Volkstheater* movement; see Gerhard Fischer and Bernhard Greiner (eds), *The Play within the Play: The Performance of Meta-Theatre and Self-Reflection* (New York: Rodopi, 2007), p. xv.

6. Of the time and place of writing: 19 February 2018, Titirangi, Auckland, New Zealand.
7. Thomas Nashe, *Haue with you to Saffron-Walden, Or, Gabriell Harueys hunt is up* (London: John Danter, 1596), p. 106, <http://gateway.proquest.com/openurl?ctx_ver=Z39.88-2003&res_id=xri:eebo&rft_id=xri:eebo:citation:99845702> (last accessed 20 February 2018).
8. His fee being the 'thirty pieces of silver' (Matt. 26: 15)
9. Nashe, *Haue with you to Saffron-Walden*, p. 106.
10. Nashe, *Haue with you to Saffron-Walden*, p. 106.
11. George Fox, *The devil was and is the old informer against the righteous* (London: John Bringhurst, 1682), n.p., <http://gateway.proquest.com/openurl?ctx_ver=Z39.88-2003&res_id=xri:eebo&rft_id=xri:eebo:citation:11327409> (last accessed 20 February 2018).
12. George Fox, *The Journal of George Fox* (Cambridge: Cambridge University Press, 1924), pp. 139, 325, 458.
13. George Whitehead, *Judgment fixed upon the accuser of our brethren* (London: Andrew Sowle, 1682), <http://gateway.proquest.com/openurl?ctx_ver=Z39.88-2003&res_id=xri:eebo&rft_id=xri:eebo:citation:14582034> (last accessed 7 February 2018).
14. Anon., 'The Informers answer to the late character vindicating themselves from the scandalous truths of that unlucky pamphlet' (London: T.C., 1675), p. 5.
15. Lionel Abel, *Tragedy and Metatheatre: Essays on Dramatic Form* (New York: Holmes & Meier, 2003), p. 113.
16. 'il dénonce . . . de manière détournée, les motivations et les identités de ceux qui le mettent en place'. Georges Banu, *La Scène Surveillée* (Paris: Actes Sud, 2006), p. 79 [trans. France Grenaudier-Klijn].
17. John Stephens, *Essayes and characters* (1615), <http://gateway.proquest.com/openurl?ctx_ver=Z39.88-2003&res_id=xri:eebo&rft_id=xri:eebo:citation:99853040> (last accessed 10 February 2018).
18. Joseph Hall, *Cases of conscience practically resolved* (1654), <http://gateway.proquest.com/openurl?ctx_ver=Z39.88-2003&res_id=xri:eebo&rft_id=xri:eebo:citation:11415099> (last accessed 2 February 2018); Francis Lenton, *Characterismi: or, Lentons leasures* (London: I[ohn] B[eale] for Roger Michell, 1631), n.p., <http://gateway.proquest.com/openurl?ctx_ver=Z39.88-2003&res_id=xri:eebo&rft_id=xri:eebo:image:9918:68> (last accessed 13 February 2018).
19. Henry Chettle, *Kind-harts Dreame* (London: William Wright, 1592), p. 34, <http://gateway.proquest.com.ezproxy.massey.ac.nz/openurl?ctx_ver=Z39.88-2003&res_id=xri:eebo&rft_id=xri:eebo:image:17363:19> (last accessed 23 February 2018).
20. Chettle, *Kind-harts Dreame*, p. 38.

21. Thomas Overbury, *Sir Thomas Ouerburie his wife with new elegies vpon his (now knowne) vntimely death* (1611), n.p., <http://gateway.proquest.com/openurl?ctx_ver=Z39.88-2003&res_id=xri:eebo&rft_id=xri:eebo:citation:20234643> (last accessed 2 December 2017).
22. Overbury, *Sir Thomas Ouerburie his wife with new elegies*, n.p.
23. Thomas Dekker, *Lantern and Candlelight or The Bellman's Second Walk* (1608), in A. V. Judges (ed.), *The Elizabethan Underworld* (London: Routledge & Kegan Paul, 1965), p. 320.
24. Chettle, *Kind-harts Dreame*, p. 10.
25. Sandra Clark, *The Elizabethan Pamphleteers: Popular Moralistic Pamphlets 1580–1640* (London: Bloomsbury, 2015), p. 154.
26. Thomas Nashe, *Pierce Penilesse, His Supplication to the Divell*, ed. G. B. Harrison (London: Bodley Head, 1924), p. vi.
27. Clark, p. 154.
28. Chettle, *Kind-harts Dreame*, p. 10.
29. Dekker, *Lantern and Candlelight*, pp. 320–1.
30. Dekker, *Lantern and Candlelight*, p. 321.
31. Dekker, *Lantern and Candlelight*, p. 321.
32. Dekker, *Lantern and Candlelight*, p. 321.
33. Dekker, *Lantern and Candlelight*, p. 321.
34. Thomas Dekker, *Lantern and Candlelight*, p. 321.
35. Luke Hutton, *The Black Dog of Newgate* (1596?), in A. V. Judges (ed.), *The Elizabethan Underworld* (London: Routledge & Kegan Paul, 1965), p. 273.
36. Hutton, p. 275.
37. Hutton, p. 276.
38. Hutton, p. 282.
39. Hutton, p. 280.
40. Hutton, p. 265.
41. Hutton, p. 265.
42. Dekker, *Lantern and Candlelight*, p. 328.
43. Dekker, *Lantern and Candlelight*, p. 328.
44. Dekker, *Lantern and Candlelight*, p. 323.
45. Dekker, *Lantern and Candlelight*, pp. 347, 365.
46. Dekker, *Lantern and Candlelight*, p. 365.
47. Bible, The Authorised Version (1611), Ephesians 6:12.
48. Bible, The Authorised Version (1611), Colossians 1:16, 2:15.
49. Bible, The Authorised Version (1611), Titus 3:1.
50. Dekker, *Lantern and Candlelight*, p. 363.
51. Dekker, *Lantern and Candlelight*, p. 365.
52. This is besides an accusation of plagiarism from Thomas Harman's *A Caveat or Warning for Common Cursitors, Vulgarly called Vagabonds* (1566); see Samuel Rid, *Martin Markall, Beadle of Bridewell* (1610), in

A. V. Judges (ed.), *The Elizabethan Underworld* (London: Routledge & Kegan Paul, 1965), pp. 389, 392.
53. John Harington, 'A Preface, Or Rather a Briefe Apologie of Poetrie', *Orlando Furioso in English Heroical Verse* (London: 1591), sig. Ii.
54. Charles Nicholl, *The Reckoning* (London: Vintage, 1992), p. 130.
55. See Angus, pp. 1–40.
56. R. A. Roberts (ed.), 'Cecil Papers: August 1594', *Calendar of the Cecil Papers in Hatfield House: Volume 4, 1590–1594* (London: Her Majesty's Stationery Office, 1892), pp. 575–601; *British History Online*, <http://www.british-history.ac.uk/cal-cecil-papers/vol4/pp575-601> (last accessed 24 February 2018).
57. P. M. Tillott (ed.), 'The seventeenth century: Civic government', *A History of the County of York: the City of York* (London: Victoria County History, 1961), pp. 173–86, *British History Online*, <http://www.british-history.ac.uk/vch/yorks/city-of-york/pp173-186> (last accessed 24 February 2018).
58. Annie I. Cameron (ed.) 'James VI, March 1594', *Calendar of State Papers, Scotland: Volume 11, 1593–1595* (Edinburgh: 1936), pp. 280–303; *British History Online*, <http://www.british-history.ac.uk/cal-state-papers/scotland/vol11/pp280-303> (last accessed 24 February 2018).
59. I. B., *The Copy of a Letter, Lately Written by a Spanishe Gentleman, to His Freind in England: In Refutation of Sundry Calumnies, There Falsly Bruited, and Spred emonge the People* (Antwerp: Ioachim Trognaesius, 1589), pp. 5–6.
60. I. B., pp. 5–6.
61. I. B., pp. 5–6.
62. Misha Teramura, 'Richard Topcliffe's Informant: New Light on *The Isle of Dogs*', *Review of English Studies*, Vol. 68 (2017), pp. 44–59, at pp. 46–7.
63. Annie I. Cameron (ed.), 'James VI, May 1593', *Calendar of State Papers, Scotland: Volume 11, 1593–1595* (Edinburgh: 1936), pp. 85–95; *British History Online*, <http://www.british-history.ac.uk/cal-state-papers/scotland/vol11/pp85-95> (last accessed 24 February 2018).
64. G. Dyfnallt Owen (ed.), 'Cecil Papers: December 1610', *Calendar of the Cecil Papers in Hatfield House: Volume 21, 1609–1612* (London: Her Majesty's Stationery Office, 1970), pp. 262–72, *British History Online*, <http://www.british-history.ac.uk/cal-cecil-papers/vol21/pp262-272> (last accessed 26 February 2018).
65. Dyfnallt Owen (ed.), pp. 262–72.
66. Dyfnallt Owen (ed.), pp. 262–72.
67. Dyfnallt Owen (ed.), pp. 262–72.
68. Dyfnallt Owen (ed.), pp. 262–72.

69. Dyfnallt Owen (ed.), pp. 262–72.
70. Dyfnallt Owen (ed.), pp. 262–72.
71. Dyfnallt Owen (ed.), pp. 262–72.
72. *House of Commons Journal*, Volume 1: 28 April 1621 (London: His Majesty's Stationery Office, 1802), p. 596; *British History Online*, <http://www.british-history.ac.uk/commons-jrnl/vol1/pp596> (last accessed 26 February 2018).
73. *House of Commons Journal*, Volume 1: 17 February 1621 (London: His Majesty's Stationery Office, 1802), pp. 525–6; *British History Online*, <http://www.british-history.ac.uk/commons-jrnl/vol1/pp525-526> (last accessed 26 February 2018).
74. *House of Commons Journal*, Volume 1: 17 February 1621, pp. 525–6.
75. *House of Commons Journal*, Volume 1: 17 February 1621, pp. 525–6.
76. Sophie Crawford Lomas (ed.), 'Elizabeth: April 1586, 6–10', *Calendar of State Papers Foreign: Elizabeth, Volume 20, September 1585–May 1586* (London: His Majesty's Stationery Office, 1921), pp. 523–40; *British History Online*, http://www.british-history.ac.uk/cal-state-papers/foreign/vol20/pp523-540.
77. *House of Commons Journal*, Volume 1: 16 March 1621 (London, 1802), p. 557; *British History Online*, <http://www.british-history.ac.uk/commons-jrnl/vol1/pp556-560> (last accessed 24 August 2017).
78. Arthur John Butler (ed.), 'Elizabeth: December 1580, 11–20', *Calendar of State Papers Foreign: Elizabeth, Volume 14, 1579–1580* (London: His Majesty's Stationery Office, 1904), pp. 508–20; *British History Online*, <http://www.british-history.ac.uk/cal-state-papers/foreign/vol14/pp508-520> (last accessed 21 February 2018).
79. Arthur John Butler (ed.), 'Elizabeth: December 1580, 11–20', pp. 508–20.
80. Nicholl, p. 135.
81. Anon., 'The Informers answer', p. 4.
82. John Bakeless, *The Tragicall History of Christopher Marlowe* (Cambridge, MA: Harvard University Press, 1942), p. 160.
83. See Ben Jonson, *Poetaster*, ed. Tom Cain (Manchester: Manchester University Press, 1995) (Ind. 23–6).
84. Faithful Teate, *The uncharitable informer charitably informed, that sycophancy is a sin, pernicious to all, but most of all to himself* (Dublin: William Bladen, 1660), p. 52, <http://gateway.proquest.com/openurl?ctx_ver=Z39.88-2003&res_id=xri:eebo&rft_id=xri:eebo:citation:99868810> (last accessed 4 January 2018). Hutson describes plays making 'greater use, in particular, of narration to convey (often misleading) accounts of unstaged events'; see Lorna Hutson, *The Invention of Suspicion* (Oxford: Oxford University Press, 2007), p. 106.
85. 'Promoter' is a synonym for 'informer'; Ben Jonson, *Poetaster*, p. 14.

86. R. A. Roberts (ed.), 'Cecil Papers: January 1602, 16–31', *Calendar of the Cecil Papers in Hatfield House: Volume 12, 1602–1603* (London: His Majesty's Stationery Office, 1910), pp. 22–43; *British History Online*, <http://www.british-history.ac.uk/cal-cecil-papers/vol12/pp22-43> (last accessed 30 January 2018).
87. R. A. Roberts (ed.), 'Cecil Papers: January 1602, 16–31', pp. 22–43.
88. Joseph Chitty, William Newland Welsby and Edward Beavan, *Chitty's Collection of Statutes: With Notes Thereon Intended as a Circuit and Court Companion*, Volume 1 (London: S. Sweet, 1854), p. 475.
89. Chitty, Welsby and Beavan, pp. 476–7.
90. Chitty, Welsby and Beavan, p. 476.
91. Chettle, *Kind-harts Dreame*, p. 44.
92. Anon., *The life and death of Griffin Flood informer*, pp. 2–3.
93. Chitty, Welsby and Beavan, p. 476.
94. Chitty, Welsby and Beavan, p. 477.
95. Chitty, Welsby and Beavan, p. 478.
96. Chitty, Welsby and Beavan, p. 478.
97. Chitty, Welsby and Beavan, p. 478.
98. Chitty, Welsby and Beavan, p. 479.
99. Chitty, Welsby and Beavan, p. 479.
100. Robert Greene, *A quip for an vpstart courtier* (London: Iohn Wolfe, 1592), <http://gateway.proquest.com/openurl?ctx_ver=Z39.88-2003&res_id=xri:eebo&rft_id=xri:eebo:citation:99841591> (last accessed 21 February 2018).
101. *House of Commons Journal*, Volume 1: 8 February 1621 (London: His Majesty's Stationery Office, 1802), pp. 513–14; *British History Online*, <http://www.british-history.ac.uk/commons-jrnl/vol1/pp513-514> (last accessed 21 February 2018).
102. Nicholl, p. 125. Banu also points this out: 'la surveillance, chacun le sait, n'est pas gratuite . . . elle implique des retombées financières': 'surveillance, as everyone knows, is not free . . . it involves financial benefits', p. 55 (my translation).
103. R. A. Roberts (ed.), 'Cecil Papers: March 1599, 16–31', *Calendar of the Cecil Papers in Hatfield House: Volume 9, 1599* (London: His Majesty's Stationery Office, 1902), pp. 107–26; *British History Online*, <http://www.british-history.ac.uk/cal-cecil-papers/vol9/pp107-126> (last accessed 21 February 2018).
104. Nicholl, pp. 47–50.
105. *House of Commons Journal*, Volume 1: 8 February 1621 (London: His Majesty's Stationery Office, 1802), pp. 513–14; *British History Online*, <http://www.british-history.ac.uk/commons-jrnl/vol1/pp513-514> (last accessed 21 February 2018).

106. Jane Humphries and Jacob Weisdorf, 'The Wages of Women in England, 1260–1850', <https://www.economics.ox.ac.uk/materials/papers/13260/jhreplacement.pdf> p. 8 (last accessed 21 February 2018).
107. This was known as a *qui tam* action. See Maurice W. Beresford, 'The Common Informer, the Penal Statutes and Economic Regulation', *Economic History Review*, Vol. X (1958), pp. 221–38, at p. 225.
108. *House of Commons Journal*, Volume 1: 21 November 1606 (1802); *British History Online*, p. 170, <http://www.british-history.ac.uk> (last accessed 3 January 2018).
109. John Bakeless, *The Tragicall History of Christopher Marlowe* (Cambridge, MA: Harvard University Press, 1942), p. 160.
110. Janet Clare, *'Art made tongue-tied by authority': Elizabethan and Jacobean Dramatic Censorship* (Manchester: Manchester University Press, 1999), p. 33.
111. W. R. Streitberger, *The Masters of the Revels and Elizabeth I's Court Theatre* (Oxford: Oxford University Press, 2016), p. 223.
112. See Jonathan Dollimore, *Radical Tragedy: Religion, Ideology and Power in the Drama of Shakespeare and His Contemporaries* (Brighton: Harvester Press, 1984), p. 24.
113. Richard Dutton, *Mastering the Revels* (Basingstoke: Macmillan, 1991), pp. 8, 126.
114. William Cobbett, Thomas Bayly Howell, Thomas J. Howell and William Jardine, *Cobbett's Complete Collection of State Trials and Proceedings for High Treason and Other Crimes and Misdemeanors from the Earliest Period to the Present Time*, Volume 8 (London: R. Bagshaw, 1810), p. 113.
115. Cobbett, Howell, Howell and Jardine, p. 113.
116. Cobbett, Howell, Howell and Jardine, p. 114.
117. Cobbett, Howell, Howell and Jardine, p. 114.
118. Cobbett, Howell, Howell and Jardine, p. 114.
119. Cobbett, Howell, Howell and Jardine, p. 114.
120. Dutton, p. 59.
121. Ian Donaldson, *Ben Jonson, A Life* (Oxford: Oxford University Press, 2011), pp. 111–12, 114, 146. This intelligencer was likely to have been the highly disreputable William Udall: see Teramura, pp. 44–59.
122. Dutton, pp. 119–22; Streitberger, p. 230.
123. George Chapman, *The Conspiracy and Tragedy of Byron*, ed. John Margeson (Manchester: Manchester University Press, 1988), p. 25.
124. Dutton, pp. 193, 186.
125. See Ethyn Williams Kirby, *William Prynne: A Study in Puritanism* (Cambridge, MA: Harvard University Press, 1931).

126. John Webster and William Rowley *A Cure for a Cuckold* (London: Thomas Johnson, 1661), <http://gateway.proquest.com.ezproxy.massey.ac.nz/openurl?ctx_ver=Z39.88-2003&res_id=xri:eebo&rft_id=xri:eebo:image:180072:19> (last accessed 25 February 2018).

127. Anon., *The life and death of Griffin Flood informer Whose cunning courses, churlish manners, and troublesome informations, molested a number of plaine dealing people in this city of London. Wherein is also declared the murther of Iohn Chipperford Vinter, for twich fact the said Griffin Flood was pressed to death the 18. day of Ianuary last past* (London: [G. Eld] for I. T., 1623), <http://gateway.proquest.com/openurl?ctx_ver=Z39.88-2003&res_id=xri:eebo&rft_id=xri:eebo:image:17716:10> (last accessed 16 February 2018).

128. Edward Ward, 'A walk to Islington with a description of New-Tunbridge-Wells and Sadler's musick-house' (London: 1699), pp. 15–16, <https://quod.lib.umich.edu/e/eebo/A67529.0001.001?rgn=main;view=fulltext> (last accessed 16 February 2018).

129. John Day, *Isle of Guls* (London: Iohn Hodgets, 1606), n.p., <http://gateway.proquest.com/openurl?ctx_ver=Z39.88-2003&res_id=xri:eebo&rft_id=xri:eebo:citation:99840846> (last accessed 2 February 2018).

130. Catherine Keane describes the satirist Horace wishing to distance himself from 'informers who stalk Rome with notebooks in hand, identifying potential victims'; Catherine Keane, *Figuring Genre in Roman Satire* (Oxford: Oxford University Press, 2006), p. 79.

131. Chettle, *Kind-harts Dreame*, p. 32.

132. Chettle, *Kind-harts Dreame*, p. 32

133. T. G., pp. 116–17.

134. Chettle, *Kind-harts Dreame*, p. 34.

135. Thomas Dekker, *The Bellman of London* (1608), in A. V. Judges (ed.), *The Elizabethan Underworld* (London: Routledge & Kegan Paul, 1965), pp. 303–4.

136. Dekker, *The Bellman of London*, p. 304.

137. Dekker, *The Bellman of London*, p. 306.

138. Dekker, *The Bellman of London*, p. 307.

139. Dekker, *The Bellman of London*, p. 307.

140. See Jonson, *Poetaster* (4.7.9–10) and Angus, pp. 115–35.

141. Lorna Hutson, 'Civility and Virility in Ben Jonson', *Representations*, Vol. 78, No. 1 (Spring 2002), pp. 1–27, at p. 14.

142. Thomas Nabbs, *Covent-Garden* (London: R. Oulton, 1639), <http://gateway.proquest.com/openurl?ctx_ver=Z39.88-2003&res_id=xri:eebo&rft_id=xri:eebo:citation:99848292> (last accessed 12 December 2017).

143. Dekker, *Lantern and Candlelight*, pp. 347, 365.
144. See Angus, esp. pp. 1–40.
145. See Nicholl, pp. 111, 121ff. See also John Michael Archer, *Sovereignty and Intelligence: Spying and Court Culture in the English Renaissance* (Stanford, CA: Stanford University Press, 1993), pp. 69, 92ff.; Helen Ostovich (ed.), *Ben Jonson, Four Comedies* (London: Longman, 1997), p. 12; Archer, p. 26; David Riggs, *The World of Christopher Marlowe* (London: Faber & Faber, 2004), p. 155; R. Warwick Bond, *The Complete Works of John Lyly*, Vol. 1 (Oxford: Clarendon Press, 1902), p. 14; Daphne Du Maurier, *Golden Lads: A Study of Anthony Bacon, Francis and Their Friends* (London: Gollancz, 1975), pp. 60, 64, 71, 97–8.
146. Nicholl, pp. 376–80, 82.
147. I treat the structures, forms and implications of metadrama in some detail in Angus, esp. pp. 24–31.
148. François Laroque, *The Show Within: Dramatic and Other Insets* (Montpellier: Publications de l'Université Paul-Valery, 1990), p. 42.
149. As in instances above also, 'oversight' here means 'seeing from a privileged position' with resonances of supervision, not its other sense of missing something.
150. As with Middleton and Dekker, *The Roaring Girl* (1.2.14–30ff.).
151. See Alan Sheridan, 'Translator's Note', in Jacques Lacan, *Écrits: A Selection* (New York: Norton 1977), p. xi. Lacan himself aligned it with *scotoma* (a blind spot) in his description of the *mirror stage*. See 'The mirror stage as formative of the function of the I', in Lacan, *Écrits*, pp. 93–100.
152. See William Nelles, *Frameworks: Narrative Levels and Embedded Narrative* (New York: Lang, 1997), p. 155.
153. Jacques Derrida uses this term to describe voyeurism, a concept related to the mechanisms here described; see Jacques Derrida, *Memoirs of the Blind: The Self-Portrait and Other Ruins*, trans. Pascale-Anne Brault and Michael Naas (Chicago: University of Chicago Press, 1993), p. 68.
154. Jacques Lacan, *The Seminar, Book XI, The Four Fundamental Concepts of Psychoanalysis*, trans. Alan Sheridan (New York: Norton, 1981), pp. 72–3ff.
155. Sight itself is not fundamental to this theory since the mechanism works with merely 'a rustling of branches or the sound of a footstep followed by silence, or the slight opening of a shutter, or a light movement of a curtain'; Jean-Paul Sartre, *Being and Nothingness: An Essay on Phenomenological Ontology*, trans. Hazel E. Barnes (London: Methuen, 1958), pp. 256–7; Bruce R. Smith describes early modern

theatre as an 'auditory field'; an audience's engagement with a play is formed in the imagination, and thus the Sartrean 'look' includes this 'auditory field' which bears an imaginary relation also to metadramatic and diegetic structures; see Bruce R. Smith, *The Acoustic World of Early Modern England: Attending to the O-Factor* (Chicago: University of Chicago Press, 1999).

156. Dylan Evans, *Dictionary of Lacanian Psychoanalysis* (Hove and New York: Brunner-Routledge, 2003), p. 72.

Chapter 1

'Subtle sleights': Amity and the Informer in *Damon and Pithias*

> What subtle sleights are wrought by painted tales' device . . .
> Trust words as skillful falconers do trust hawks that never flew
> Richard Edwards, 'Fair words make fools fain'[1]

Richard Edwards's *Damon and Pithias*, first performed in 1564 and published in 1571, is an early example of a play that registers the increasing awareness of the ubiquity of the intelligencer in its metadramatic devices. As an instance of how the early modern theatre responds to the shifting paradigms of power, the play offers a typology of the kinds of illegitimate oversight associated with the informers and intelligencers of the day. It also suggests its own solution to this perceived abuse of authority, in the form of classical Ciceronian amity, a subject close to the heart of the Erasmian programme of humanist education in the grammar schools of the day. 'Amity' is defined by Cicero in *De Amicitia* as 'an accord in all things, human and divine' and is a quality than which, the author claims, 'with the exception of wisdom, no better thing has been given to man by the immortal gods'.[2] Thomas Elyot's enormously influential educational treatise *The Governour* (1531) devotes three whole chapters to the concept of amity, set in the context of the manual of training for statesmen.[3] Joseph Hall's *Characters of Virtues and Vices* (1608) attests to the persistence of this ideal throughout the period, referring to the friend's willingness to 'lift up his friend to advancement, with a willing hand, without envie, without dissimulation'.[4] The faithful friend's 'charitie' in Hall's description serves to 'cloake noted infirmities, not by untruth, not by flattery, but by discreet secrecie'.[5] In relation to each of these descriptions, the friend serves as the diametric opposite of the popularly understood figure of the intelligencer, who is typically characterised by anything but the constancy and unswerving faithfulness we see here. It is easy to understand why this plain affirmation of the 'virtue associated with mutual trust and friendship', as Quentin Skinner terms it, should be offered as an antidote to the vicious scheming and promotion of self-interest which was felt to be tainting contemporary social relations in the latter half of the sixteenth century.[6]

Regarding the evident proliferation of metadrama from this time onwards, it may not be entirely coincidental that 1564, the year of the play's first performance, also witnessed the expansion of the Privy Council's policy of arresting and imprisoning people for recusancy, and was thus a significant year in terms of the work of Francis Walsingham's network of intelligencers.[7] Robert Cecil, the inheritor of Walsingham's and William Cecil's system, wrote of the extensive and 'diverse' nature of the informers bequeathed to him 'that doe as occasione serves', as he says, responding to circumstances as necessary, and 'as a due to my place, advise mee of occurrents.'[8] But the royal spymasters did not have a monopoly on the use of intelligencers; rather, any person of influence might be able to arrange a flow of information from servants and inferiors acting as informers and intelligencers in return for considerations of one kind or another. These reflections pervade the atmosphere of Edwards's fictional Syracusa, as the play's protagonists find to their cost.

The frequency with which characters move to the wings, or hide behind curtains or partitions, standing aside to collect useful information that might be passed on and thus offering the offstage audience an alternative perspective, is remarkable in the drama of this era. One might only need pause to consider the effect of a character like Carisophus on this play, or Sejanus, Iago, Rosencrantz and Guildenstern, or Bosola on theirs, to appreciate what dramatic force can be exerted by an onstage intelligencer in search of incriminating evidence. The plots of many early modern plays are driven by such onstage plotting of characters who are either facilitated by intelligencing or are intelligencers themselves. The perception of the intelligencer thus may be said to permeate the conditions of early modern dramatic production and moreover to haunt the vagaries of its reception. The metadrama that arises from this, with its various modes of self-reference and its structures of oversight and overhearing involving role play about role play, plays within plays or audiences watching audiences, mirrors the eavesdropping and hidden oversight that constitute this insidious societal malady. In this intimidating political milieu, it is quite possible that a play might be misinterpreted as seditious and, whether the misprision is deliberate or not, that this might result in 'death, mutilation or prolonged imprisonment' for the unhappy author of the drama, as we have seen.[9] These concerns are most clearly reflected where early modern theatre reflects upon its own dramatic register and it is in the 'subtle sleights' to which Edwards refers, facilitated by the 'painted tales' devices' of the era's metadrama, that these fears are embodied and contained. These devices are often designed to manipulate the parameters of audiences' perspectives, interpretations and responses in defensive gestures which serve to suggest their own necessity. The central issue in all of this is the contested status of authority as a whole in a system reliant upon the unreliable, deceitful or even treacherous assertions of a widely reviled class of interpreter. Alongside discourse around the legitimacy of theatre, this informs the post-Reformation debate around the crisis of authority itself.[10]

The fear of the insidious figure of the intelligencer as a malevolent construer of words is at play then in the general social discourse of the era. Hutson identifies the contemporary conscious sense of menace around merely informal chat with what she calls its 'interpretative openness and liability to circulate maliciously, as malevolently construed evidence against the speaker.'[11] It was no wonder that 'all men behold [the informer] with indignation', as Francis Lenton said.[12] The casual pervasiveness of these figures might be exemplified by Daniel Tuvill's *The Dove and the Serpent* (1614) which sarcastically recommends to potential intelligencers that the 'procuring of better information' might be achieved by hanging around in taverns until people's tongues are loosened by alcohol.[13] This is obviously a very familiar case, and an informer appears in a public house to the great consternation of the inhabitants and guests in Thomas Nabbs's *Covent-Garden* (1638).[14] The Irish informer James Patricke, who, William Cecil writes, 'hath money of me without agreement', gathered his information by loitering every day by the Thames, 'at the privye keies at the water syde to see passengers that lande.'[15] Such commodification of the normal relations of patronage not only adds potential suspicion to any observing or lingering person, but also effectively puts a price on any incriminating interpretation that might occur to the viewer or listener in any context, including that of a dramatic transaction. The dread and loathing of informers being all but universal, such negative constructions are pervasive in the era and the serious possible consequences involved mean that it is small wonder that these predatory and insidious characters figure in the preoccupations of many early modern writers and dramatists.

Critical readings of *Damon and Pithias* have typically focused on the traditions of humanist drama offered in celebration of the classical ideals of friendship outlined above, an approach Laurie Shannon has developed significantly.[16] G. K. Hunter refers to *Damon and Pithias* in generic terms as 'a play about friendship, tyranny and flattery'.[17] In this vein, Robert Stretter identifies the continuation of this tradition throughout the period, noting that 'the Admiral's Men ... in 1594 performed a play entitled *Palamon and Arset* and obtained rights from Henry Chettle to a *Damon and Pythias*.'[18] J. E. Kramer takes a slightly different tack and argues that the play presents what he suggests is 'an early critical defense of poetry (in the dramatic mode)'.[19] Kramer places it in the lineage of plays like *A Midsummer Night's Dream*, *Hamlet*, *The Knight of the Burning Pestle* and *The Roman Actor*, which he rightly argues 'investigate the relation of drama to society', adding that the play's self consciousness is also about 'the power of art to combat ... abuses and to transform the society in which they are allowed to flourish.'[20] In this regard, however, one might pause to consider the undermining paradox of a defence of the stage delivered from the stage itself. I would agree with the suggestion that questions of ideal friendship are rooted in practical concerns and questions over legitimate social authority, but rather than seeing theatrical self-consciousness of metadrama as simply a defence of theatre, as Kramer does, I would suggest that it in fact registers the nature of these 'abuses' in its own dramatic bones, so to speak. It succeeds in reflecting its own disturbing conditions of production while challenging these social conditions with its assertion of the impossible ideal of an equalising friendship.

Its origin as a production within the auspices of the Chapel Royal places the play within a context which takes for granted the underlying structures of power the play's metadrama delineates. Richard Dutton notes the 'extremely close relationship' which pertained between the Children of the Chapel and the Court, and one can assume that in this context very little subversion was either intended or felt.[21] But its performance at Lincoln's Inn suggests a different potential context and an alternative audience perspective. The Inns of Court at this time were to some extent understood as the 'suburbs of the court itself', as J. R. Dasent called them, and were regarded as 'seminaries and nurseries wherein the gentry of the kingdome and such as serve his majesty in the common wealth are bredd and traÿned upp'.[22] However, there was a clearly seditious element to these institutions too and they often paralleled the theatres themselves in their potential for unrest and subversion.[23] Significantly for the purpose of this argument it is evident that they were also a hotbed of informers. Since the Inns were perceived to be breeding grounds for sedition, the Elizabethan regime was particularly determined to enforce social compliance among their lawyers (such as largely comprised the audience for *Damon and Pithias* at some performances) and schoolmasters (such as Edwards). Further testament to the subversive undercurrents of the Inns of Court at this time is that the Elizabethan government wanted to restrict their growth, due in part to 'Catholic proselytising among the junior members'.[24] And the members themselves were not the only problem. According to W. R. Prest, a contemporary reported that the Inns of Court 'always harbored a large and shadowy population of non-members; domestic staff, personal servants, lawyer's clerks, seminary priests, bankrupts and debtors, which make here their subterfuges from arrests'.[25] Coupled with the relative ease of access to the authorities and the potential financial rewards involved, these conditions are likely to produce as ripe a crowd of potential informers as any other early modern institution. Indeed Prest notes that the bulk of the extant evidence about Catholics around the Inns of Court in the late sixteenth century comes directly from the reports of informers.[26] As a noted insider in Mary Tudor's Catholic court, Edwards himself may well have been familiar with the experience of being observed in such a way.[27] In this case, the early modern friendship doctrines modelled in *Damon and Pithias*, presenting what Laurie Shannon calls 'a vision of . . . a virtually civic parity', form an ideal which these social climbers and ambitious politicians must have found both challenging and highly appealing.[28]

To summarise the primary plotline: when Damon and Pithias, two idealistically true friends in the Ciceronian model, travel as tourists to Syracusa, a scheming informer to the local tyrant Dionysius falsely interprets Damon's innocent sightseeing as intelligencing on the defences of the town and reports this to the authorities. With his good friend sentenced to death for espionage, Pithias offers his own person to act as security until Damon returns from home, having been given leave to settle his affairs before his death sentence is carried out. Since his friend's return is unavoidably delayed beyond the allotted time, Pithias consents to die in his place, and in the confusion of Damon's timely re-entrance, each one begs to be allowed to die instead of his friend. Witnessing this astonishing display of amity Dionysius undergoes a sudden metamorphosis from tyrant to friendly and tolerant ruler.

In a play which deals with a society suffering an interpretative malaise, it is significant that the play's Prologue aims to preclude and dispense with certain types of interpretation. Despite it operating within the usual apologetic mode, its very conventionality should not blind us to the textual detail of the appeal itself. Initially in this case, the Prologue addresses the audience in terms of their expectations of the drama, which, apparently, they must expect to be frustrated:

> On every side, wheras I glance my roving eye,
> Silence in all ears bent I plainly do espy:
> But if your eager looks do long such toys to see,
> As heretofore in comical wise were wont abroad to be:
> Your lust is lost, and all the pleasures that you sought,
> Is frustrate quite of toying plays.
>
> (Prol. 1–6)[29]

They are informed further that 'our author's muse, that masked in delight, / Hath forc'd his pen against his kind no more such sports to write' (Prol. 7–8) and that the reason for this is 'for that to some he seemed too much in young desires to range', adding 'in which, right glad to please: seeing that he did offend, / Of all he humbly pardon craves: his pen that shall amend' (Prol. 11–12). This writing therefore seems to be predicated upon the declaration and disclaiming of a previous dramatic transaction in which the author has overstepped his authorial authority. In this, even within the parameters of the licence sanctioned by the genre of comedy, it seems that he has unadvisedly allowed his 'young desires to range'.[30] This Prologue very much speaks to confirm, as Dutton notes, that Edwards was 'well aware of the danger that his plays would be ransacked for "applications"'. Dutton muses, 'had there been comment at court . . . Or was Edwards simply worried that what might be unexceptionable to an educated audience could be misconstrued elsewhere?'[31] Either way the Prologue invites the audience to react to this play at least partly as a corrective to a previous textual misdemeanour. It is clear also that the audience are to think of themselves to some extent as complicit in this transgression, since the Prologue also makes it plain that they 'do long such toys to see' (Prol. 3). The implication here is that the audience have been culpable participants in an illegitimate transaction of some kind, and that they have at least a potential appetite for more.

As the argument of the apology develops, however, Edwards begins to place a hierarchical structure of dramatic authority on this complicity, addressing his 'worshipfull Audience' and declaring

> thus much I dare avouch,
> In comedies the greatest skill is this, rightly to touch
> All things to the quick: and eke to frame each person so,
> That by his common talk you may his nature rightly know.
> (Prol. 13–16)

The author here asserts the legitimacy of the mimetic properties of his medium, and, in claiming the ability 'rightly to touch / All things to the quick', establishes, by this authoritative distancing from his subject, his own discursive and satiric power. Only then does he go on to make it clear that anyone who questions the legitimacy of this aspect of the generative process is disagreeing with the ancient authorities (the Chaucerian 'auctoritees'[32]) by proclaiming that 'if this offend the lookers on, let Horace then be blamed, / Which hath our author taught at school, from whom he doth not swerve' (Prol. 24–5). As a classical satirist of the humanist canon, Horace is widely respected at this time, among other things, for his criticism of sedition.[33] Positioning himself thus firmly in the established tradition of Horace and others, he writes defensively, 'thus much for his defence (he saith), as poets erst have done, / Which heretofore in comedies the self-same race did run' (Prol. 27–8). In this reference, Edwards follows the practice of earlier authors in English who, as Andrew Galloway notes, display a general predilection 'to cite ancient and patristic *auctores* to authorise their writing'.[34] However, what distinguishes this prologue from such conventions is its deployment of the ancient authority not simply to authorise itself by invoking a revered predecessor, but rather to designate the precedent to be referred to in the event of a denunciation.

This may be explored in a closer look at Edwards's usages of the word *author*. In the first usage, 'our author's muse, that masked in delight' (Prol.7), where his muse 'hath forc'd his pen against his kind, no more such sports to write' (Prol. 8) in an act of apparently forced conformity to moral consensus, the designation of the writer is plainly single, as line 8 indicates. In the second, which asserts 'if this offend the lookers on, let Horace then be blamed, / . . . from whom he doth not swerve' (Prol. 24–5), he recruits Horace as *auctor* in order to defend himself against potential accusations of offence, and it remains singular.[35] In the third usage, however, 'the time, the place, the authors here most plainly shall it find' (Prol. 42), where it becomes necessary to assert that 'talking of courtly toys – we do protest this flat! – / We talk of Dionysius' Court, we mean no court but that' (Prol. 39–40), the origin of the pronoun is suddenly pluralised in what seems to be an implicitly defensive move. The Prologue here performs the conventional dispersal of the responsibility for the creation of the piece but also declares specifically that this is spoken 'for our defence, lest of others we should be shent' (Prol. 43) and begs that the 'worthy audience . . . take things as they be meant' (Prol. 44). The possibly unconscious shift to the plural pronoun reinforces the sense that the author is on the defensive here. On the whole, this prologue seems to be concerned not merely to argue that Edwards's writing is legitimated by the ancient *auctoritees*, or that it is simply a declaration of submission to the conventions of form, but it seems further to posit an appropriation of the authoritative status of 'Horace' as a defence against an empowered and critical audience. This complicates the notion of a simple focus for earlier 'pre-commercial' Tudor drama, playing merely to please patrons and factions; the author's preoccupation here, rather, reveals the necessity of self-preservation in what must be to some extent a potentially volatile interpretative environment. It is my contention that these concerns are borne out through the rest of the play.

In *Damon and Pithias*, three sites of authority are at variance: that of the author, that, most pertinently, of the audience and that pertaining to the court. These are all both dramatic representations of authority and real sites of authority, and in this the boundaries of the real and the depiction of the real are sometimes fluid. The actors in performance form the node of intersection between these discourses and boundaries and consequently in this exposed position often bear the brunt of adverse reaction to a play.[36] A conventional hierarchical sequence for the control and regulation of discourse might entail the authority of the court operating through the office of the Master of the Revels, and any potential informers on the author, actor and audience in turn. The concern of the Prologue here has been that the sequence has become disrupted, with the authority of the audience also somehow having become a force that is operating upon the author and actors. The author's appropriation of *auctorial* legitimacy as a defensive weapon against this is evidence of a perception that the audience might misinterpret the message of the play and hence misrepresent it to the courtly authorities. The Prologue's metadramatic acknowledgement of the audience's complicity in the process of meaning-making (over what is plainly 'meant') is significant here because it both connects this empowered role with interpretative agency and marks them out as potential informers. This implicit acknowledgement of the discursive power of the audience is an indication of anxiety around the negotiable nature of legitimate perspectives and sets the scene in this play for some revealing metadramatic transactions.

Throughout the play, the dramatic narrative and the structures it sets up offer its offstage audience a number of ways of perceiving itself. These are desirable or undesirable in varying degrees, and the play goes on to suggest by the end an ideal interpretative position, as seen of course from the author's point of view. The first of these ways is to be found modelled in Damon's statement upon arriving in Syracusa as a tourist to view the town and its people:

> Pythagoras said, that this world was like a stage,
> Whereon many play their parts: the lookers on, the sage
> Philosophers are, saith he, whose part is to learn
> The manners of all nations, and the good from the bad to discern
> (346–9)

Within the milieu of the *theatrum mundi*, the audience, or 'lookers on', are initially characterised in this case as 'sage philosophers' whose job is primarily to 'learn'. This interpellation dignifies them as another respectable body, which though wise is essentially passive. However, this also alludes strongly to the overall metadramatic environment of the play in which the audience will be invited to identify with (at least) one of four approaches to authority, as instanced by either Aristippus (the social climber), Diogenes (the philosopher), Carisophus (the informer), or Damon and Pithias (the exemplary friends), in order that they might be able 'the good from the bad to discern'.

Aristippus, the play's 'pleasant gentleman', discussing the nature of his own character, describes himself as a philosopher and asks appealingly that, if 'lovers of wisdom are termed philosophy – / Then who is a philosopher so rightly as I?' (7–8). His humorous form of 'philosophy', however, is not by any means a reasoned asceticism; rather it aims at material preferment through flattery. This is an accusation much levelled at informers and intelligencers, who are perceived to be like obsequious dogs bending to the will of their masters. And in fact Aristippus reveals as much as he comments on the many differences between himself and the true philosopher Diogenes:

> Some philosophers in the street go ragged and torn,
> And feed on vile roots, whom boys laugh to scorn:
> But I in fine silks haunt Dionysius' palace . . .
> And I profess now the courtly philosophy,
> To crouch, to speak fair, myself I apply
> To feed the king's humour with pleasant devices,
> For which I am called *Regius canis*:
> But wot ye who named me first the king's dog?
> It was the rogue Diogenes, that vile grunting hog.
> Let him roll in his tub, to win a vain praise:
> In the court pleasantly I will spend all my days.
>
> (13–15, 19–26)[37]

Here, Aristippus is offering the audience either of two unattractive philosophical options or viewpoints. The first is that of 'courtly philosophy', which, as he says, implies to 'crouch, to speak fair [and] / To feed the king's humour with pleasant devices', in short to become, as he aims to be, 'the king's dog', and here the term 'philosophy' is applied with much irony. The second is that of Diogenes the Cynic, whom he says 'boys laugh to scorn' and who lives in a tub merely 'to win . . . vain praise'. This is a choice between two dog-like positions the second of which is also reminiscent of the self-pleasing 'hog', each of them disgustingly bestial in its own way.[38] Aristippus clearly expects that his own position is the preferred option, but the fact that such dog-like fawning as he describes is one of the common accusations levelled at sycophantic intelligencers suggests that even his form of relatively mild courtly ambition is tainted by association with corrupt forms of empowerment.

The play's explicit informer Carisophus, meanwhile, offers another approach to authority in happily admitting that 'there was never rumour, / Spread in this town of any small thing, but I / Brought it to the king in post by and by' (62–4). The reference here to 'any small thing' is calculated to cause annoyance and raise the hackles of the original audience who might themselves have been subjected to such petty sniping. Aristippus' description of Carisophus may ring with hypocrisy when he calls him a 'flattering parasite, a sycophant also', but his mind is very much on the person of the intelligencer when he calls him out as 'a common accuser of men, to the good an open foe', and claims that 'of half a word he can make a legend of lies'; he makes explicit also the connection with theatre when he tells us that Carisophus 'will avouch' his lies with 'tragical cries' (105–8). As the more pleasant and appealing character, Aristippus of course wants to distinguish his own 'courtly philosophy' from that of the dangerous, conniving influence of Carisophus. His own philosophy may be merely the search for courtly preferment, and it may cause him to 'crouch' and 'speak fair' and use 'pleasant devices' in order to 'feed the king's humour', but it stops short of endangering the lives of others in the process. However, despite the reluctance of this middling figure to admit so, there is plenty of common ground between these two inveiglers seeking advancement in the court of the tyrant.

The two eponymous friends Damon and Pithias, however, model a comparatively desirable type of audience engagement in which discernment is unpolluted by self-promotion. Their perspective argues for a dramatic and political ideal: the possibility of pure disinterested observation, in contradistinction to the distorted representations offered by Aristippus, Diogenes and Carisophus. In the city of a tyrant, however, even pure observation is hazardous. When his master Damon is wandering around Syracusa innocently observing the town and its people, his servant Stephano pleads with him to be more attentive to the reflexive tenability of his viewpoint, advising him, 'I pray you, sir, for all your philosophy, / See that in this court you walk very wisely', going on to observe that 'many eyes are bent on you in the streets as ye go: / Many spies are abroad, you can not be too circumspect' (337–41). Damon replies to this with reckless self-confidence, saying:

> Stephano, because thou art careful of me, thy master, I do thee praise:
> Yet think this for a surety: no state to displease
> By talk or otherwise my friend and I intend: we will here
> As men that come to see the soil and manners of all men of
>   every degree.
>
> (342–5)

Despite what he and his friend might intend, with the 'many eyes' that are bent on them 'in the streets' Damon and Pithias are thus both observers and the observed. This metadramatic state of affairs mirrors the Sartrean reciprocal gaze implied by the Prologue's curious opening lines claiming that 'on every side, wheras I glance my roving eye, / Silence in all ears bent I plainly do espy' and supposing 'your eager looks do long such toys to see' (Prol. 1–3). Stephano is persistent in warning Damon and Pithias, however, that

> ... concerning the people they are not gay,
> And as far as I see, they be mummers; for nought they say,
> For the most part, whatsoever you ask them.
> The soil is such, that to live here I can not like.
>
> (350–3)

The townsfolk they are observing are silent like the audience described by the Prologue; as 'mummers', they are also actors, but most significantly they are spies and potential informers. Their silence could be read as an act of resistance to the mechanisms of surveillance which bind them, but the context suggests it is potentially menacing. Elizabeth's own motto was *video et taceo* – 'I see and keep quiet' – and this also contains an implicit threat. Damon and Pithias here simultaneously stand in the place of the offstage audience, watching the drama of the town and the crowd, and are themselves watched by the ominously soundless audience of the townsfolk.

Damon's response to this revelation is to assert his immunity as a mere observer whose subject-position, he would like to believe, affords him the luxury of being fully detached from the object of his gaze, claiming that 'a wise man may live everywhere' and foolishly continuing to suggest to his 'dear friend Pithias' that they should 'view this town in every place, / And then consider the people's manners also' (356–8). On one level, this is offered to the offstage audience as a kind of interpretative ideal, a pure and wise perspective which contrasts with the dangerous reciprocity of the gaze offered by the spying townsfolk, the 'many eyes . . . bent on you'; but on the other, and overall, it is an appeal for common sense to apply to the ways in which authority structures itself.

In an early modern theatre which offers a more significantly aural experience than later versions, this play's distinction between the silence of 'mere observation' and a conspiratorial whispering plays out in the metadramatic relationships of Damon and Pithias, the townsfolk of Siracusa and the offstage audience.[39] The Prologue confidently proclaims, and in a certain sense requires, of the audience that 'silence in all ears bent I plainly do espy' (Prol. 2); this is a silence required in order to facilitate the correct hearing of the Prologue's crucial message. The metadramatic form here works to delineate a particular response. Later in the play, after a lengthy aside, Aristippus warns the audience to be silent as the informer approaches: 'mumbudget, for Carisophus I espy, / In haste to come hither' (492–3). This is also a silence required in order to avoid misinterpretation. However, though they are themselves espied like actors, the metaphorical 'mummers' of Syracusa are neither wholly silent observers nor do they express themselves openly. Their whispering is neither open speech nor silence and, as Stephano perceives, seems menacingly to relate to himself and the other observing visitors:

> I like not this soil, for as I go plodding,
> I mark there two, there three, their heads always nodding,
> In close secret wise, still whispering together.
> If I ask any question, no man doth answer:
> But shaking their heads, they go their ways speaking.
>
> (246–50)

These metadramatic interrelations between points of observation and interpretation betray a number of concerns with regard to both dramatic production and reception. In the first instance the observed silence is being required of the offstage audience in order to facilitate correct interpretation of the author's meaning (delivered by the Prologue). In the second it is required in order to avoid misinterpretation, by the informer Carisophus, of their own imaginary conversation with Aristippus. The first of these requires passivity; the second, implicitly, activity. Each of these, however, reflects an audience model in which silence is the key to avoiding misinterpretation.

The silence of the 'mummers', however, in response to Stephano's questions entails a mistrust of even the ideal pure interpretative audience that Damon and Pithias, these strangers to Syracusa, model. This profound suspicion may be expedient under tyrannical authority, but, further, the townsfolk's whispering suggests disturbing possibilities of deliberate and venal misinterpretation. Both the silence and the whispering of the citizen-mummers, these spies which may be 'espied', are infused with that which typically augments the informer figure in a tyrannous state: fear of wild or unremittingly violent authority. In his later critique of the contemporary courts of justice, William Lambarde laments the purposes of what he calls the 'whisperious informer', whose voice is 'the very quintessence of abuse and corruption'.[40] Hence it seems that to give any answer at all to Stephano's questions would be to risk subjecting themselves to the same potentially vicious scrutiny with which they threaten Damon and Pithias. This is precisely the kind of contemporary wresting and false application that the Prologue wants to obviate in asserting that 'wherein talking of courtly toys, we do protest this flat, / We talk of Dionysius' court, we mean no court but that' (Prol. 39–40).

Voluntarily active within this tyrannical system of authority is the explicitly parasitic intelligencer Carisophus. In common with other audiences represented here, Carisophus is also a viewer-auditor of a kind, but he is one with specifically author-like powers. Aristippus' claim that 'of half a word, he can make a legend of lies, / Which he will avouch with such tragical cries, / As though all were true that comes out of his mouth' (107–9) resounds with an assertive authorship and a theatricality which he believes will serve his courtly ambitions. The power relations between Carisophus and whatever or whoever he is viewing are thus framed in suitably 'tragical' terms, and the contemporary sense of this implies that his interaction is not only theatrical but also voluble and unwelcome. But further than this, the implication of the claim that 'of half a word' he is able to make 'a legend of lies' suggests that he is fundamentally an augmenter or embellisher of the truth, and in sixteenth-century terms this identifies him as both informer and author. The play has more to say in this connection. Moreover, his operation of this profitable role as augmenter is fully dependent upon his position as a corrupt and explicitly predatory observer, as pirate-like he announces 'in hope of good wind, I hoise up my sail', and goes 'into the city to find some prey for mine avail' (367–8), admitting to his voracity in these matters, saying 'I hunger while I may see these strangers' (369) and confessing openly to the audience that 'for profit I will accuse any man, hap what shall' (374). He continues conspiratorially:

> But soft, sirs, I pray you hush: what are they that comes here?
> By their apparel and countenance some strangers they appear.
> I will shroud myself secretly, even here for a while,
> To hear all their talk, that I may them beguile.
>
> (375–8)

Thus, in the course of the narrative, Damon and Stephano are now overlooked by Carisophus, and he invites the offstage audience to collude in his vice-like malefactory perspective as he shrouds himself 'secretly' and enjoins them again to silence with 'soft, sirs, I pray you hush'. This effectively means that the offstage audience is watching (with) Carisophus, watching Damon and Stephano. Depending on the staging they all may be also watching the 'mummers' of the town whose silence is imposed by the authority for whom Carisophus is intelligencing. Here the audience are foregrounded as themselves, but the manner of the appeal implies a certain amount of common ground with the intelligencer, and thus with the tyrant his information benefits and upholds. This metadramatic mode operates via a shift in the perception of the authoritative viewpoint within the diegetic strata and provides a moment of synchronic reflection in which the interpretative freedom this allows the audience is initially tainted by the shared perspective of the informer. However, the effect of this type of metadrama is to draw the authoritative viewpoint of the audience inwards as they momentarily become co-audience with Carisophus of Damon and Pithias, and then co-audience with Damon and Pithias of the mummer-people of the city. The audience are drawn into sharing this subject-position via the subtle centripetal motion of its concentric metadrama – the effect of watching (with) someone watching (with) someone watching someone and so on produces a diegetic gravity which impels the view inwards through each successive framing device to the inmost centre of focus. In this way, the offstage audience are afforded a salutary ethical shift from the predatory position of Carisophus to that of Damon and Pithias, the pure observers. Reinforcing this movement, the prayer to the audience, 'worthy audience, we you pray, take things as they be meant, / Whose upright judgement we do crave with heedful ear and eye' (Prol. 44–5), becomes an implicit warning in the mouth of Carisophus the insidious watcher who deliberately intends 'to creep into men's bosoms, some talk for to snatch, / By which, into one trip or other, I might trimly them catch / And so accuse them' (160–2). What is 'meant' is of primary importance, and those under observation depend on 'upright judgement' to defend their vulnerability.

This warning against misinterpretation and augmentation is exemplified when Damon's innocent geographical comment that 'the seat is good, and yet not strong; and that is great pity' (412) is deliberately misperceived as an intelligencer's appraisal of the defensive capacities of the city. Carisophus has thus caught his prey, exclaiming with collusive satisfaction, 'I am safe, he is mine own' (415) and thus needs only to augment the information Damon has given him with meanings of a sinister character in order to profit from the transaction.[41] He hints strongly he will do this in the wording of his response to Damon's assertion that he likes to 'see the state of countries' (446): 'You do wisely to search the state of each country / To bear intelligence thereof, whither you lust' (449–50). This will turn out badly for Carisophus nevertheless, since his reputation as an informer already means that, as he says, 'not with one can I meet, / That will join in talk with me, I am shunn'd like a devil in the street, / My credit is crack'd where I am known' (162–4). Moreover, the purity of the two friends' amity causes even the corrupt court to reject him, as Aristippus exclaims 'to live in court not beloved, better be in hell: / What crying out, what cursing is there within of Carisophus, / Because he accused Damon to King Dionysius!' (1017–19). Shunned like an intelligencing devil and then better off in hell, Carisophus has become the accuser of the brethren, and although he is manifestly operating as the powerful vice-character of the piece, ultimately he is disenfranchised and bereft of his informing and authorial influence.

By these subtle metadramatic devices the audience is steered towards a particular interpretative position: that of disinterested, uncritical and impartial observer, a position which promises safety for all honest participants. This approach, centred on Damon and Pithias themselves, contrasts primarily with Carisophus' tenuous position in relation to authority, which is explicitly connected to his financial motivation and his voracious mendacity. The feebleness of Carisophus' connection to the authority for whom he ostensibly works is displayed in his abortive and painful attempt to steal Damon's property, to which as an informer he in fact has some entitlement in both Roman and English law.[42] Carisophus says that 'the king gave me the spoil: to take mine own wilt thou let me?' and when Stephano replies 'thine own villain! where is thine authority?', Carisophus responds, somewhat optimistically, 'I am authority of my self; dost thou not know?' (921–3). It is clear here how far Carisophus has fallen: from a position of power dependent upon his ability to provide a service of information to the tyrant, to a situation which necessitates such an empty boast as being the 'authority of my self'. In this the informer reaches further than the legitimate author and is thus exposed, in a salutary way, as not only illicit but also unprotected by his putative employers.

Such a disinterested and impartial interpretative position as Damon and Pithias offer also contrasts with that of Aristippus, who, despite his moderate character, is himself reliant upon the information of intelligencers for the maintenance of his position at court. At one point he instructs his servant Will, 'learn thou secretly what privily they talk / Of me in the court: among them slyly walk, / And bring me true news thereof' (268–70). Will replies: 'I will sir, master thereof have no doubt, for I / Where they talk of you, will inform you perfectly' (271–2). Aristippus' use of these tactics for purposes of personal empowerment is developed into a mocking of those who appeal the authority of *auctors*: 'the king's praise standeth chiefly in bountifulness: / Which thing though I told the king very pleasantly, / Yet can I prove it by good writers of great antiquity' (477–9), which may be somewhat self-deprecating on Edwards's part. Justifying Aristippus' sycophantic flattery in this way must draw attention to the moral emptiness of the gesture, even as it marks him out from Carisophus' self-authorisation.

With these intelligencing aspects as the background to the character, Aristippus, at a crucial point in the narrative, is overlooked by Pithias alone. At this point, Pithias suggests to the audience, 'let us slip aside his talk to hear' (652). The conventional metadramatic device of the aside, which usually acts as a vehicle for the disturbing empowerment of the watcher over the watched, is in this case made benign as Pithias discovers that Aristippus may be a potential ally in his quest to save Damon. Though the end justifies the means in this small instance, Pithias has set up a little scopic hierarchy in which the audience takes part. The subtle invitation of complicity which Pithias offers the audience here may be rendered harmless by its employment in a good cause, but this simply serves to normalise the structure further. Pithias subsequently pleads for Damon, asserting to Aristippus that 'nought hath he done worthy of death; but very fondly, / Being a stranger, he viewed this city: / For no evil practices, but to feed his eyes' (684–6). This plea in the familiar vernacular of appetite complicates somewhat the idea of a truly pure perspective. Nevertheless, this appeals to the voracious Aristippus and leads indirectly to Pithias making his substitutionary bargain with the King, allowing Damon to return to Greece to order his estate. This process begins with another metadramatic overlooking as Dionysius enters and Aristippus advises Pithias and Stephano that since the king is at hand, they must 'stand close in the prease. Beware, if he know / You are friend to Damon he will take you for a spy also' before he makes a quick getaway, bidding them, 'farewell, I dare not be seen with you' (715–17). Ultimately, through all of this, unadulterated observation (that is the disinterested perspective of the non-informer) is shown to have positive instrumental effects in terms of the diachronic action of the narrative. The audience are again drawn into sharing this relatively favourable subject-position and in the same motion they are drawn away from the subject-position of the despised intelligencer Carisophus, the demon of the piece.

Of note here is the tendency for the informer to function as an author in a text, something which, as mentioned, often causes authors themselves to be anxious to draw clear distinctions.[43] It is Stephano who makes explicit Carisophus' authoring of the tragic narrative by spinning his 'legend of lies' for financial reward; he refers to him as 'cursed Carisophus, that first moved this tragedy' (905). Though a prime mover, however, he is not in control of the narrative which issues from his scheme. It is Pithias' exemplary conduct in relation to the tragic narrative Carisophus has caused that gives Eubulus cause to lament, 'O heavy hap hadst thou to play this tragedy' (1501). These metadramatic gestures serve to reinforce the sense of constructedness which pervades the play from the outset, at the Prologue's mention of 'our author's . . . pen' (Prol. 7–8).

This type of metadrama, connecting the outer play with the informer-authored inner tragedy, reveals anxieties over the misinformation of potential intelligencers. As just such a vicious figure, Carisophus admits openly the fear which is encoded in the defensive conventions of the prologue when he says 'for profit I will accuse any man, hap what shall' (374). Since Carisophus is author, audience and informer, this seems not only to express concern both that the author himself may be so accused by an audience member, but also that the author may be perceived himself as accusing real members of the court of being the self-seekers, sycophants and intelligencers that some undoubtedly were. As the author and eventual victim of the inner tragedy, Carisophus embodies the structural contradictions inherent in authorship in this period and acts perhaps as an object of transference for authorial angst over perceived legitimacy and the dangers inherent in writing and playing. In this sense then Carisophus functions as Edwards's whipping boy.

When Damon makes his belated entrance at the planned execution of Pithias he defines another stage and, by implication, another audience, when he exclaims 'O my Pithias, my noble pledge, my constant friend! / . . . Give place to me, this room is mine, on this stage must I play, / Damon is the man, none ought but he to Dionysius his blood to pay' (1596, 1598–9). The dramatic stage is thus shifted on to the scaffold – traditionally the place of the final dramatics of royalty and the nobility – in order to play out the remaining elements of this struggle for representative autonomy before the tyrant Dionysius.

Earlier in the play Stephano reports the intelligence he has gained to Pithias, saying:

By friendship I gat into the court, where in great audience
I heard Dionysius with his own mouth give this cruel sentence
By these express words: that Damon the Greek, that crafty spy,
Without further judgement tomorrow should die.
(638–41)

Dionysius is the author and the leading actor here, and the kind of audience he is used to holding is one where the implicit power relations are explicitly expressed as power over life and death, as Stephano hears. As the ultimate authority, Dionysius here becomes briefly the instigator of the ensuing narrative in order to take up a spectatorial position himself. He thus instructs the hangman Gronno, 'do my commandment: strike off Damon's irons by and by. / Then bring him forth, I myself will see him executed presently' (719–20). Dionysius authors this inner drama of execution in order to be its audience, yet its metadramatic power is that it is actually an unruly and open-ended frame-narrative which manages to spill over into the world of the play, refusing to be contained by the spectacular conventions the tyrant intends to have performed.

Although he is both empowered author and audience member in this situation, the show Dionysius receives is of a kind he has not anticipated, and is in a sense inexpressible. His expected power over interpretation diminishes as the action proceeds beyond familiar parameters, and he is prompted to remark in recognition of this that 'the immortal gods above / Hath made you play this tragedy, I think, for my behoof' (1679–80), thus rescinding any claim to authorship in favour of the gods themselves. As now a mere audience to Damon and Pithias' powerfully dramatic friendship ideal, he too feels the pressure of silence required, complaining that 'my spirits are suddenly appalled, my limbs wax weak: / This strange friendship amazeth me so, that I can scarce speak' (1661–2). The normally vocal Eubulus to whom he exclaims this also seems affected by this scarcity of speech in relation to the model of authority this friendship generates, eulogising it as simply 'unspeakable' (1665). These silences are not so much demanded in order to circumvent misinterpretation, but because the strength of this classical amity performs an ideal that transcends representation and interpretation. At one point Carisophus asks 'what is the perfectest friendship among men that ever grew?', and Aristippus replies, 'where men loved one another, not for profit, but for virtue' (1423–4). It is this immaterial perfection that requires the virtual silence of the tyrant, whose almost involuntary response bespeaks an authority discomposed. 'Virtue' here is a recollection of the ambitions and conventions of courtly love which, rather than reinforcing a feudal outlook, will be somewhat paradoxically employed in the conclusion as a levelling device between the 'friends', now including, at his own request, the King himself. This will suggest an ideal prospect in which the tyrant is offered the security of mutual commitment in return for the abandonment of the status afforded him by the remote power he exerts through the mistrust engendered by structures of informing. Thus the very basis for Dionysius' authority contrasts unfavourably with Damon and Pithias' 'unspeakable friendship' of classical amity (1665) which bespeaks a moral authority which is more equitable since it is based on a vision of the world unclouded by the desire of private gain at any cost.

The implications of these powerful early modern doctrines of friendship in relation to a monarch's necessary isolation have been skilfully articulated by Shannon, who argues that public sovereignty and private friendship are thought by the early moderns to be highly incompatible. She argues convincingly that the very precondition of the 'king's function as an emblem of public sovereignty' is what she calls his 'emphatic and comprehensive preclusion from exercising the very gestures and capacities friendship celebrates.'[44] With this in mind, the 'sudden change' in Dionysius' attitude to the friends and their relationship is detected in the king's conduct of his own private business by Aristippus even before being fully articulated by the king himself. As he explains, exclaiming:

O perfect amity!
Thy force is here seen, and that very perfectly.
The king himself museth hereat, yet is he far out of square
That he trusteth none to come near him: not his own daughters
  will he have
Unsearch'd to enter his chamber.
                                                    (1046–50)

Aristippus notes that the 'force' of this friendship is something that 'the king himself museth hereat' and perhaps it is this sense of genuine puissance in the concept that causes him to be so 'far out of square'. It is certain that he is feeling threatened to the extent of the amplification of his already extremely untrusting and private nature, which is used to dealing only with and within a world of predation. The 'devices' of the play argue that it is this stark but simple contrast between differing modes of human relationship, encapsulated in the phrase 'not for profit, but for virtue' (1423–4), that makes Dionysius repent of his judgement and pardon Damon. This he does even to the hyperbolic extent of offering the friends an equal share in his kingship:

> Damon, have thou thy life, from death I pardon thee;
> For which good turn, I crave, this honour do me lend.
> O friendly heart, let me link with you, to you make me the third friend
> My court is yours; dwell here with me, by my commission large,
> Myself, my realm, my wealth, my health, I commit to your charge:
> Make me a third friend, more shall I joy in that thing,
> Than to be called, as I am, Dionysius the mighty king.
>
> (1688–94)

He is so impressed with the self-sacrificial nature of the friends' relationship that he is not only moved to request of them 'make me a third friend', but he is prepared to surrender his authoritative superiority to achieve that objective.

Damon's response to this is quite specific, and fits with early modern views of monarchical authority, as he says 'for my part, most noble king, as a third friend, welcome to our friendly society; / But you must forget you are a king, for friendship stands in true equality' (1699–1700). Dionysius' response is similarly specific: 'unequal though I be in great possessions, / Yet full equal shall you find me in my changed conditions' (1701–2). 'Full equal' they shall indeed find him, as such an arrangement undermines the separateness which is the precondition of kingship, as much as it does the structure of power and authority which upholds it.

The great ideal theme of friendship here, in the form of classical amity's love, mutual vulnerability and a willingness to die in a substitutionary surrender of power, is eventually what conquers the predatory power structures of the despot. It is a friendship that entails the equality implied by interchangeability which causes Dionysius to conceive a desire for the extinction of his tyranny, a tyranny whose very distinction is predicated above all things on the craving for invulnerability, founded on the work of informers, which drives his prosecution of Damon in the first place. His willingness to give up his kingship in exchange for this is a humanist version of a fantasy of Christian repentance brought on by the devilishly informer-authored 'tragedy' Damon and Pithias have played out before him.[45] In this way the friends' personal, subjective interchange becomes a metadramatic exchange in which the enabling structure of authority itself is being explored. This tragedy, of which Dionysius is the empowered and participatory audience, feeds into a fantastical discourse of political transformation, the 'fantasy of agency' Shannon identifies in early modern discourses of amity.[46] She suggests further that early modern friendship 'imagin[es] what a politics of consent might look like'; this consent is what Damon imagines is possible before the text's informers and intelligencers intrude upon his idealism.[47] It is also confirmed in the vindicating outcome of the play in which the typical characteristics of the intelligencer are negated by the celebration of the opposite characteristics in the doctrine of the friends, and their acceptance as virtues by the chief beneficiary of the intelligencers' work.

In terms of the play's metadramatic structures, in the outermost stratum of the play, Damon and Pithias are presented to the offstage audience as mere cultural tourists, a neutral, purely observational model in strict contrast to the self-serving Aristippus and the vicious Carisophus. Their goal is solely and innocently to see the 'soil and manners of all men of every degree' (342–5). In the interplay between the outer play and the inner tragedy authored by Carisophus, however, Damon and Pithias are made to represent the two possible selves of the audience in relation to the potential effect of the authoritative viewpoint – on the one hand the morally dubious and politically dangerous informer and on the other the legitimate observer and impartial judge. As these selves interplay according to the authoring and direction of Carisophus they expose the illegitimacy of Dionysius' exaggerated authority. Finally, having been seen to represent the ideal point of pure observation, the redeemed Damon and Pithias represent an ideal audience – impartial, self-confident, self-sacrificial, loving, quiescent and justified – performing therefore an exemplary role, and inviting the offstage audience to exhibit the same commendable properties. It is these qualities which finally convince the king to renounce his authority in favour of the friendship of which these attributes consists.

Dionysius meanwhile functions as the tyrant authority, who, despite his authoritarian and totalitarian perspective, is not immune to transformative exempla, here presented to him in the form of a dramatic tragedy playing out in his everyday world. In his responses to this, he is exemplary in his willingness to use his authority to overturn his previous authoritative pronouncements; he is also generous in rewarding the players of this tragedy and reinforcing his commitment accordingly with significant sumptuary gifts: 'your instruction will I follow, to you myself I do commit / Eubulus, make haste to fet new apparel fit / For my new friends' (1717–19).[48] In this way the tyrant, as both actor in, and audience to, the tragedy authored by the author-informer Carisophus takes true control of the narrative for the first time when he shows mercy and, eventually, moves to relinquish his kingship to take on the equality inherent in the contemporary status of the friend. In both cases the authorship of Carisophus is rejected in order to gain control of a discourse wildly disorientating to the tyrant's psyche.

So at the end of the narrative, an ideal of the audience meets an ideal of authority. The function of Carisophus' tragedy has been to bring them together and to acknowledge, or at least suggest, their conceptual and authoritative equality. The fantasy here is that amicable equity is possible in the turbulent dramatic and political spaces between the ultimate narrative authority of the court, the subjectivity of the audience and the good intent of the players. In this discursive space of moral and social fantasy, Edwards's 'subtle sleights' and their 'painted tales' devices' argue for a dramatical 'friendly society' in which mutual observation is unadulterated by predatory self-promotion and where 'painted speech, that gloseth for gain, from gifts is quite debarr'd' (1755). Here both the author and the audience are liberated from the contained and self-destructive influence of the culture of informing. This implies a kind of freedom from discursive obligations to higher authorities and provides access to the utopian possibilities of self-authorised transformation. In sharp contrast to the 'sudden change . . . wrought' by the audience response to Edwards's previous production, this transformation is one of idyllic authorly empowerment.

Notes

1. Richard Edwards, 'Fair words make fools fain', lines 11, 30, in Ros King, *The Works of Richard Edwardes* (Manchester: Manchester University Press, 2001), pp. 201–2.
2. *Cicero, De Amicitia*, trans. William Armistead Falconer (Cambridge, MA: Harvard University Press, 1923), p. 131.
3. Sir Thomas Elyot, *The Book Named the Governor* [1531], ed. S. E. Lehmberg (London: Everyman's Library, 1962), chapters 11–13, pp. 132–54.

4. Joseph Hall, *Characters of Virtues and Vices* (1608), pp. 46–7, <http://gateway.proquest.com.ezproxy.massey.ac.nz/openurl?ctx_ver=Z39.88-2003&res_id=xri:eebo&rft_id=xri:eebo:image:3779:31> (last accessed 5 February 2018).
5. Hall, *Characters*, pp. 46–7
6. Quentin Skinner, *Reason and Rhetoric in the Philosophy of Hobbes* (Cambridge: Cambridge University Press, 1996), p. 79.
7. Curtis C. Breight, *Surveillance, Militarism and Drama in the Elizabethan Era* (Basingstoke: Macmillan, 1996), p. 107.
8. Breight, p. 109.
9. Dollimore, p. 24; Dutton, p. 126.
10. See Joel Hurstfield (ed.), *The Reformation Crisis* (London: E. Arnold, 1961), p. 1.
11. Hutson, 'Civility', p. 15.
12. Lenton, n.p.
13. Daniel Tuvill, *The Dove and the Serpent* (London: 1614), p. 43.
14. Nabbs, *Covent-Garden* (London: R. Oulton, 1639), n.p.
15. Breight, p. 109. See also pp. 102, 273, n. 13.
16. See Laurie Shannon, *Sovereign Amity: Figures of Friendship in Shakespearean Contexts* (Chicago and London: University of Chicago Press, 2002).
17. G. K. Hunter, *John Lyly: The Humanist as Courtier* (London, 1962), p. 80.
18. R. Stretter, 'Cicero on Stage: "Damon and Pithias" and the Fate of Classical Friendship in English Renaissance Drama', *Texas Studies in Literature and Language* [serial online], Vol. 47, No. 4 (2005), pp. 345–65, at p. 351.
19. J. E. Kramer, '*Damon and Pithias*: An Apology for Art', *English Literary History*, Vol. 35, No. 4 (1968), pp. 475–90, at p. 475.
20. Kramer, p. 475.
21. Dutton, p. 33.
22. J. R. Dasent (ed.), *Acts of the Privy Council of England* (London: Eyre & Spottiswood, 1890), p. 145.
23. Wilfrid R. Prest, *The Inns of Court 1590–1640* (London: Longman, 1972), p. 223.
24. Prest, p. 18.
25. Prest, p. 18.
26. Prest, p. 177.
27. King, p. 26.
28. Shannon, p. 2. If there is any doubt that a children's company could be accused of subversive representations, Heywood's *Apology for Actors* mentions 'the liberty which some arrogate to themselves, committing their bitternesse, and liberall invectives against all estates, to the

mouthes of Children, supposing their juniority to be a priviledge for any rayling, be it never so violent.' See Thomas Heywood, *An Apology for Actors* (London: 1612) n.p.; see also Dutton, p. 128.
29. Richard Edwards, *Damon and Pithias: The Dramatic Writings of Edwards, Norton and Sackville* (Guildford: Charles W. Traylen, 1966), pp. 3–84.
30. Possibly what Turberville refers to as his 'sugred Songs'; 'An Epitaph of Maister Edwardes sometime Maister of the Children of the Chappell, and Gentleman of Lyncolns Inne of Court', George Turberville, *Epitaphes, epigrams, songs and sonets with a discourse of the friendly affections of Tymetes to Pyndara his ladie* (London: Henry Denham, 1567), <http://gateway.proquest.com/openurl?ctx_ver=Z39.88-2003&res_id=xri:eebo&rft_id=xri:eebo:citation:99846797> (last accessed 28 January 2018).
31. Dutton, p. 38.
32. Geoffrey Chaucer, *The Canterbury Tales* (Ware: Wordsworth Editions, 1995), p. 291.
33. See, for example, Aristotle, *Aristotle's politiques, or Discourses of gouernment*, trans. Loys Le Roy (London: Adam Islip, 1598), <http://gateway.proquest.com/openurl?ctx_ver=Z39.88-2003&res_id=xri:eebo&rft_id=xri:eebo:citation:99842553> (last accessed 16 February 2018).
34. Andrew Galloway, 'Authority', in Peter Brown (ed.), *A Companion to Chaucer* (Oxford: Blackwell, 2000), p. 30.
35. The alteration in spelling in the original may be significant to the concept of authority with regard to shifts of meaning in the transition from the spelling of *auctor* to *author*. This may merit further study. The *Shorter OED* lists the etymology of 'author' as: *Author*: Middle English 'autour' adopted from Anglo-French [i.e. Anglo-Norman] 'autour' / Old French 'autor' adopted from Latin 'auctor', formed on Latin 'augere / auct-', 'to increase promote, originate'. It adds that the Latinised spellings 'aucto(u)r' were 'usual' in the fifteenth and sixteenth centuries, and that 'aucthor' and 'autho(u)r' appear in the sixteenth, 'with the graphic variant "th" for "t", which finally influenced the pronunciation.' This suggests that a loss of the Latin '-c-' occurred when the word was borrowed into French implying that the '-c-' was reintroduced when it was borrowed into Middle English. However, the *OED* proper points out that it was 'already in fourteenth [century French] occasionally written *auct-* after [the Latin]'. The Latinised English forms usual in the fifteenth and sixteenth centuries then would have been the factitious product of writers tutored in Latin, who perhaps felt that the Latin spelling was a more appropriate scholarly form. The pressure this exerted on pronunciation may have been similar to the varying ways people currently pronounce the French loan word 'homage': in normal usage, it has an

Anglicised pronunciation, where the 'h-' is pronounced and the word ending rhymes with 'ridge'; however, when referring to a work of art (especially film) the French pronunciation is more common (where the 'h-' is silent and the word rhymes with 'fromage'). Interestingly, though 'homage', like 'autour', was borrowed from French during the Middle English period and has, therefore, been an English word for hundreds of years, a French pronunciation is still thought to be appropriate in certain contexts. This is evidence of a hangover in which French is perceived to be the most appropriate language of culture. It would seem reasonable to assume, then, that the choice of the Latinised spelling (and possibly pronunciation) indicates the ongoing perception of Latin, with its ancient religious connections to the concept of received truth, as the appropriate language of authority. I am indebted to Dr Adam Mearns of the University of Newcastle for discussion of the above.

36. See Clare, pp. 160–1.
37. In John Lyly's *Campaspe*, Alexander tells Diogenes, 'I will haue thy / Cabin remoued neerer to my Court, because / I will be a Philosopher.' Diogenes replies to this: 'And when you haue done / so, I pray you remoue your Court further / from my Cabin, because I will not / be a Courtier' (5.4.103–5).
38. *OED*, 2nd edition notes for *cynic*: 'In the appellation of the Cynic philosophers there was prob. an original reference to the κυνοσάργες, a gymnasium where Antisthenes taught; but popular use took it simply in the sense "dog-like, currish", so that κύων, "dog" became a nickname for "Cynic".'
39. *OED*, 2nd edition notes that 'whispering' may be 'itself in opposition to truth', citing Anthony Munday's 'Aduertisement and defence for Trueth against her Backbiters, and specially against the whispring Fauourers ... of Campians.'
40. William Lambarde, *The courts of justice corrected and amended. Or the corrupt lawyer untrust, lasht and quasht. Wherein the partiall judge, counsellour, great mover, whispering informer, favourite at the bar are fully displayed, convicted, and directed* (London: George Lindsey, 1642; originally published in 1631 as *The just lawyer his conscionable complaint against auricular or private informing and soliciting of judges*), p. 7, <http://gateway.proquest.com.ezproxy.massey.ac.nz/openurl?ctx_ver=Z39.88-2003&res_id=xri:eebo&rft_id=xri:eebo:image:124077:5> (last accessed 23 February 2018).
41. See Alan G. R. Smith, *The Emergence of a Nation State: Commonwealth of England, 1529–1660* (London: Longman, 1988), p. 112, for reference to the Tudor anxiety over the insecurity of border defences which Carisophus plays upon here.

42. In terms of payment, successful informers could earn themselves a very good purse indeed, as the introduction suggests. Contemporary legal statutes dictated that the informer should receive a portion of whatever fine was imposed, with the rest going to the crown; a common share was a third to a half of the value of the goods informed upon. See Angus, p. 9ff.; Beresford, pp. 232–3.
43. This may be exemplified in Ben Jonson's eminent desire in his *Poetaster* to differentiate the flattering 'fawn' from the nobly satirical 'satyr' and to consolidate his own legitimacy by aggressively representing his fellow poets in the former category as informers. See Ben Jonson, *Poetaster*, ed. Tom Cain (Manchester: Manchester University Press, 1995), n. 4.7.9–10.
44. Shannon, pp. 2–3.
45. Contrast the consequences of Iago's informing 'work' in *Othello* (see 5.2.363–5).
46. Shannon, p. 2.
47. Shannon, p. 10.
48. Players would often receive gloves at court performances and this might be an occasion to do just that.

Chapter 2

The Parasites of Machiavel

In Christopher Marlowe's *The Jew of Malta* (1589–90), Thomas Middleton/Cyril Tourner's *The Revenger's Tragedy* (*c*.1602) and John Marston's *The Malcontent* (1605), as in many other plays of the period, intelligencer characters perform as exemplary dysfunctionals. They are not only the inheritors of the function of the Vice and demonic provocateurs of the medieval dramas, but now their meaning includes an implicit satirical social critique as they operate as metaphors for perceived inconsistencies in the authority structures of their societies. More so, as scapegoats, they offer the dramatist both an easy target and a deniability which allows for a broad critique of the dysfunction of authority while avoiding the accusation of attaching that to persons of social power. Who, after all, would like to associate themselves with the 'hellish detested *Judas* name of an Intelligencer' by assuming that such a figure represented them on the early modern stage?[1]

In the early morality plays of the medieval church, the attributes of the Christian Devil are often personified as individual vices, but around the middle of the sixteenth century, this mutated into a 'single representative figure of evil', or the Vice, as Antony Hammond notes, whose method is always 'deceit and guile'.[2] This often metadramatic figure attracts the audience's sympathy both by 'embodying its own destructive and anti-authoritarian impulses, and by engaging the audience in a conspiratorial relationship'.[3] These functions can be made to serve highly metadramatic purposes, while also being apt for the depiction of underhand characters. As plays evolved a progressively secular character, the collusive aspects of this relationship became increasingly empathetic and resulted in the kinds of villain figures that carry the characteristics of the informer and intelligencer.

It is arguable that the popular awareness of Niccolò Machiavelli's *The Prince* (1514) not only developed alongside the evolution of this Vice figure, but inflected its development in the English theatre.[4] In *The Prince*, pragmatism rather than morality is the primary virtue and this view suggests a situation in which a ruler might feel justified in discarding their moral principles in defence of their supremacy. The moral compromise associated with dealing with informers then would be a non-issue, and the sense of moral outrage felt in a society subject to their corrupted ministries would be of little concern. Like the work of the intelligencer, Machiavellian realpolitik is specifically perceived as anti-Christian at this time, even perhaps essentially malevolent.[5] George Abbot's *Exposition upon the Prophet Jonah* (1600) expresses Machiavelli's fashionable reputation at this time, describing him as being 'most fit for euill . . . a professed politician, whose preceptes closely couched, haue filled the world with the deuill.'[6] The demonic element figures largely in the imagination of this character in the texts of the period, accompanied by the menace of occulted motives and manipulative politicking.

Marlowe's Barabas fits these transforming characteristics, both as a Vice figure 'in the tradition of the morality play' as David Bevington affirms and what I would describe as a very Machiavellian 'anticipation of Shakespeare's Richard III, Iago, and Edmund'.[7] Throughout this process of the development of the stage villain, an apparent contradiction grows between the Vice's character as an anti-authoritarian, devilish malcontent and the same as a tyrannous, Machiavellian authority. The connecting factor is often the theatrical figure of the informer or intelligencer, who feeds into both of these narratives, variously performing, among other things, as an actor, an author, a malcontent, a plotter, an evil adviser or a 'politician' in George Abbot's sense of that word. Everard Guilpin's 'Skialetheia' (1598) draws on these attributes when he describes one who

> like the vnfrequented Theater
> Walkes in darke silence, and vast solitude,
> Suited to those blacke fancies which intrude,
> Vpon possession of his troubled breast.
>
> ('Satyre V', 84–7)

The poem continues in this mode to declare that 'he is a malecontent: / A Paipst? no, nor yet a Protestant, / But a discarded intelligencer'

('Satyre V', 93–5), the 'blacke fancies' clearly being a reference to the melancholic aspect of the stage malcontent. Further theatrical connections are drawn when the text identifies one that it calls 'vizarfac't pole-head dissimulation', who is cursed as a 'parrasite' and a 'squynt-eyde slaue, / which lookes two wayes at once' ('Satyre I', 56–60).[8] This Janus-faced street-wanderer, it says, 'hath so bereyde the world with his foule myre, / That naked truth may be suspect a lyer' ('Satyre I', 61–2); he is a frustrated intelligencer who is infecting his society with misinformation and bile. But more than this, Guilpin declares that

> he is the deuill,
> Brightly accoustred to bemist his euill:
> Like a Swartrutters hose his puffe thoughts swell,
> With yeastie ambition: *Signior Machiauel*
> Taught him this mumming trick, with curtesie
> T'entrench himselfe in popularitie.
>
> ('Satyre I', 70–5)

The ambitious intelligencer here is a devil figure, associated with the blackened faces and black clothes of the marauding Dutch swartrutters and the foreign influence of the Machiavel, but in the speaker's paranoid construction this only adds to his popularity. And he has achieved this dangerously popular theatrical status not only through lying but also through bribery, such that 'no broome-man that will pray for him, / Shall haue lesse truage then his bonnets brim' ('Satyre I', 66–7). In the tradition of the vice which precedes them, and of which they take their essence, these stage Machiavels very often invite the structures of metadrama, as both plotters of dramatic narratives and deceitful, malcontent schemers. Although they are figures popularly identified as informers or intelligencers, they also carry something of the identity of the satiric commentator on society, though this is tainted by its association with the pursuit and disbursement of filthy lucre.

These issues inflect our plays in differing ways. Although popular perceptions of Machiavellianism infect Marlowe's Malta in all its political and personal dealings, *The Jew of Malta*'s self-conscious prologue of Machiavel attributes its malaise to the Jew alone. In that sense, Barabas plays the scapegoat for a society entirely entranced by the ministrations of money and the kinds of policy and plotting which are oiled by it. In Middleton/Tourner's *The Revenger's Tragedy*, Vindice, having been drawn into the role of informing and plotting parasite, wholeheartedly embraces his social function, and his subsequent downfall exemplifies its critique. Like Webster's Bosola, he is an indispensable outsider operating inside the political establishment, but unlike Bosola he takes the heat for a society which is dysfunctional in its own imperatives and mechanisms of control, without finding his own sense of redemptive agency. *The Malcontent*'s equally parasitic Malevole is also both a metadramatic actor and a satiric exemplar of the decadence and corruption of his society. Thought by some contemporaries to offer a critique of the court of James I, this figure resounds with the popular image of the Machiavel and functions within recognisably metadramatic modes, the natural province of the intelligencer. Moreover, his fate is tied in with that of the structures which choose to employ his dubious talents.

In the defining Prologue of Machiavel to *The Jew of Malta*, it is of course not the real Florentine courtier but the Machiavelli of the popular imagination that Marlowe draws upon to frame the world in which the stereotypically usurious Barabas operates. Here, and throughout this play, Marlowe deals with fashionable perceptions of Machiavellianism which seem to resonate with the consciousness of political life in Britain at the time. These are particularly related to the ways in which the personal aspects of plotting and policy are delineated by the prospects of financial gain.[9] There is some debate about the extent to which the play depicts any authentic Machiavellian concepts. Irving Ribner sees the play as a 'classic example of Elizabethan "Machiavellianism"', but argues that it 'contains absolutely no reflection of Machiavelli's own ideas.'[10] Luc Borot, however, has persuasively argued otherwise.[11] Though Machiavelli's ideas may have been circulating in university coteries, as Margaret Scott has argued, the play's original audience probably had little or no access to Machiavelli in their own language.[12] N. W. Bawcutt agrees that in the late 1580s knowledge of Machiavelli 'began to percolate outwards from the learned controversialists to a wider audience', but asserts that this was 'often at a very superficial level'.[13] For the purpose of developing an understanding of the play's impact, however, this debate is somewhat beside the point, since the Machiavel operates here, as in many contemporaneous plays, as a political bogeyman. The fact that his reputation therefore suffers from hyperbole and an infamy born of ignorance does not diminish the impact of the popular Machiavelli on European culture, but rather, on the contrary, seems to enhance it.

It is perhaps unnecessary to rehearse here Marlowe's own probable connection with the Machiavellian Elizabethan underworld as an agent, but suffice it to say that if, as seems likely, his premature death was linked to this work, then he may have been implicated in various intelligencing projects, not merely as an occasional outing but 'throughout his playwriting years', as Lisa Hopkins says.[14] His capacity to articulate the performance aspects of the intelligencing vocation may be related to his own ability to 'pass amongst those who believed without actually sharing their belief', as Hopkins suggests.[15] This situation was further complicated at the time by the fact that the government was especially 'sensitive about the theatrics of recusants' and their shifting disguised natures, as Arata Ide notes.[16] It is likely in this situation that Marlowe would at least be required to be plastic enough to play 'Catholic' or 'Protestant' as required.

As we have seen, the dependence on informers and intelligencers by those who would paint their authority with a moral legitimacy was troubling to the early modern mind. So, in as much as his dramatis persona exhibits both intelligencing and theatrical dispositions, Barabas plays the scapegoat for perceived anomalies in the conceptual and material structures of social authority. Like most stage informers and intelligencers, he is simultaneously 'cunning, ruthless [and] a practised deceiver', and 'a superb actor able to play whatever role suits his purposes', as David Bevington says.[17] Ide notes Barabas's 'remarkable dexterity as a player of roles'.[18] With a sheer metadramatical delight, he revels in his in boastfulness and bluster to the audience about his mutable nature and takes pride in what Bevington calls the 'sheer versatility of his machinations'.[19] Ide meanwhile sees him in a dark mould, as a 'protean monster'.[20] In this case, the Machiavel that declares 'I count religion but a childish toy, / And hold that there is no sin but ignorance' (1.1.14–15) speaks more loudly of the feared machinations of the intelligencer and informer than of the perception of the perfidious Hebrew at this time, although the two may be conflated to some extent in the popular reputation of the Jew for both incestuous secrecy and cony-catching usury. In his misfortune, Barabas thinks of himself as a 'sad presaging raven' (2.1.1), a typically avian image of the intelligencer in texts of the time, here found spreading 'contagion from her sable wings' (2.1.4), until the return of his gold converts him to a lark 'singing' over his money (2.1.63). He exhibits another popularly remarked quality of the intelligencer when, in moving from avian to canine imagery, he claims 'we Jews can fawn like spaniels when we please' (2.3.20), and his various metadramatic asides simultaneously theatricalise this fawning function to an offstage audience whose sympathies may be elsewhere. In his compact with Ithamore, he also represents the necessary financial aspect of the bond between the employing authority and the intelligencing agent when he promises 'be true and secret, thou shalt want no gold' (2.3.219).

Not content of course to be merely the author of his own tragic story, Barabas takes care to plot, scheme and stage-manage the narratives of those around him in a most authorial fashion, and with what was at the time disparagingly termed 'policy'. When he alludes to a cosening device delivered in a letter that might be 'cunningly performed', his iniquitous Ithamore is keen to take the role, exclaiming keenly 'Oh, master, that I might have a hand in this' (370–1). Ithamore celebrates this as what he describes as 'villainy / So neatly plotted and performed' (3.3.1–2), concluding that 'my master has the bravest policy' (3.3.13). 'Policy' here and throughout is a term freighted with associations around plotting, double-dealing and intelligencing, as it is when *1 Henry IV*'s Hotspur describes it as 'bare and rotten policy' (1.3.108).[21] These words then allude to a venomous atmosphere suffused with the taint of plotting intelligencers. In this world of 'policy', Ithamore of course both betrays Barabas's confidence and is intended to be betrayed in his turn by Pilia-Borza (4.4.27), until Barabas rounds off this circle of betrayal by attempting to poison the lot (4.4.44). His intent also to poison the entire convent which takes in Abigail mirrors a real-life Machiavellian episode in which Richard Baines, Marlowe's erstwhile companion on foreign governmental work and later enemy, plotted to poison the whole seminary of Rheims.[22] Barabas's own credentials as a Machiavellian intelligencer are confirmed when Calymath the Turk asks 'whom have we there, a spy?', and he answers in the affirmative. Furthermore, when he is made Governor of Malta in return for leading the Turks into the city, he muses openly 'since by wrong thou got'st authority, / Maintain it bravely by firm policy' (5.2.35–6) in an admission of the nature of the relationship between the popular Machiavel and raw power, unbounded by moral considerations. When Barabas's attempt backfires and he is caught in the trap intended for Calymath he boils to death in a cauldron for his trouble, but he is nevertheless found unrepentantly railing to the last, 'tongue, curse thy fill and die' (5.5.88), the tongue being the intelligencer's best and most feared weapon. Unlike Faustus, he does not repent of the bargain he has made with money and power and seems therefore to retain the integrity of his own hell-bent and devilish agency, despite the extremity of his punishment.

In considering the destabilising elements of this form of Machiavellianism on early modern structures of authority, it might be useful to see the imperatives of the Machiavel as a form of *virtu*, that is the expression of a certain masculine power, and very much in contradistinction to virtue in the common sense of the word. As Bevington says, in this respect 'virtu was a trade name for the Machiavellian'.[23] So, it can be argued that the figure of the popular Machiavel exposes an anxiety that the social qualities of the politicking intelligencer are actually significantly personally empowering, despite the informer's low reputation. In this respect alone, therefore, they are potentially destabilising to traditional top-down hierarchies of divinely endorsed authority structures. So, when the Prologue's Machiavel declares that 'many will talk of title to a crown' yet asks 'what right had Caesar to the empery?' and concludes that 'might first made kings' (1.1.18–20), this is more than a mere challenge to divine right: it is an assertion of a truth almost universally acknowledged but that few dare to speak out loud at this time. The Machiavel then becomes an indicator of the nakedness of the vain emperor in procession and perhaps even something of a weathervane for the coming destabilisation of authority that will manifest through the increasingly desperate hubris of the reigns of James and Charles Stuart. The fact that Barabas is punished in the most obvious way for one of such roiling ambition seems not to diminish this aspect of the role. And this is the case for its multifarious iterations at the time, all of which seem to have the potential to destabilise the moral core of authority structures and therefore their claim to divine sanction.

The metadramatic parasite Malevole in John Marston's *The Malcontent* (1604) also resonates with the popular figure of the Machiavel and through this provides a boldly satirical mirror for the decadence and corruption of his society. The play's metadramatic modes are the natural province of the staged informer and intelligencer, as we may by now perceive, but its apparently ambiguous perspective on this suggests a complex moral position regarding the boundaries of legitimate social critique and malicious informing.

The Malcontent has long been thought to offer a critique of the court of James I, although it seems somewhat early in James's reign for the author to intend it to do so. However, the fact that Marston clearly seems to have expected trouble from the printing may go some way towards confirming this, as his preface To the Reader suggests: 'I understand some have been most unadvisedly over-cunning in misinterpreting me, and with subtlety (deep as hell) have maliciously spread ill rumours' (12–15). This concern with legitimate versus 'over-cunning' interpretation is reflected in Condell's metadramatic speech in the Induction, in which he speaks as himself and complains that 'there are a sort of discontented creatures that ... will wrest the doings of any man to their base malicious applyment' (Ind. 54–6). The 'Imperfect Ode' which probably preceded the Blackfriars performance of the play puts the concern thus: 'to wrest each hurtless thought to private sense / Is the foul use of ill-bred Impudence' (Prol. 1–2), and complains that 'immodest censure now grows wild, / All over-running' (Prol. 3–4). These desperate sentiments echo Hall's description of a 'Male-content' in *Characters of Virtues and Vices* (1608), who 'speaks nothing but *Satyres*, and libels, and lodgeth no guests in his heart but rebels.'[24] The artist here may run the knife edge of satire and libel himself, but the overdetermination of the admonitory apology in this case certainly suggests that Marston is also deeply troubled by the potential for an unpredictably volatile interpretation by some defamatory audience malcontent.

Marston's pseudonym, 'W. Kinsayder', appearing in *The Scourge of Villainy* (1598) and in the anonymous academic drama *2 Return from Parnassus* (c.1598–1602), puns on *kunikos*, the Greek root of the canine-associated cynic and satirist. This fits with the image of Marston as one 'lifting up [his] leg and pissing against the world' (lines 267–8).[25] He was no stranger to controversy and his play *2 Return from Parnassus* was one of those caught up in the Bishops' ban on satire in 1599. The image of the dog, however, is not only linked with the satirical cynic, but also widely employed of informers and intelligencers, for both dissimilar reasons, to do with informers' fawning and bestial voracity, and similar, related to their caustic, critical barking at perceived iniquities. Hall's malcontent mirrors exactly these traits as he is described as a 'querulous curre whom no horse can passe by without barking at.'[26]

In this play, Malevole has much more to incentivise him than simply 'a passion to smell out corruption', as George K. Hunter puts it, and is obviously also playing a role aimed at redressing the wrongs he has suffered.[27] Just as it contains elements of the Machiavel, this social function has an outstandingly metadramatic quality. Critics have long noticed that Malevole's particular quality as a dramatis persona 'springs from the fact that he is acting', as A. H. Gilbert may exemplify, and this self-consciousness fits with his surroundings.[28] This seems entirely fitting, since *The Malcontent*'s ruling court, as much as any other early modern court, works as a 'self-presentational game centered around the getting and keeping of power', as Douglas Lanier presents it.[29] In relation to this theatrical configuration of power, however, Malevole's thoroughly metadramatic aspect is combined with that of the malcontent, which can envision morality only 'on the far side of cynical disillusion and the Machiavellian tactic', as Hunter argues.[30] In Machiavelli's advice on the creation of conspiracies, he offers a warning directive about working with malcontents: 'So soon as thou hast discover'd thy self to a malcontent, thou giv'st him means to work his own content, for by revealing thy treason, he may well hope for all manner of favour.'[31] This indicates the potential necessity to work with such treacherous figures in any deep intrigue, although it is presented as a caution. Malevole's own metadramatic personal conspiracy sidesteps this anomaly in the fact that his malcontentment is an act and he is actually Altofronto, the Duke of Genoa, in disguise. This reconfigures the trope of the disguised authority figure going about its own intelligencing, in a role which mirrors Duke Angelo in *Measure for Measure* and which will be repeated in Jonson's *Bartholomew Fair* with Justice Overdo, making the authorities' dependence on the Machiavellian tactics of malcontents for their intelligence much more explicit.

It may be argued that Marston displays in this character the deeply ambiguous common trait of the satirist as one 'committed to what he condemns', as Hunter describes it.[32] In his dual nature, Malevole is in a sense a dramatised version of this ambiguity and exposes the anxious connection between social power and the immoral structures which affirm and undergird its authority in his unity with Altofronto. Given this, we may question the extent to which Marston is condemning the theatre of intelligencing through this character. Intelligencing is of course a difficult field to critique, since it risks drawing the unwanted attention of those it condemns or the powers that benefit from their actions. Part of the answer to this may reside in the very theatricalisation of the figure, which seems to offer a kind of deniability, since then any critique offered can be said at least to be inclusively self-deprecating. The satire-speaking malcontent of Hall's *Characters* is similarly imaged as 'the wheel of a well-couched fireworke that flies out on all sides, not without scorching it selfe', though this may be accidental.[33] But equally, since 'the sine qua non of statecraft is stagecraft, the skillful management of self-disclosure and self-concealment', as Lanier says, the play's corrupt court is one in which the satirist is exceptionally fitted to prosper.[34] The conflation of satirist and intelligencer as critical voices may prove a benefit to a dramatic narrative, but it can only reflect negatively on an authority structure which does the same. From these materials, the play will set up an opposition between performance and authority which it will then proceed to demolish.

This duality may be perceived in Webster's highly metadramatic Induction, which sees the actor Will Sly playing himself and insisting on setting himself up as an onstage audience, although this seems to have been a practice common at the private theatres only. He then refers to himself to ask 'where's . . . Will Sly?' (Ind. 11–12), in a way that sets up the self-conscious frame requisite for the structural exposition of intelligencing to come. Sly plays on this connection specifically when he refuses the Tire-man's attempts to shoo him from the stage, offering 'I am one that hath seen this play often, and can give them intelligence for their action' (Ind. 15–16). When Sinklo, the usurer's son and Sly's onstage companion, says 'I durst lay four of mine ears, the play is not so well acted as it hath been' (Ind. 88–9), he alludes to the ear-cropping which might be meted out to the satirist who goes too far in his critique of social power, risking the ire of the Machiavellian informer. This is an odd thing for a dangerously morally compromised audience-figure like this to say, since he would be more likely to be perceived as a threat in this regard rather than a potential victim. These issues are taken to a further remove when Sly and Sinklo are ushered from the stage, finally, by another famous actor, John Lowin, who is again playing himself. The metadramatic self-consciousness of this episode is remarkable because of the clear connection drawn between metadrama and the malcontent intelligencer, and because the framing device that Sly proposes, one that would normally offer an extra level of fictionality and therefore deniability, is rejected, thus reinforcing the case for a reading of the play's themes as openly critical rather than guardedly defensive.

The immoral context of the Genoan court is made plain to see here, with specific warnings about instances of informing and politicking throughout, as Malevole's caution to Celso suggests: 'speak low; pale fears / Suspect that hedges, walls, and trees, have ears' (3.3.2–3), and this is always an opportunity for an audience to construct themselves metonymically as the 'ears' referred to. The anxiety of the bond between political power and the corrupted social configurations upon which it is established may be revealed in the hypostatic union of Altofronto with Malevole. The surname of Giovanni Altofronto suggests association with the highbrow, the high fronted and the noble-looking; his given name is shared with Christ's most beloved and 'spiritual' disciple; he is married to a Maria, and he is friended by Celso, which name speaks of the 'high, famous [and] eminent'.[35] But, depending on one's perspective, his true nature may be revealed when these aspirations are seen in combination with the 'Malevole' facet: the one of bad volition, the ill-wisher, echoing the Satanic accuser of the brethren: one who is 'more discontent than Lucifer when he was thrust out of the presence' (1.2.19–20). This hybridity may be described as a metacharacterisation or metadramatis persona, that is not simply a figure disguised, but an expression of the full nature of both. This dual-natured dissonance is mirrored in the discord of his music, a metaphor for his personality which is the first we hear of him as he celebrates his own malcontentment, saying 'discord to malcontents is very manna' (1.4.38). As Pietro expresses it, 'the elements struggle within him; his own soul is at variance within herself' (1.2.26–7). However, there is a positive aspect to this, as one might expect when a satirist is depicting a satirist, as Pietro again says, 'I like him, faith; he . . . makes me understand those weaknesses which others' flattery palliates' (1.2.28–9), and is thus depicted as a plain speaker. But even this is qualified by Pietro referring explicitly to his function as an intelligencer, as he adds, 'he gives good intelligence to my spirit' (1.2.28–9). One contemporary reputed to exhibit a similar duality would be Christopher Marlowe, being perceived as 'at once an agent of the establishment and deeply subversive', as Stephen Orgel suggests.[36] Through these complexities, the offstage audience must find their loyalties drawn towards Malevole in his place at the intersection of these lines of power and performance.

Malevole's first appearance is invited by Pietro in terms often reserved for informers and satirists: 'come down, thou ragged cur, and snarl here ... trot about and bespurtle whom thou pleasest' (1.2.10–12). This resounds with the satirical image offered of Marston himself, 'like a dog with its urine' pissing on the leg of the world, a clear indication that the expected role of the micturating malcontent is to besmirch or bespatter those around him with contaminating words.[37] If he functions as Marston's *raisonneur* in this play, this dramatis persona carries a level of self-deprecation that may be unsafe, except that there is some justification for the critical view this authorial perspective embodies. When Malevole replies 'I'll come among you ... I'll fall like a sponge into water, to suck up, to suck up' (1.2.13–15), he alludes again to the popular image of both the intelligencer and the social critic, in this case soaking up information in a given situation for squeezing out elsewhere. Ben Jonson's characterisation of Horace in *Poetaster* exemplifies this where he is described as 'a mere sponge, nothing but humours and observation ... [who sucks] from every society, and when he comes home squeezes himself dry again' (4.3.104–7).[38] At this point, Malevole, declaring himself weary of religious 'policy', wishes he were 'one of the Duke's hounds' (1.3.16) and Pietro continues this canine metaphor for the intelligencer when he enquires for the 'common news abroad' (1.3.17), as an intelligencer should know, in asking, 'thou doggest rumour still?' (1.3.18). This metaphor may be continued obliquely by Ferneze when he invokes 'the scorching heat of heaven's dog' (1.6.40), using the dog star's heat as a metaphor for the 'enforcing eyes' (1.6.41) of the beloved Aurelia, another possible link to the dangerously scorching eyes of the intelligencer.

Unfortunately for Pietro, Malevole's first piece of information concerns him closely, as it suggests that Pietro is being cuckolded by Mendoza (1.3.81). Despite his ostensibly restorative imperative, it seems Malevole may be doing this parasitically for reward, or, so to speak, out of the badness of his heart. Either way he is rewarded materially for his work (1.3.153–4, 1.4.62). Even as he sighingly muses on the unhealthiness of this situation, lamenting the acquisitive ambitions that are 'heaved to them are minions to a crown' (1.4.78), it is exemplified in the meretricious Maquerelle, who demands 'jewels of your ears to receive my enforced duty' (1.6.6–7) when asked by Aurelia for information on Mendoza. This might serve to emphasise the ubiquity of the servitude and patronage systems which underpin contemporary networks of intelligence at all levels.

Pietro's detailed introductory appraisal includes lamenting that Malevole's speech is 'halter-worthy at all hours' (1.2.27–8), as Malevole himself admits in his metadramatic confession to the audience of his disguise: 'this affected strain gives me a tongue / As fetterless as is an emperor's' (1.3.164–5). In this expression, too, it seems that the high and low are unified. This is implied again when he alludes to his position and his current role, asking Celso in a metadramatic moment, 'play I well the free-breathed discontent?' (1.4.31), determining that 'he's resolute who can no lower sink' (1.4.43). Throughout, his free-flowing intelligencing is linked with both incontinence and predatory hunger, as Pietro finds and declares 'his appetite is unsatiable as the grave' (1.2.20–1). Although Altofronto/Malevole's banishment has come, he claims, because he had a deficit of the Machiavellian mechanisms of governance, so 'wanted those old instruments of state, / Dissemblance and suspect' (1.4.9–10), and was thus usurped by 'the crowd' (1.4.14), he is certainly making up for that lack of suspect dissembling in his present role. Mendoza is his exemplar for this kind of conduct, as may be seen when he asks, in a deeply ironic passage aimed at justifying himself to Pietro, 'hath my intrusion / To places private and prohibited, / Only to observe the closer passages / . . . Made me suspected . . . deemed a villain?' (1.7.25–7, 29). As Mendoza plots to dupe the cuckold Pietro and kill Ferneze as Aurelia's lover, he declares alone to the offstage audience that, 'as bears shape young, so I'll form my device' (1.7.87), and the typical bestial and theatrical aspects of intelligencing are again expressed here. His moral imperative as a device-maker is found in his statement that there is 'nothing so holy, no band of nature so strong, no law of friendship so sacred, but I'll profane, burst, violate, 'fore I'll endure disgrace, contempt, and poverty' (2.1.15–17). When Malevole is proposing friendship to Mendoza, and agrees to come to his chamber 'as a raven to a dunghill' (2.5.115), he is following his path and switching the dog metaphor to a simile of the other main image of the intelligencing type: the carrion bird. The connection with his metadramatic status is further established when, after rescuing Ferneze, he comments, 'now 'gins close plots to work; the scene grows full' (2.5.160). These connections between the metadramatic and the intelligencing function of the character are the natural stage for the outworking of Malevole's duality.

The almost fully metadramatic scene where Mendoza and Malevole converse about their natures is witnessed by various audiences. Firstly there is the onstage audience of Celso, who 'retires' at Malevole's request to 'give place' (3.3.37). Here Malevole is ironically accused of being noble, which of course he is, and thus affirms his hybridity, if somewhat obliquely, in the seemingly radical words of Seneca channelling Plato: 'there is no slave but may derive from kings, no king but may derive from slaves'.[39] It is then that he is suborned to 'murder the Duke!' (3.3.74), and of course money is again involved in the exchange (3.3.72). Then, when Malevole is quick to plot a better death than Mendoza suggests for the impedimentary Duke, Mendoza declares him a 'god of policy!' (3.3.115), which is, as we have seen, a synonym at this time for Machiavellian plotting and politicking. As Malevole invites Celso out from his hiding place onstage and asks him whether he heard this, he also asks 'Heaven' the same, and thus conjures God as his ultimate offstage audience, asking him why he suffers the world to 'carouse damnation even with greedy swallow' (3.3.128) without thundering his displeasure. Depending on the production, this may equally be addressed to the offstage audience, although this would have been an unlikely choice at the time. In this holistic metadramatic atmosphere, Malevole informs Pietro of the plan to kill him and makes his own intelligencing and authorial plot to disguise Pietro as a hermit to witness the guilt of Mendoza first hand. When this is witnessed, and Pietro and Malevole are severally enjoined by Mendoza to kill one another, Pietro rants and Malevole responds with a characteristically metadramatic turn, 'do not turn player; there's more of them than can well live one by another already' (4.3.4–5). In these ways, Malevole exemplifies all the characteristics of the informer and intelligencer. He is the eponymous malcontent with a reputation tending towards the melancholic; he is in disguise, playing a role within a role as a metadramatic character; and he is learning a Machiavellian practice from an expert. He also uses dog and bird imagery and has the reputation for hunger that the voracious parasite deserves. His one dissent from this pattern is in the vice of flattery, which is a delinquency he does not exhibit, declaring he 'had rather follow a drunkard, and live by licking up his vomit, than by servile flattery' (4.5.66–8). This seems set up to contrast with jaded types like Bilioso, mentored by Aurelia's handmaid Bianca, who boasts 'see the use of flattery. I did ever counsel you to flatter greatness, and you have profited well' (3.1.45–6), and the reply comes 'thou art ever my politician!' (3.1.50). Further, Malevole curses Bilioso as a 'whoreson flesh-fly' (4.5.105), another common image of the parasitic courtier, who often exhibits intelligencing tendencies along with his sycophancy. In this, Marston the satirist may be reflected, with this essentially linguistic resistance to the typical model of the intelligencer perhaps being the key to his restoration. This may sound ironic coming from the metadramatic hybrid of Altofronto/Malevole, but then, as he says, 'there goes but a pair of shears betwixt an emperor and the son of a bagpiper; only the dyeing, dressing, pressing, glossing, makes the difference' (4.5.116–19).

In the final metadramatic scene, where the masque is to be the inner play that resolves and puts an end to the play's playing within roles, Mendoza cries out 'Malevole!' and the eponymous hero replies simply 'no' (5.6.113–14). Malevole's reversion to the noble state here is accompanied by a statement about 'great ones' which has an anti-Machiavellian bent, that 'when they observe not Heaven's imposed conditions, / They are no kings, but forfeit their commissions' (5.6.148–9) and he rather peremptorily sorts out his friends from his foes, ending by asserting 'the rest of idle actors idly part' (5.6.163) and dismissing the offstage audience with a breezy 'good night' (5.6.165). This breaks the spell of the character's hybridity and his power to straddle the worlds of authority and intelligencing. Here, the Epilogus, having the last word, offers the audience 'art above Nature, Judgement above Art' and asks that they 'receive this piece, which hope nor fear yet daunteth', declaring finally, that 'he that knows most knows most how much he wanteth' (Epi. 16–18). This oblique appeal for favourable interpretation and sober self-assessment is couched in the vocabulary of assertion, a nod back to the careless pisser on the leg of the world perhaps, but may be somewhat superfluous. After all, this is already a forthright argument: a Machiavellian character has rejected the world of the Machiavel and all its associated typologies for a merciful restoration of judgement over artifice. The performative theatre of intelligencing has been superseded again by the theatre of authority, purged of the influence of the Florentine courtier and thus relegitimised as an ideal. In this process, the intelligencer has been performing the role of the satirist, merely offering physic to a sick society. If this ideal seems too easy an answer, the extent to which it can hold may be apparent from the proliferation of other texts and characters of the period which cover the same ground.

In *The Revenger's Tragedy* (1607), the very idea of representation itself is being represented, not merely relating to the theatrical experience but also in terms of the ways in which authority represents and justifies itself. To an extent, the play deals with the issue of revenge by contraposing the concept of honour and integrity with the purely corrupting power of money, but this quickly devolves into power plays of courtly intrigue around intelligencing for sex and power. Typically, the play frames these ubiquitous Machiavellian manoeuvres metadramatically and these then form part of the critique of representation.

If he had any part in the authorship of the play, Cyril Tourneur's life is largely obscure to us. We may, however, conjecture an understanding of the kind of characters drawn here from the general environment of the Jacobean court, and in Tourneur's case his association with the Cecil family. Tourneur was arrested on the orders of the Privy Council in 1617, but released after intervention by Sir Edward Cecil, nephew of the spymaster Robert Cecil, of whom Tourneur may have written a 'character' in 1612. He died from disease contracted onboard a ship of Edward Cecil's fleet on the loot-hunting raid at Cadiz in 1625. Moving in these circles, it seems safe to assume the author's familiarity with the forms of authority under scrutiny here. If the authorship rests with Thomas Middleton, we have no evidence of similar connections, but it is nevertheless certain that his association with other poets and players whose lives were more overtly entwined with the world of intelligencing would have furnished him with plenty of material in this regard. His own experiences of falling foul of the Bishops' ban on satire in 1599 would have also given him an understanding of the nature of the resistance of authority to critique, as might later the closing down of *A Game at Chess* after just nine performances for inflaming the ire of the Spanish Ambassador.[40] For both of these writers, representation seems to have been problematic.

The beginnings of plays are always very revealing and in this case Vindice, the title's eponymous revenger, enters to witness the passing over the stage of the guilty characters, metadramatically, at a distance and by torchlight. He is therefore immediately presented as an onstage audience, and his first words are to interpret these dramatis personae and represent them as lecherous, impious and evil, sarcastically declaring them to be 'four ex'lent characters' (1.1.5).

The fact that he does this while holding the skull of his girlfriend, Gloriana, who we find was poisoned by the Duke when she rejected him (1.1.32–4), may also serve a metatheatrical function in referring to *Hamlet*, another play entirely suffused with intelligencing and metadrama.[41] Vindice's brother Hippolito calls the skull 'Death's vizard' (1.1.49), implying a theatrical or masquing element to this memento mori over which Vindice is sighing. In his opening lament over the loss of this lover, Vindice claims vengeance is what he calls a 'tenant to Tragedy' (1.1.40) in a further metadramatic moment which signals that the play will deal not only with the revenge of the title, but also with the act of representation itself, within its critique of contemporary authority structures. Vindice's character then is forged in the furnace of metadrama, which suits his intelligencing status. In as much as this play is a post-Shakespearean meditation on the genre of revenge tragedy itself, this crucial theatrical and intelligencing element has long been neglected.[42]

Vindice's brother Hippolito's introduction encompasses the complaint that the Duke's aptly named son Lussurioso attempted 'by policy to open and unhusk me / About the time and common rumour' (1.1.67–9), and this tells us that he has narrowly avoided being used as an informer. Instead, as he says, he 'had so much wit to keep my thoughts / Up in their built houses, yet afforded him / An idle satisfaction without danger' (1.1.70–2), indicating both the hazardous nature of that territory and Hippolito's reluctance to entertain this function. When Lussurioso asks Hippolito instead to recruit a 'base-coined pandar' (1.1.80) to procure a certain woman, however, he recommends his brother Vindice and does so with the quite damning claim that 'this our age swims within him / . . . He is so near kin to this present minute' (1.3.24, 26). This may be merely playing the linguistic game of the court and nepotistically bargaining for a favour, but it nevertheless contains a clear critique of the understood immorality of the contemporary social moment, at least as a concept.

Unfortunately for Vindice, the object of his pandering is to be his own sister, Castiza (1.3.128), but the very fact that he is willing to play this game suggests a patent connection between morally dubious intelligencing and the business of acting. Moreover, when Lussurioso gives him gold for this immoral service, saying 'gold though it be dumb does utter the best thanks' (1.3.29), it plays to the typical understanding, and theatrical representation, of the particular nature of the intelligencer at 'this present minute' as a parasitic, grasping and lying danger to the commonweal. This is confirmed in the most personal of terms as, immediately after Lussurioso and Vindice have been discussing sex and the strange lusts that Vindice pretends he has witnessed as a pander, Lussurioso gives him more money and provocatively asserts 'thus I enter thee' (1.3.88). Such a venal and venereal sense of money is emphasised when Lussurioso relates Castiza's chastity to money for spending (1.3.116–19). The job at hand involves Vindice metadramatically acting within the act and disguising himself appropriately, as he tells the audience in a parting aside, 'I'll quickly turn into another' (1.1.134), one whose name is to be 'Piato'. This theatrical employment may have an immoral aim, but it also affords Vindice a window of opportunity to revenge his poisoned lover, by intelligencing his way into the right sphere in which to perform his vengeance. In this process, metadrama and intelligencing are presented as two sides of the same coin, and thus representation itself is proposed as a particular problematic.

Initially, however, Vindice performs a mockery of intelligencing, whose ostensible aim for him at least is to test Castiza's chasteness. This is a bare defence which very quickly runs into mortal trouble when he discovers that his mother, Gratiana, is not only biddable in this case but is very much willing to help persuade Castiza to prostitute herself for the sake of Lussurioso's money. His seemingly better intentions as something of a mock intelligencer are thus corrupted by one he could hope to act in a less corrupt manner. Gratiana's response to Vindice's suggestions on behalf of Lussurioso sets the moral context for these personal dilemmas. Gratiana, whose name means 'grace', works as a travesty of the divine mother, and thus stands for the deeply corrupted nature of a society which sells its integrity to the highest bidder.

This is a context which is mirrored in the circumstances of a court where the Duchess herself lusts incestuously after Spurio, the Duke's own bastard son (1.2.110), and where one of the Duchess's sons, known as Younger Son, has raped and killed Lord Antonio's revered wife (1.2.43). Moreover, he has done this using a masque to cover the crime and while acting like an intelligencer, 'full of fraud and flattery' (1.4. 29–31). When Vindice has made this first assay on the pimping of his sister, reporting back his mother's disturbingly encouraging speech, Lussurioso tells him to kneel and beg an office, and Vindice replies 'I would desire but this, my lord; to have all the fees behind the arras' (2.2.79–80), which has been glossed as 'a tax on lovemaking' or 'fees for making assignations'.[43] The nuance of this, however, is far more likely to reference the intelligencer's potentially hefty fees, which would also be generated by behind-the-arras activities, as the informing devices of very many contemporary plays bear out. The play's personal Machiavellian intrigues are thus presented within morally dissolute authority structures that support a normative framework of depraved and parasitic personae and financial relations which are associated with intelligencing. They are also largely metadramatic in nature.

It is clear that Vindice still feels at this stage the moral dishonour of the job of intelligencer-pander (2.2.89–103) and throughout the following scenes the structures of intelligence and metadrama threaten to overwhelm as they pile up, one on the next, in various ways. Firstly, Hippolito informs Vindice of the bastard Spurio's virtual incest, of which he has been given intelligence by 'stair-foot pandars' (2.2.111) in the household. Then when Spurio enters, he is just in the process of being informed of Lussurioso's pursuit of their sister by a servant, who was informed of it in turn by someone 'most inward' with Lussurioso's lusts (2.2.119). Entirely appropriately, Hippolito says 'there's a wicked whisper; hell is in his ear / Stay, lets observe his passage' (2.2.114–16) and they 'retire' (2.2.116 s.d.) to overhear this intelligence. Here, one informer gives information to another informer who passes it to Spurio while overheard by two other informers in the hidden audience, one of whom informs his own patron. Next, when Lussurioso enters, Vindice says 'Brother fall back / And you shall learn some mischief' (2.2.150–1), and Hippolito again stands aside to watch Vindice play his role and inform Lussurioso of what he has just heard about Spurio from Hippolito. So, in this case the hidden informer is an onstage audience that watches another informer, who is playing a role within his role, passing on incriminating information that the hidden informer was informed of by another informer. The hyperbolic and self-conscious nature of the overdetermination of these multiple strata of theatrical representation serves to suggest the proliferation of intelligencing, and this can only operate as a satirical critique of the society which produces it.

The outcome of all this hyperbolised intelligencing is simply Lussurioso's passionate anger, until, losing control, he runs off with

Vindice to the Duchess's bedroom to catch the unhappy couple at it. But his rash action on this spurious basis results only in disaster as he catches the Duke and Duchess in bed instead, and is accused of wanting to murder them. He fails to inform the Duke of Spurio's sins because he is dragged out peremptorily and is thus put in some danger of serious punishment himself until the Duke pardons him, and this only because his other sons so clearly do want him dead, although they plead otherwise (2.3.80–8ff.). As a further consequence of this misapplication of intelligence, although the Younger Son, the rapist offspring of the lusty Duchess, is to be sprung from confinement by his brothers Ambitioso and Supervacuo (who have, they inform him, 'thought upon a device to get thee out by a trick' (3.4.13)), the gaoler's wires are crossed and the death warrant they deliver for Lussurioso, not knowing he has been freed, is instead enacted upon the Younger Son. These farcical cross-plots, it may be asserted, are just the primary consequences of a system of authority based on the depravity of both the Machiavellian political milieu and the individual actions of the self-interested intelligencer.

Other intelligencing forms, expressed through such metadramatic structures as onstage audiences, operate when Hippolito again 'retires' (3.5.119), this time to see the old Duke kiss the poisoned skull of Gloriana, Vindice's betrothed, in a device of Vindice's making (3.5.144). Here it is disguised as some shadowy female in a move which would surely pose a challenge for any production. Next the Duke is violently silenced and made to oversee Spurio's incestuous relationship with the Duchess as a passively subdued hidden audience and in revenge for his own original poisoning of Gloriana, before being allowed to die (3.5.216). This hints at a fantasy of authorial control over the offstage audience which is often an element in metadrama, which testifies to the instability of the structures of interpretation to which authors themselves were sometimes subject, and which certainly seems to impend heavily in their imaginations and the dramatic plots and structures which express them.

For instance, there is considerable metadramatic irony generated in the fact that Lussurioso casts off the disguised Vindice for seemingly falsely accusing Spurio and getting Lussurioso into trouble, but unknowingly re-employs him, this time undisguised, to kill himself in the person of his previously disguised persona. This structure sets up the offstage audience to share a critical perspective on these deceptive forms. The immanent dramatic irony is amplified in an aside to the audience as Lussurioso confides in them his 'deep policy' that he will kill Vindice for knowing too much, once the murder is done (4.2.191–2). Money of course changes hands again in these transactions (4.2.114).

The audience here in fact, along with both Vindice and Hippolito, already know far more than Lussurioso about every convoluted turn of events and murderous self-interested ambition and this places them in an authoritative interpretative position. However, Vindice has another metadramatic 'device' (4.3.207) in which he proposes to dress up the Duke's undiscovered corpse as himself to fool Lussurioso that the deed has been done as ordered. This is the second such device in the play, after the scene kissing Gloriana's skull. Here the corpse of the victim of the first device is used in the second to convince his son that the intelligencer, on whose faulty information the son rashly endangered his own life, has been killed by his next intelligencer, who is in fact the same person. In disguising the Duke as himself, the intelligencer thus uses one authority figure to undermine the safety of another in a theatrical and intelligencing interchange which speaks to the connection of both. This very clearly conflates the complexities of the metadramatic plotting business of the intelligencer with the demise of legitimate authority which has allowed itself to be undermined by its own corrupt underlings. These intelligencing matters are also alluded to when Vindice says that the Duke died 'like a politician, in hugger-mugger' (5.1.17–18), that is 'covertly'. Such complications can only multiply in what are dangerous times for those who employ these parasitic 'flesh flies' (5.1.12), self-interested, subversive and vengeful sycophants and inappropriately empowered audiences. This no doubt works as a powerful pre-emption of the interpretative responses of the play's offstage audiences.

Furthermore, when the old Duke is discovered dead and Lussurioso inherits, he orders revels and the other nobles make preparations for a masque (5.2.13) in which Supervacuo plans to get rid of Spurio. In this, he is witness to the connection of drama and plotting when he says, 'in this time of revels, tricks may be set afoot . . . / A masque is treason's license' (5.1.173, 177). At the same time, Vindice and Hippolito plan to use the revels to conceal their swords and kill the new Duke and his nobles in a general rebellion involving 'five hundred gentlemen' (5.2.28), the conspirators aiming to make those 'few nobles that have long suppressed you / . . . sigh blood' (5.2.11, 22). After the dumb show of the coronation, Vindice and Hippolito dance in the masque of revengers and kill Lussurioso and three nobles. In this way theatre becomes the explicit setting for a very pointed plot of revenge, which echoes metadramatic elements in Kyd's *Spanish Tragedy* and prefigures them in Massinger's *The Roman Actor*. Their act is marked by thunder. As Vindice says: 'Dost know thy cue, thou big-voiced crier?' (5.3.43), carrying on the metadramatic metaphor by claiming: 'When thunder claps, heaven likes the tragedy' (5.3.48). Here God appears to applaud the act with his own 'claps' of thunder, approving of the play and by extension the deed, and playing the ultimate offstage audience as he does in *The Malcontent*. To the extent that he is cued in by the 'Duke's groans' which are 'thunder's watch words' (5.3.46), as Vindice says, God himself is further acknowledged as an actor in the tragedy. This works as a vindication of the theatrical project to some extent, and affords it a certain validity, or even reality, which may act as an apologetic. But it does implicate God himself in the grubby transactions of a Machiavellian concept of authority.

As the play draws to a conclusion with the second masque, Ambitioso and Supervacuo arrive to kill Lussurioso and are killed in their turn. Vindice next elects the wronged Antonio to the dukedom, in the process confessing to the murder. Significantly, Vindice and Hippolito are then taken away to be executed as scapegoats for the authority structures which necessitated their services. This series of disastrous outcomes arises from a few simple acts of overhearing, overseeing and passing on of information. The masque within the play thus acts as a medium for the resolution of the plot in revenge and turns out to be the most apt vehicle for the actions of the venal, murderous intelligencer. It also provides an effective modern medium for the telling of an urgent story: the use of intelligencers undermines the moral authority of the social formation they support, even to the extent of tainting the role of God in human institutions. In as much as Vindice embraces the parasitical intelligencing roles his social order offers him, his ultimate ruin illustrates its inherent dysfunction. On a personal level, the demise of the intelligencing Machiavellian politician shows that, despite the promise of great reward or even restitutive justice as here, their own fate is tangled with the deceptive representational sphere they promote, and that those who live by the deceiver's word will die by the deceiver's word.

Notes

1. Nashe, *Haue with you to Saffron-Walden*, p. 106.
2. William Shakespeare, *Richard III*, ed. Antony Hammond (London: Methuen, 1981), p. 100.
3. Hammond, p. 100.
4. See Niccolò Machiavelli, *The Prince* (1514), trans. George Bull (Harmondsworth: Penguin, 1961).
5. For the influence of other Machiavellian ideas and rhetoric on Iago, see Ken Jacobsen, 'Iago's Art of War: The "Machiavellian Moment" in *Othello*', *Modern Philology*, Vol. 106, No. 3 (February 2009), pp. 497–529.
6. George Abbot, *An exposition vpon the prophet Jonah* (1600), <http://gateway.proquest.com/openurl?ctx_ver=Z39.88-2003&res_id=xri:eebo&rft_id=xri:eebo:citation:99836358> (last accessed 11 February 2018).
7. Christopher Marlowe, *The Jew of Malta*, ed. David Bevington (New York and Manchester: Manchester University Press, 1997), p. 8.
8. Edward Guilpin, *Skialetheia. Or, A shadowe of truth, in certaine epigrams and satyres* (London: Printed by I[ames] R[oberts] for Nicholas Ling, 1598) <http://gateway.proquest.com/openurl?ctx_ver=Z39.88-2003&res_id=xri:eebo&rft_id=xri:eebo:citation:99841568> (last accessed 8 March 2018).
9. Christopher Marlowe, *The Jew of Malta*, in David Bevington (ed.), *English Renaissance Drama* (New York and London: W. W. Norton, 2002).
10. Irving Ribner, 'Marlowe and Machiavelli', *Comparative Literature*, Vol. 6 (1954), pp. 348–56, at p. 353.
11. Luc Borot, 'Machiavellian Diplomacy and Dramatic Developments in Marlowe's *The Jew of Malta*', *Cahiers Elizabéthains*, Vol. 33 (1988), pp. 1–11, at p. 2.
12. Margaret Scott, 'Machiavelli and the Machiavel', *Renaissance Drama*, Vol. 15 (1984), pp. 147–74, at p. 151.
13. Christopher Marlowe, *The Jew of Malta*, ed. N. W. Bawcutt (Manchester: Manchester University Press, 1978), p. 13.
14. Lisa Hopkins, *Christopher Marlowe: A Literary Life* (Basingstoke: Palgrave, 2000), p. 40.
15. Hopkins, p. 68.
16. Arata Ide, '*The Jew of Malta* and the Diabolic Power of Theatrics in the 1580s', *Studies in English Literature, 1500–1900*, Vol. 46, No. 2, Tudor and Stuart Drama (Spring, 2006), pp. 257–79, at p. 258.
17. Marlowe, *The Jew of Malta*, ed. David Bevington, p. 2.

18. Ide, p. 259.
19. Marlowe, *The Jew of Malta*, ed. David Bevington, p. 8.
20. Ide, p. 259.
21. William Shakespeare, *King Henry IV, Part 1*, ed. David Scott Kastan (London: Arden, 2002); see also Angus, pp. 136–60.
22. Nicholl, p. 179.
23. Marlowe, *The Jew of Malta*, ed. David Bevington, p. 6.
24. Hall, *Characters*, p. 105
25. Janette Dillon, *Theatre, Court and City, 1595–1610: Drama and Social Space in London* (Cambridge: Cambridge University Press, 2000), p. 86.
26. Hall, *Characters*, p. 105.
27. John Marston, *The Malcontent*, ed. George K. Hunter (London: Methuen, 1975), p. lxvii.
28. A. H. Gilbert, *Literary Criticism, Plato to Dryden* (Detroit: Wayne State University Press, 1962), p. 186.
29. Douglas Lanier, 'Satire, Self Concealment, and Statecraft: The Game of Identity in John Marston's *The Malcontent*', *Pacific Coast Philology*, Vol. 22, No. 1/2 (1987), pp. 35–45, at p. 37.
30. Marston, *The Malcontent*, p. lxviii.
31. See Niccolò Machiavelli, *The Prince* (1640), p. 148, <http://gateway.proquest.com/openurl?ctx_ver=Z39.88-2003&res_id=xri:eebo&rft_id=xri:eebo:image:12126:8> (last accessed 12 December 2017).
32. Marston, *The Malcontent*, p. lxviii.
33. Hall, *Characters*, p. 105.
34. Lanier, p. 37.
35. Marston, *The Malcontent*, p. 36, n. 49; p. 17, n. 5.
36. Stephen Orgel, *Impersonations* (Cambridge: Cambridge University Press, 1996), p. 48.
37. Marston, *The Malcontent*, p. 22, n. 12.
38. Ben Jonson, *Poetaster*, ed. Tom Cain (Manchester: Manchester University Press, 1995).
39. Marston, *The Malcontent*, p. 94, n. 60.
40. Loxley, p. 22; Thomas Postlewait, 'Theater Events and Their Political Contexts: A Problem in the Writing of Theater History', in Janelle G. Reinelt and Joseph R. Roach (eds), *Critical Theory and Performance* (Ann Arbor: University of Michigan Press, 2007), pp. 198–222, at p. 200.
41. Cyril Tourneur, *The Revenger's Tragedy*, ed. Bryan Gibbons (London: A & C Black, 1991). Unless otherwise noted, this is the edition cited throughout.

42. Aimee Ross-Kilroy, '"The Very Ragged Bone": Dismantling Masculinity in Thomas Middleton's *The Revengers Tragedy*', *Renaissance and Reformation/Renaissance et Reforme*, Vol. 33, No. 4 (2010), pp. 51–71, at p. 53.
43. Tourneur, *The Revenger's Tragedy*, ed. Bryan Gibbons, p. 41, n. 79; Cyril Tourneur, *The Revenger's Tragedy*, ed. R. A. Foakes (London: Methuen, 1975), p. 47, n. 81.

Chapter 3

The Knight of the Burning Pestle and the Menace of the Audience

In Francis Beaumont's *The Knight of the Burning Pestle* (1607), the metadramatic field of representative play and social commentary includes a very obvious example of an onstage audience, comprising a Citizen and his wife Nell, who emerge from offstage to interfere with the performance. These metadramatis personae are clearly meant to offer an ironic and entertainingly chaotic element, but their constant interferingly critical observation of each passing scene suggests something more serious may be going on. Their intrusive presence in this play seems a very apt mirror for the widely felt sense of continuous scrutiny by potential intelligencers in early modern society and, more particularly, in relation to a significant anxiety over the interpretation of the fictional worlds of the theatre.

When this hyper-vigilant onstage Citizen judges that there is 'abomination knavery in this play' (1.61), to which he is a very visible audience, his response is to utter darkly suggestive threats about what he might do with such information. These murmurings appear to cow the actors in the midst of their performance and place informing at the metadramatic centre of the offstage audience's experience of the play. In Ben Jonson's *Bartholomew Fair* (1614), other unsafe or threatening onstage audiences appear, as may be exemplified by the self-informing overseer Justice Overdo or the hypocritically moralistic puritan Zeal-of-the-land Busy. Their metadramatic interactions also suggest a concern with a general malaise affecting interpretation and authority, one which is somehow putting the seemingly natural connection between the legitimacy of each out of joint. Jonson's onstage watchers seem very much cast in the mould of the interrupting citizens of this, his Mermaid Tavern companion's earlier metadramatic play, except for the fact that Jonson's onstage audiences are often allowed only ridiculous or overblown reactions, a kind of didactic dysfunction, while remaining entirely under the control of the author. Although *The Knight of the Burning Pestle* stages a similar disjunction, Beaumont's onstage audience are allowed a much more actively intrusive role, as they attempt to control both the writing and the production of the play they inhabit. Unlike in many other metadramatic interactions, in this case the players are forced to react to these unruly disruptions and alter the play as they go along, extemporising in response to the ugly incursions they encounter. Beaumont's play therefore stages a kind of dramatic authorship which seems to feel itself under siege by an unruly form of audience empowerment, and one very much associated with the social pressures of intelligencing and informing.

The onstage presence of Beaumont's disruptive citizens might be perceived as merely playful in the generic context of a fairly farcical comedy, but the menace of their threats has, like all good comedy, some sound basis in reality. In his poem 'An Epistle to a Friend', Jonson expresses the common unease around the fact that 'flatterers, spies, / Informers, masters both of arts and lies; / [are] . . . easier far to find / Than once to number.'[1] Jonson, who had been imprisoned just three years previously with Chapman for *Eastward Ho*, was beleaguered by informers when inside, but this was not his only such experience. As I have argued throughout, this perception is borne out in wider society at the time, where there is a rising sense of the ubiquity of informers employed on an ad hoc basis to feed administrations and individuals of influence with information.[2] The possibly hefty payments that contemporary legislation specified for such information, with the intelligencer potentially receiving a significant portion of any fine imposed, dangerously commercialised any detrimental interpretation such an informer might desire to construct.[3] It seems, further, that the profusion of metadramatic forms at this time itself registers heightened concerns, even one might say fears, of the hidden watching, eavesdropping and tale-bearing which is associated with intelligencers and informers.[4] Beaumont's dangerously intrusive citizens, straddling dramatic strata so theatrically, may be exemplary in this respect.

KBP's metadramatic playfulness therefore shades into a more disturbing narrative where the figure of the intelligencer lurks as a significant element in the dramatic figuring of an audience and, by extension, an authority which is tainted by the connection with such despised individuals. Furthermore, contemporary metadrama often aims to manipulate the parameters of an audience's interpretation and this desire for control suggests a defensive preoccupation with the boundaries and mechanisms of authority. In this way the play's metadramatic structures are a window onto the strictures within which early modern authors like Beaumont feel themselves constrained to write.

Within a culture permeated by the practice of informing, the shifting contemporary hierarchies of city authority, which to some degree the citizens represent, may also at this time be perceived as untrustworthy. This may be the case even to the extent of fostering 'charlatans, liars and frauds', as Janette Dillon has claimed.[5] This sense of unsound authority is carried onto the stage here in a structure which offers a metadramatic parody of audience engagement and draws in actors, authors, citizens and servants, and the authorities of the City which loom in the background. The knockabout interplay of these various authorities in *KBP* seems as much concerned with material jurisdiction as with the politics of dramatic representation. Thus the Prologue enters and begins by situating the play geographically: 'From all that's near the court, from all that's great / Within the compass of the city walls, / We now have brought our scene' (Ind. 1–3).[6] Beaumont's Prologue is careful to distinguish city authorities from courtly ones by defining his own boundaries within the 'compass of the city walls'. On one level, the Citizen and his wife who comprise this onstage audience signify the city's desire to intrude upon the Blackfriars' liberty; this encroachment was finally granted by James in 1608, the year after the play's first performance, as Dillon also notes.[7] At the time of the performance, however, the Blackfriars' Dominican monastic history still rendered it free of city jurisdiction, lending a relatively safe ambiguity to the authoritative position of plays produced there. Bearing in mind these geographical and authoritative considerations, we encounter in this case an audience that crosses the boundaries of performance and representation and steps up into the world of the play itself, where states of watching and being watched are foregrounded as modes of subjectivity and authority. At the same time, the contemporary offstage audience of 1607 is foregrounded metadramatically, both explicitly as a play-going audience with all its interpretative power and implicitly in the negative onstage model of the citizens.[8] The results of such metadrama are twofold, both giving a sense of the necessary negotiation between these sites of early modern narrative authority in the creation of meaning and dramatising an implicit correlation between them. In this case, the shadow of the reviled intelligencer that an onstage audience may conventionally harbour is further cast over the city authorities as a whole.

These issues are not limited to parodic dramatis personae, but seriously affect the pressures that bear upon both authorship and performance at the time. After its apparently conventional apologetic, making it explicit that 'the author had no intent to wrong any one in this comedy',[9] in the printing at least, the play begins with a further familiar plea against misinterpretation, here drawn from John Lyly's *Sappho and Phao* (1584):

> Where the bee can suck no honey, she leaves her sting behind; and where the bear cannot find origanum to heal his grief, he blasteth all other leaves with his breath. We fear it is like to fare so with us, that seeing you cannot draw from our labours sweet content, you leave behind you a sour mislike, and with open reproach blame our good meanings because you cannot reap the wonted mirth . . . We have endeavoured to be as far from unseemly speeches . . . as we hope you will be free from unkind reports or, mistaking the author's intention – who never aimed at any one particular in this play. (Prol. 1–7, 14–18)

This should not be dismissed lightly as a mere convention, since the nature of conventions is that they come to seem self-perpetuating or even 'natural' when in fact their very conventionality often masks an ongoing political or material reality. Here, the ground of contention is within a contrast which is drawn between the 'honey', 'sweet content', 'mirth', 'good meaning' and avoidance of 'unseemly speeches' which the author promises, and the potential 'sting', blasting 'breath', 'sour mislike', 'open reproach', 'unkind reports' and 'mistaking the author's intention' which he attributes as potential actions of the offstage audience. This is the same 'fond and merely literal interpretation or illiterate misprision' (22–3) over which Walter Burre expresses his concern in the play's dedicatory epistle to Master Robert Keysar.[10] With this in mind it is significant that a hostile audience is allowed onto the stage itself, bearing all of these menacing characteristics and potentialities with them.

The opening of the play comedically explores the nature of the offstage audience's authority, as the interrupting Citizen enters from the audience and debates with the Prologue upon a fitting subject for the play.[11] Invading thus the space of the stage, the Citizen first commands silence, and when asked what he means by this, replies 'that you have no good meaning: These seven years there hath been plays at this house; I have observed it, you have still girds at citizens, and now you call your play *The London Merchant*. Down with your title, boy' (Ind. 6–9). This interjection relates directly to the prefatory apologetic: the Citizen questions the 'good meaning' which the Prologue has promised and accuses the house of having 'girds at citizens' which, he says, he has 'observed'. Boundaries between dramatic fictions in the two plays – *The Knight of the Burning Pestle* and *The London Merchant* – are thus destabilised, with the acting company struggling to perform their play in the face of the chivalric story which is requested by the onstage audience of the Citizen and Nell, and meant to be acted by their servant Rafe. This explicit representation of the audience is visible at all times in this play and acts as a constant self-referentially metadramatic mode throughout. Once the audience is established onstage, they frame an inner narrative which they are then able largely to dominate. Initially, it is the jurisdiction of the city itself which is at stake here, and it is to this that the Prologue alludes as he questions the citizen's social status as 'a member of the noble city' and a 'freeman' (Ind. 10, 12). The Citizen asserts that he is also a grocer, and the Prologue responds 'so, grocer, then by your sweet favour, we intend no abuse to the city' (Ind. 14–15). Standing outside the jurisdiction of the city authorities, this theatrical 'we' seems nevertheless to embody an authorship feeling the pressure of social forces beyond its control.

Throughout this episode, the Prologue attempts to reassert theatrical control over a world in which authoritative representation seems to have become diffuse and promiscuous, as the invasive audience continually requires their input into the authoring of the play, or at least to augment what is already there. When the Citizen demands that the play contain a grocer, his wife Nell, who is at this point still offstage, has her own idea for the narrative, shouting 'let him kill a lion with a pestle, husband; let him kill a lion with a pestle'; the Citizen agrees: 'so he shall, I'll have him kill a lion with a pestle' (Ind. 42–4). To 'kill a lion with a pestle' is, on one level, a figure of usurped authority, a triumph of the quotidian over the majestic. This image of the powerful pestle incorporates both the idea of a grocer's guild and his wife's specifically domestic sphere.[12] It also usurps the authoritative positions of the player and the author, to whom this proposed narrative element is at no point referred. With his wife now also on the stage, this metadramatic Citizen sets out his own stage, commands, 'boy, let my wife and I have a couple of stools, and then begin,' and orders 'let the grocer do rare things' (Ind. 55–6). When the Prologue objects to these amendments on the simple ground of a lack of sufficient actors, Nell has a further suggestion, which is to 'let Rafe play him', and to declare 'beshrew me if I do not think he will go beyond them all' (Ind. 59–60). Thus Rafe, the couple's indentured serving man, having been reluctantly accepted by the Prologue, also mounts the stage and crosses the boundary into the world of the drama, the Prologue even promising him 'a suit of apparel if he will go in' (Ind. 87) presumably to the tiring-house, the heart of the dramatic operation. This onstage audience therefore take on the additional roles of dramatic author and actor and, while Rafe exits to be costumed and thus be assimilated further into the dramatic frame, they continue to straddle representational boundaries, sitting upon their stools on the stage.

Thomas Dekker may well have had this play partly in mind in his contemporary parody of rank and convention, *The Gull's Hornbook* (1609), when he suggests that the fashionable place to be seen at the theatre was no longer above the tiring-house but 'on the very rushes where the comedy is to dance', a position simultaneously honoured, expensive and ridiculed. As Dekker points out, such an onstage audience must be 'planted valiantly, because impudently, beating down the mews and hisses of the opposed rascality.'[13] These citizens are certainly valiant and impudent in their interactions. Dekker images one thus seated onstage as either a 'feathered estrich' or a 'piece of ordnance', neatly encapsulating the extent to which such a position is fraught with ambiguities and contradictions.[14] Moreover, Dekker identifies reasons other than self-display for sitting on the stage: by this practice, he adds, 'you have a signed patent to engross the whole commodity of censure, may lawfully presume to be a girder, and stand at the helm to steer the passage of scenes.'[15] Again, this seems a perfect fit for Nell and her censorious husband as they attempt to 'steer the passage of scenes' in this play. Just as *KBP*'s metadramatic passages satirise the negotiation between the different sites of authority necessary to writing for the early modern stage, Dekker also satirises one practical method by which the author and the audience may be associated in this process: 'if you know not the author, you may rail against him; and peradventure so behave yourself, that you may enforce the author to know you.'[16] He further parodies the kind of authority which this spectatorial position affords by describing its correlation with both venal interpretative dissection of texts and bawdy tavern-talk:

> By spreading your body on the stage, and by being a justice in examining of plays, you shall put yourself into such true scenical authority, that some poet shall not dare to present his muse rudely upon your eyes, without having first unmasked her, rifled her, and discovered all her bare and most mystical parts before you at a tavern.[17]

This violent dis-covering of the secret parts of the poet's muse is reminiscent of the informers Rosencrantz and Guildenstern's bawdy response 'faith her privates we' and reflects the distaste and fear with which such critical and informing 'private' practices were regarded in the dramatic community.[18] The misogyny of these metaphors attaches to both the 'scenical authority' of the potentially misinterpreting audience and the implicit intelligencer as incontinent users of language and inappropriate revealers of what should be concealed. The very public interpretative position of the onstage audience is also one which Dekker caricatures as 'being a justice in examining of plays', and there is a danger inherent in occupying such a ridiculous and unstable place of representation which Dekker identifies:

> Whether you be a fool, or a justice of peace; a cuckold, or a captain; a Lord Mayor's son, or a dawcock; a knave, or an under-sheriff; of what stamp soever you be; current or counterfeit; the stage, like time, will bring you to most perfect light, and lay you open.[19]

The stage here is itself presented as a catalyst for the exposure of what is hidden and thus acquires an authority resounding with the revelatory power its apologists might desire. Its propensity to lay open what is concealed, however, parallels the feared interpretative authority of the onstage audience, which demands the discovery of 'all [the muse's] bare and most mystical parts', and the rifling of the poet's muse by this theatricalised 'justice' is thus connected with both the incontinent tongue of the intelligencer, which makes public what is 'private', and the idea of the theatre as moral arbiter for the nation.[20] It is an oblique apology for his trade and a defensive invective against inappropriate audience power.

This kind of overt onstage audience is also very much in a liminal position, sitting across two fields of visual and auditory perception, which in fact metadrama often transcends, though not always simultaneously as here. Also, the onstage audience ranting and interjecting on their stools are both watchers and watched, but doubly so, both from the perspective of the actors and that of the offstage audience. It remains to be conjectured whether the dramatic onstage audience here may have shared that space with a real onstage audience, as was possible. If so, these may be the primary 'gentlemen' to which the citizens and actors occasionally refer and would add an extra layer of dramatic structure. However, this would surely add a level of complexity to the performance that any professional company would have wished to avoid, and this present argument assumes that to be the case. Either way, in *KBP* the practice of stage-sitting, with all its disturbing ramifications, is obviously being held up for public ridicule.

In the course of the narrative, the offstage audience should be aware not far into the play that the Citizen and his wife, although having elevated themselves out of the offstage audience, are actors, a move which sets up the whole area of dramatic practice as a spectacle of possible subversion by its audience. To some extent, this subversive potential is an illusion since this is a dramatised audience whose unruly incursion is in fact scripted and therefore ultimately under the control of the author. With this in mind, it is worth considering the view of comic illusion which M. T. Jones-Davies describes as 'not so much a question of belief or unbelief in a false reality as the acceptance of a theatrical convention making of the spectator an accomplice with the actors.'[21] Here the sense of complicity is entirely compromised by the activities of the metadramatic onstage audience. As they disrupt both the inward pull of the offstage audience's view and the diegetic strata of the narrative, the 'illusions' of the inner play become largely irrelevant to the performance and the Citizen and his wife become themselves the focus of attention. Although the offstage audience presumably knows their metadramatic input is pre-scripted, this in no way tempers the negative form the citizens offer, since we are in no doubt by this stage that a significant element of the model is the implicit threat of informing which underlies their every interpolation. In this way the offstage audience is implicated in the depictions of informing occurring in the play and, given contemporary attitudes to intelligencers, would certainly want to distance itself from this.

The Citizen and Nell make their first truly menacing hints of possible informing after the acting proper begins when, in the dramatic context, the frustrated lovers Jasper and Luce make plain that they have been scheming dramatically: 'you know the plot / We both agreed on?' and Luce declares that she will 'will perform / [her] part exactly' (1.56–8). When the alert Citizen asks 'What a matter's here now? ... I'll be hanged for a halfpenny if there be not some abomination knavery in this play ... let 'em look to't, Rafe must come', he adds with a menacing pause 'and if there be any tricks a-brewing –' and Nell completes the thought, 'let 'em brew and bake too, husband, a'Gods name. Rafe will find all out, I warrant you' (1.61–6). The couple's response here is due to a mistaken perception that Jasper and Luce's 'plotting' and Luce's performing of a 'part' are inherently suspicious. The Citizen's apprehension that there may be 'some abomination knavery in this play' is obviously parodic of over-zealous puritanical responses to such plays, like Zeal-of-the-Land Busy's infuriated reaction to cross-dressing and abomination in *Bartholomew Fair*'s metadramatic puppet-show. Nell's response to this is also characteristic of Justice Overdo's preoccupation with correct weights and measures in that play, and both obviously have specific expectations of Rafe in relation to their interpretation of the unfolding drama. In this circumlocutory way, it is fairly clearly implied that Rafe is, or has been, an informer, himself a discoverer of abominations, and both responses again speak of a culture suffused with expectations of intelligencing and informing. This may then form a significant element in the willing readiness of the players to have Rafe join them. The fact that it is plausible within the dramatic context that no objection is raised suggests an all-pervading atmosphere in which any reluctance to be open to observation signals guilt. Nell further draws attention metadramatically to the fictional nature of the whole performance, including her own, when she interrupts, questioning the actors: 'were you never none of Mr. Monkester's Scholars?' (1.96–7). This allusion to Richard Mulcaster, whose students included Edmund Spenser, Thomas Kyd and Thomas Lodge, may be merely incidental, but it may also allude to Mulcaster's rehabilitation of the acting company of Paul's Children who, for more than ten years after the season of 1589–90, had been banned from appearing in London, possibly for becoming involved in the Martin Marprelate controversy.[22] This would reinforce the underlying mistrust of the actors which these characters bring to the stage. As an allusion to a previous misdemeanour, its metadrama would also underline the material dangers inherent in an audience's interpretation.

The aggressive control of representation that such potential danger seems to necessitate is depicted in various ways. When Rafe reappears, the metadramatic Citizen attempts to control the onstage activity by both silencing his wife and advising Rafe on his delivery: 'peace fool. Let Rafe alone. – Hark you, Rafe, do not strain yourself too much at the first. – Peace! – Begin, Rafe' (1.213–15). Rafe then begins to deliver a part whose provenance is a text recently translated from the Spanish by Anthony Munday, a noted 'plotter' in his own right, and which fits only tenuously with the main plot.[23] Depending upon whether the audience accepts that his part has been hastily written for him on demand, his piece about the lack of 'fair well-spoken knights in this age' (1.244–5) may play on the comedic idea of a character taking control of the narrative. Hence Rafe asks (and asserts, rhetorically), 'why should not I then pursue this course, both for the credit of myself and our company? For amongst all the worthy books of achievements, I do not call to mind that I yet read of a grocer errant. I will be the said knight' (1.259–62). The concept of a 'grocer errant' is of course a joke, but the idea of citizens and grocers exerting pressure on the processes of representation is plainly familiar enough to the early modern audience to merit a parody of this kind. When Nell, needing reassurance at Rafe's self-assertion, asks, 'do the gentlemen like Rafe, think you, husband?', the Citizen replies, 'ay, I warrant thee, the players would give all the shoes in their shop for him' (1.280–3). Although this contains a pejorative reference to the players, a pun on both their status and their sexuality, the 'shoe' being both an example of an everyday piece of merchandise and a euphemism for female genitalia, Nell's primary metadramatic reference here is to the reaction of 'the gentlemen' of the offstage audience to Rafe's performance. Coming from a parodic simulation of an audience, this simultaneously foregrounds and undercuts the interpretative role of the real audience. As a supposed audience member, Nell is taking on the concerns particular to the acting company and the offstage audience are thus momentarily invited to consider this from both angles. In this case, comedy does what comedy does best: it addresses with some bathos what is clearly an area of anxiety – here the potential consequences of the response of an audience to an actor upon the overall interpretation of the play.

At first, aside from Rafe and the Prologue, the actors themselves ignore the often quite considerable interjections of these disruptive metadramatis personae, as when Nell attempts to intervene in the Merrythoughts' marital wrangling and is pointedly ignored (3.542–61). However, after Jasper has beaten the hapless suitor Humphrey, Nell forces herself into the dramatic scene in comforting him physically, saying 'come hither, Master Humphrey. Has he hurt you?' and insisting on medicating him: 'here, sweetheart, here's some green ginger for thee' (2.261–3). This marks a shift in the citizens' relationship to the dramatic action. Standing for the offstage audience but nevertheless able to comfort a fictional character, Nell's interaction with the universe of the play draws the real and fictional worlds into a commonality of experience. This sense of complicity may provide a persuasive apologetic, though that would depend upon the offstage audience's response to Nell's liminal position in this metadramatic structure. Much possibility of sympathetic connection is again lost, however, when the critical Citizen once more tries to rewrite the play to suit his and his wife's preferences and to arrange revenge for the beaten Humphrey, saying, 'I'll ha' Rafe fight with him, and swinge him up well-favouredly' and insisting 'Sirrah boy, come hither. Let Rafe come in and fight with Jasper' (2.267–9). Moreover, when the boy makes the entirely fair objection that 'the plot of our play lies contrary, and 'twill hazard the spoiling of our play' (2.271–2), the Citizen misconstrues his meaning and makes an oblique threat which is at the crux of the issue of metadrama and informing in this play, warning 'plot me no plots. I'll ha' Rafe come out. I'll make your house too hot for you else' (2.273–4). This metaphor of heat is employed specifically as an intelligencer's threat to the theatrical 'house' in which 'plots' are concocted, such as we have already seen, the implication being that the Citizen will claim to have discerned in the play some 'plot' against person, government or monarch. This is a threat felt deeply enough that the boy immediately acquiesces to the Citizen's demands and draws the audience into the transaction: 'Why, sir, he shall; but if any thing fall out of order, the gentlemen must pardon us' (2.275–6). For this scene to be dramatically plausible, the offstage audience must recognise their own circumstances or issues in the dramatic action, which may be cathartic or disturbing for them, but which is at least an acknowledgement of this social pressure.

It is at this juncture that the metadramatic strata which have been loosely maintained up to this point begin to break down. Having been 'written in' to the action by the Citizen, Rafe is unfortunately defeated by Jasper who steals Rafe's pestle. Jasper then draws attention to his own fictionality in a bizarre shift of register as he takes up the narration and declares of himself: 'with that he stood upright in his stirrups, and gave the Knight of the Calfskin such a knock that he forsook his horse and down he fell, and then he leaped upon him, and plucking off his helmet' (2.312–15). This narrative citation alludes to the metadramatic cast of the play as a whole as Rafe plays the Quixotic part of a questing knight mistaking ordinary things for the staples of heroic fiction. This also, however, has the effect of giving the rest of the play's outer frames a less fictional aspect in relation to these clearly defined textual references, drawing the offstage audience inwards to share the perspectives of the outer frames in which the onstage citizens dwell. Having the offstage audience share the perspective of the interrupting citizens might be counter-productive were it not that it is now, as the main plot and Rafe's impromptu sub-plot begin to overlap and the Citizen and his wife begin to take a more direct control of the action.

When Mistress Merrythought, who is very much a part of the main plot, comes onto the stage to move that part of the narrative forward, the Citizen and Nell object, as they are wanting the play to cut to the action between Rafe and a 'giant' he is about to fight. Here, the Citizen commands 'good Mistress Merrythought, be gone, I pray you, for my sake . . . You shall have audience presently', while Nell asks her, 'refrain your passion' (3.287–91).[24] Their persuasive authority here is based on their own growing presence not only as an inappropriately empowered audience but also as actor-authors, and between them they are successful in sending her offstage again.

They thus extend their influence directorially to include both the individual actor's 'passion' and when he or she 'shall have audience'. In a similar vein, as the boy enters again, the Citizen once more commands him to alter the substance of the play to suit their preferences, this time by bringing on Ralph's fight with the 'giant'. Again the boy protests – 'In good faith, sir, we cannot. You'll utterly spoil our play and make it to be hissed, and it cost money. You will not suffer us to go on with our plot. – I pray, gentlemen, rule him' (3.296–9). Here the boy appeals to the offstage audience, somewhat bizarrely, in order to control their own onstage avatars, these mistaken and mistaking projections who are intent on shaping the production of the play. In doing so, he incidentally alludes again to the double-meaning of 'plots', and the involvement of money in the whole process. Since the offstage audience are aware by this stage that the onstage audience are actors, and therefore they have no control over them, this merely has the effect of confirming the author's overall command of this parodic representation.

Within these strictures, the authoring Citizen gets his way and the boy acquiesces once more in the understanding that the Citizen will not trouble him again. The couple are thus allowed an initially formal input which becomes increasingly dialogic until they become complicit in the very 'plotting' which causes the Citizen such a paranoid reaction in the first place, as exemplified in the individual actor's expression of making the 'house too hot' for the players. In a sense also, the citizens license the plot, since it only goes ahead at their allowance and to their personal tastes. In these ways, while metadramatically arresting the scopic pulsion of the offstage audience's view of the inner play, and thereby overseeing the narrative, the couple become more and more implicated in the dramatic process they might wish to threaten. After Rafe has defeated the giant and freed his captives, the Citizen assures his wife of Rafe's positive reception by the audience, 'cony, I can tell thee the gentleman like Rafe'; Nell responds to this, 'Gentlemen, I thank you all heartily for gracing my man Rafe, and I promise you you shall see him oft'ner' (3.459–62), now apparently taking it upon herself to make promises to the offstage audience about future productions. This sense of interference may reference the potential for the city's expansion into this dramatic territory, figuring the city as a belligerent audience, but, in as much as it becomes an authoring authority, it is self-defeating.

The menacing nature of the citizens' authority as both authors and informers is further expressed as Nell orchestrates the reappearance of Mistress Merrythought, telling her, 'now Rafe has done, you may go on' (3.478); Merrythought, meanwhile, is so angry at the conduct of her ignorant drunken husband that she protests to the Citizen who promises again to perform the function of the anonymous intelligencer, advising: 'I have a trick in my head shall lodge him in the Arches for one year ... and yet he shall never know who hurt him neither' (4.22, 25). Thus the position of authoring interpreter is empowered by its volatile potential to develop into the position of the informer. This is alluded to throughout this play and here the correlation between metadramatic structures and an informing audience is made explicit. This is a key moment in the metadramatic foregrounding of the audience and reveals some factual knowledge of the prospective activities of informers and their possible consequences. The 'Arches' here is a reference to the ecclesiastical Court of the Arches, situated in the crypt of St Mary-le-Bow and under the jurisdiction of the Archbishop of Canterbury. This was one of the possible outlets for the kind of incriminating information the citizen is offering to provide, either against the players or Merrythought's bibulous spouse. This court is mentioned in the *Diary of Mal Cutpurse* (1662), also with reference to the activity of an informer, where she complains that 'some Promooting Apparator ... cited me to appear in the Court of the Arches, where was an Accusation exhibited against me.'[25] The roles of apparator and informer crossed over at the time. In this case, Nell shows her own potential for complicity in the process, as she is clearly in full agreement with the Citizen's casual proposal of supplying incriminating information (4.26).

Eventually, however, these shifting metadramatic structures fall apart when the narratological demands of these interloping authors and potential informers become unwieldy, with Nell demanding, that Rafe

> travel over great hills, and let him be very weary, and come to the King of Cracovia's house, covered with velvet, and there let the King's daughter stand in her window, all in beaten gold, combing her golden locks with a comb of ivory, and let her spy Rafe and fall in love with him. (4.33–8)

Although the Boy seizes upon this as an opportunity to comment upon the ridiculously misconceived nature of the couple's authorly role, nevertheless the play action shifts momentarily to Moldavia. Here, however, their demands proliferate: 'Let Rafe come out on May Day in the morning and speak upon a conduit, with all his scarfs about him, and his feathers and his rings and his knacks' (Int. 4, 9–12). The boy responds still cautiously, 'Well, sir, he shall come out. But if our play miscarry, sir, you are like to pay for't' (Int. 4.19–20), reminding the Citizen and Nell of the consequences of their interjections and amendments, and foregrounding the economics of the relationship between the dramatic producers and their audience.

Regardless of the metadramatic permeability of the acting space, the play itself seems to offer resistance to these interlopers into its perimeters. In all, the sub-narratives that the citizens engender through their intrusive audience participation turn out to be blank ends. The relatively marginal roles that Rafe is asked to play lead nowhere significant and he never gets to kill his lion. As the play ends, his 'part' has come to nothing, and the Boy rightly blames this on the couple's destructive authorship of the inner performance, saying ''tis long of yourself, sir; we have nothing to do with his part' (5.279–80). Even the fact that the couple therefore decide that Rafe's 'knight' should have at least a dramatic death, the Boy's objection that ''twill be very unfit he should die, sir, upon no occasion, and in a comedy too' (5.286–7) going unheeded, simply means that Rafe's inner-play character dies at the whim of what is a lethally authorial audience. Overall, although they exert a critical pressure on the content of the drama and share a menacing oversight connected with the figure of the intelligencer, this metadramatic onstage audience, subsumed into the object of their own critique, are finally found to be 'complicit with the transgressiveness they seek to police', as Dillon puts it, and are thus rendered harmless.[26] The conventional plea for applause is left to Nell, who leaves the stage, presumably back into the audience of the city from which she came, taking the unstable authority of the intelligencer and the undesirable model of the authoring audience with her.

The Knight of the Burning Pestle thus uses its explicit metadramatic forms to stage malconnections between various jurisdictions of social and theatrical authority. The success of its metadrama rests upon its reference to a sense of the potential for miscommunication between the producers and the receivers of dramatic representation. The violent possibilities implied by the casual inclusion of the threat of the intelligencer in even these light entertainments form a sinister element in these problematic connections. As a parody of the intended expansion of city authority, *The Knight of the Burning Pestle*'s metadramatic interlopers signify the fear of the genuinely dangerous properties of venal interpretation and misheld authority. Even though the plots of Beaumont's Citizen and his wife Nell ultimately come to nothing, the end result is a theatrical form which accurately reproduces the critical atmosphere of the drama and of the material context of its production. In offering this, Beaumont reveals the precarious nature of his own authority in relation to that of a potentially informing audience. As it turns out, the common entreaty against misconception by the bee who 'leaves her sting behind', or the bear who 'blasteth all other leaves' because he 'cannot find origanum', in fact resonates with the implicit threat of humiliating and potentially debilitating prosecution at places like the Court of the Arches, or worse. This metadrama registers, in both form and content, not only the properties of illegitimate authority, but also the solid fear that 'sour mislike' and 'open reproach' of 'unseemly speeches ... mistaking the Author's intention' by intelligencing informers may lead not only to 'unkind reports', but also ultimately to the horrors of the early modern gaol.

Notes

1. Ben Jonson, 'An Epistle to a Friend to Persuade Him to the Wars', in C. H. Herford and Percy and Evelyn Simpson (eds), *Ben Jonson*, 11 vols (Oxford: Clarendon Press, 1925–52), 8: p. 167.
2. See Angus, p. 8ff.; Beresford, pp. 232–3; G. R. Elton, *Policy and Police: The Enforcement of the Reformation in the Age of Thomas Cromwell* (Cambridge: Cambridge University Press, 1972).
3. Beresford, p. 225.
4. See Angus, esp. pp. 1–24.
5. Dillon, p. 96.
6. Francis Beaumont, *The Knight of the Burning Pestle*, ed. Sheldon P. Zitner (Manchester: Manchester University Press, 2004). Unless otherwise noted, this is the primary text for all references to this play.
7. See Dillon, pp. 99–100.

8. For the purpose of this present argument, the 'offstage' audience is presumed to be that at the first performances. Subsequent audiences might well configure these issues differently, depending on their own circumstances.
9. Beaumont, *The Knight of the Burning Pestle*, 'To the Readers of this Comedy', lines 8–9, p. 53.
10. Beaumont, *The Knight of the Burning Pestle*, p. 52.
11. See Thomas Dekker, *The Gvl's Horne-Booke* (Menston: Scholar Press, 1969), p. 26, for a humorous flavour of the oppositional character of these sites of authority:

> You that have authority under the broad scale of mouldy custom, to be called the *'gentle Audience'* [emphasis original] . . . hiss, or give plaudities; I care not a nutshell which of either: you can neither shake our comic theatre with your stinking breath of hisses, nor raise it with the thunderclaps of your hands . . . As for thee, Zoilus, go hang thyself; and for thee, Momus, chew nothing but hemlock . . . you may abuse the works of any man; deprave his writings that you cannot equal; and purchase to yourself in time the terrible name of a severe critic.

'Zoilus' is the name of a Greek critic and grammarian (fourth century BC) famous for his severe criticism of Homer, a censorious, malignant or envious critic. See the *OED*'s quotation of R. Sheldon's 1612 *Sermon at St. Martin's* (47): 'Such as are eminent should be careful of their conuersations when they are besieged with such malitious Zoiles.' For Momus, the *OED* notes: '1. a. The Greek god of censure and ridicule, who was banished from Olympus for his criticisms of the gods . . . b. A person who habitually grumbles or finds fault, a carping critic.'
12. Wendy Wall, *Staging Domesticity* (Cambridge: Cambridge University Press, 2002), p. 162.
13. Thomas Dekker, *The Gull's Hornbook*, ed. Ronald Brunlees McKerrow (New York: AMS Press, 1971), p. 50. E. K. Chambers suggests that this practice emerges around 1596: see Chambers, p. 535.
14. Dekker, *The Gull's Hornbook*, ed. McKerrow, p. 50.
15. Dekker, *The Gull's Hornbook*, ed. McKerrow, p. 50.
16. Dekker, *The Gull's Hornbook*, ed. McKerrow, p. 51.
17. Dekker, *The Gull's Hornbook*, ed. McKerrow, p. 51.
18. William Shakespeare, *Hamlet* (2.2.233).
19. Dekker, *The Gull's Hornbook*, ed. McKerrow, p. 51.

20. For the requisite silence of gentlewomen at this time see Richard Brathwaite, *The English gentlewoman* (London: Printed by B. Alsop and T. Fauucet, for Michaell Sparke, 1631) <http://gateway.proquest.com/openurl?ctx_ver=Z39.88-2003&res_id=xri:eebo&rft_id=xri:eebo:citation:20020778> (last accessed 24 February 2018).
21. M. T. Jones-Davies, '"The Players … Will Tell All," or the Actor's Role in Renaissance Drama', in Kenneth Muir (ed.), *Shakespeare, Man of the Theater* (Newark: University of Delaware Press, 1983), p. 79
22. See Michael Shapiro. *Children of the Revels* (New York: Columbia University Press, 1977), p. 21ff.
23. Anthony Munday's *Palmerin D'Oliva*. See Arthur Kinney, *Renaissance Drama: An Anthology of Plays and Entertainments* (Oxford: Blackwell, 2000), p. 397, n. 220; for the 'plotter' reference, see Francis Meres, 'Poetrie; Poets; and A Comparatiue discourse of our English Poets, with the Greeke, Latine, and Italian Poets', in *Palladis Tamia Wits Treasury* (London: P. Short, 1598), <http://gateway.proquest.com/openurl?ctx_ver=Z39.88-2003&res_id=xri:eebo&rft_id=xri:eebo:citation:99845635> (last accessed 14 February 2018).
24. The giant Barbaroso is actually a barber whose 'prisoners' are syphilitics looking for a cure and in this regard it would be coy not to mention the quibbling value of the 'burning pestle' of the play's title.
25. 'Mal Cutpurse's Diary', from Janet Todd and Elizabeth Spearing (eds), *Counterfeit Ladies: The Life and Death of Mary Frith; The Case of Mary Carleton* (London: Pickering & Chatto, 1994), pp. 33–4.
26. Dillon, p. 108.

Chapter 4

The Reluctant Informer: Humanising the Beast

Even more than Shakespeare's Iago, John Webster's Bosola seems to represent the early modern theatre's quintessential combination of actor and intelligencer. His self-consciously Machiavellian role in *The Duchess of Malfi* (1612–13) involves him in negotiating various metadramatic modes.[1] But inversely, and perhaps even ironically, these include significant reflection on the case of the actor who is condemned, or occasionally even prosecuted, for playing the part of the theatrical villain. Iago inspires our interest because 'his evil is too essential to be changed', as Robert N. Watson is representative in seeing.[2] The very idea of an essential evil here carries existential claims which are bound to certain moral effects and which are conventionally religious in nature. Bosola, on the other hand, commands our continuing interest perhaps partly because of his very human reaction to the noble conduct of the Duchess. As the Duchess's unfolding tragedy informs the development of Bosola's dramatis persona, in some way this complex character's withdrawn conscience wakes and gets the better of him until he is finally able to offer resistance to the role allotted him by circumstances and his employers. If it is his perception of the nobility of the Duchess in her suffering that 'reawakens his bitterly repressed virtues', as Watson says, this is partly to do with necessity and in reaction to the neglect of the brothers, who do not value his work to the extent of paying him in full for its execution.[3] It is therefore equally a product of his growing disaffection with the oppressive mechanisms of the state as much as his own crucial role in it which resuscitates his merits in this way.

Since his conversion from the prevailing Machiavellian role of the informing intelligencer comes too late both for the Duchess, and finally for himself, this works as a satirical commentary on the potentially lethal nature of issues surrounding informing. But perhaps more than this, the fact that Bosola's intelligencer does ultimately transform under the dictates of his conscience suggests a nuancing, perhaps even a humanising, of the figure of the informer and intelligencer. Moreover, this takes place even as Ferdinand, who is both his paymaster and the instigator of this intelligencing work, moves in the other direction, towards an increasing bestialisation. Perhaps both of these transformative models are offered as exemplary correctives to perceived anomalies in the moral authority of contemporary systems of oversight and governance. The one, a bogeyman of the day, sees the error of his ways and undergoes a metamorphosis which is in any case rendered futile by the very nature and weight of his previous sins in a transformation with Calvinist caveats. The other, meanwhile, is an exemplary tyrant whose metamorphosis is an outing of his fundamental voracity and bestial incontinence. The whole narrative of the play is keyed off reactions to the personal desires of the Duchess; this chapter explores how the intelligencing mechanisms established to contain such incorrigible unruliness consume themselves under the pressure those desires generate.

In a play which focuses on how 'words and matter change, and men / Act one another', as John Ford's dedicatory poem describes (Commendatory Verses, 35–6), the complementary worlds of metadrama and intelligencing meet and are contrasted with what the Duchess terms 'the path / Of simple virtue, which was never made / To seem the thing it is not' (1.1.446–8). Bosola's personal inauthenticity is aptly described when the Duchess forcefully wishes 'were I a man / I'd beat that counterfeit face into thy other' (3.5.118). Counterfeiting is the business of actors and intelligencers of course and, in a world where the theatre is vulnerable to the passing of misinformation, this similarity is bound to be a cause of some anxiety. It may perhaps further evidence a kind of cognitive dissonance which emerges between the social identity of players and the perception of their business.

Critical interpretations of Bosola have included the understanding that he has the characteristics of a 'chorus rather than a character' and noted his metadramatic nature as a kind of presenter of the action.[4] Yet, despite this displaced nature of the dramatis persona, he is simultaneously someone who, 'against his own will, develops from illusion to self-knowledge, from spying and cutting throats to penitence and moral purpose', as John Russell Brown describes.⁵ Ralph Berry also sees this trajectory and identifies Bosola's character as defined by his 'series of role-playing changes' but links these aspects of the character in seeing this metadramatic side as caused by his having chosen 'a course of action that is ultimately opposed to his inner values.'⁶ These allude to the two functions of Bosola's character most pertinent to this detailed study: that of his metadramatic nature, and that of his complex and slowly humanising intelligencer.⁷ It is the case, as Lee Bliss says, that sharing Bosola's viewpoint in this play results in us partaking of an understanding of 'the practical struggle for subsistence drained of all moral meaning', but it seems highly objectionable and somewhat defeatist to suggest also that Bosola 'represents the rationalizing spirit of accommodation in us all'.⁸ The figure rather exemplifies a negative model of social compromise in what never quite seems to be the face of necessity or desperation. It may also be the case, as Bliss claims, that 'to the extent that we have shared Bosola's viewpoint, we are relieved when Webster severs our dramatic intimacy', but this may be largely the effect of the interpretation of the character on the part of the actor in the role or the particular performance of a night.⁹ This personal reaction to the character of Bosola is, however, somewhat beside the point for the purpose of this argument. Bosola's belated appeal to an offstage audience is far more likely to be found in his revealing the inadequacies of the social structures that have consumed himself, the worthy Duchess and many others, rather than any emotional connection we might feel. In this case, if not in many other examples of metadramatic appeal and manipulation, the audience's sympathy with the character is to some extent superfluous.

In the context of the Malfian court, a world where information is the means of production, any political aspiration is concomitant with the contemporary pressures and seemingly indispensable structures of intelligencing. 'Ambition', Antonio says, 'is a great man's madness / . . . girt / With the wild noise of prattling visitants, / Which makes it lunatic beyond all cure' (1.1.420–4). We are thus invited to see Antonio as free of such insane ambition with its attendant 'prattling visitants' who can only be the informers and intelligencers which necessarily attend the mechanisms of power, making up the 'flatt'ring sycophants' he has described previously and contrasted with 'provident Council' (1.1.8, 17). Although the play is set in Italy, Antonio is associated with a reformed France by reference to his recent visit there. Webster's source for this passage is probably the description of the court of the Phoenician Emperor of Rome, Alexander Severus, from Sir Thomas Elyot's *Image of Governance* (1541). Elyot describes how Severus 'dyscharged all minysters . . . banyshing also out of his palaice . . . persones infamed, semblably flatterers' and thus purged it of the kinds of corruption from which Malfi clearly suffers.[10] Furthermore, as Elyot describes in his earlier book *The Governor* (1531), Severus 'used many tymes to dysguise him selfe in divers strange fashions . . . And most politikely fynd occasion to see the state of the people, with the industry or negligence of them that were officers.'[11] In this way, just like Marston's Malevole or Jonson's Justice Overdo, he operated in the mode of an intelligencer himself.[12] Like Overdo also, he presumably did this because the milieu in which he operated meant that he could not trust even his own informers to report to him accurately.

Antonio's speech here uses the word 'inform' twice in this passage, in both cases to associate it with the duty of giving good advice to princes, emphasising that it is a 'noble duty to inform them / What they ought to forsee' (1.1.18, 21–2).[13] However, it may be telling that he highlights this just before Bosola appears on stage, thus associating even good counsel with the pitfalls of intelligencing which are often seen to focus on the fallibility of the informer himself. As Antonio sees it, Bosola is a hypocrite who 'rails at those things which he wants' (1.1.25) and thus makes a virtue of a necessity. Antonio's exemplary French court still rings then with the kind of surveillance mechanisms which Bosola introduces as supposedly contrastingly corrupt in their Malfian setting, and both carry a specifically English connection which allows Webster a critical social comment by displacing it onto a foreign court.[14]

Antonio identifies Bosola, pejoratively of course, as a 'court-gall' (1.1.23), which implies he is a chafing sore, the bitter scourge of the court, exactly the malcontent, melancholic, Machiavellian informer type we may by now be familiar with. In *Troilus and Cressida*, Shakespeare identifies such 'gall' with the lying reports of one who 'coins slanders like a mint' (1.3.193) and this sense always seems applicable when the term is used as pertaining to a courtly setting. But also implicit within Antonio's critique here is a wariness of the satirical bent which is the social function of the ideal Horatian poet. It is in this particular respect that Bosola is celebrated even by Ferdinand for not flattering him, to the point of denying his mooted perspicacity and conversely informing him, 'you / Are your own chronicle too much: and grossly / Flatter yourself' (3.2.87–9). Ferdinand's proverbial response suggests an ideal of authority which is otherwise very much out of keeping with his dramatis persona, unless it serves to show his inconsistency and instability, as he declares, '*that friend a great man's ruin strongly checks / Who rails into his belief all his defects*' (3.1.92–3, italics original). The satirical and poetic model of railing which Ferdinand pins on him also fits with Bosola's identification by Antonio as the type of the foul melancholic (1.1.75) who would also typically offer unflattering critique. Delio later confirms one other characteristic association of melancholy when he asserts that Bosola has tendencies as a 'fantastical scholar' (3.3.41). This, however, he suggests, was a self-invention of Bosola who, having 'studied himself half blear-eyed to know the true symmetry of Caesar's nose', he asserts, did this merely 'to gain the name of a speculative man' (3.3.45–7). He seems very much to fit the mould of M. H. Curtis's 'alienated intellectuals of early Stuart England' whose social disaffection and discontent will contribute to the tensions eventually leading to the English Civil War not many years later.[15] But for Antonio, the melancholy of a character like Bosola is a flaw that merely feeds a moody black malcontentment (1.1.87) which, in popular thinking, can be easily tempted to politic intelligencing and seedy self-interested informing as an almost inevitable symptom of its frustrated ambition. Webster himself may have been frustrated in this way by his reliance on income from his other occupation of cartwright, although there is no indication at this point that he was involved with surveillance or intelligencing of any kind, unlike many of his contemporaries.[16] Framing Antonio's description of Bosola's melancholy, however, is the admission of his reputation as one who is 'very valiant', and the significant fear being expressed is that, regrettably, his melancholy 'will poison all his goodness' (1.1.75–6). This sets the tone for his future, if somewhat tardy, repudiation of his master's will and his own paid function, towards his own transformation into something more than a stock informer character. His dramatic destiny is not simply to personify an undesirable social function, but to bring down the system that creates him.

Bosola describes the nature of the situation in the court of Malfi, where a universal atmosphere of suspicion leads to a generalised practice of deception. As he has cause to caution, 'to suspect a friend unworthily / Instructs him the next way to suspect you, / And prompts him to deceive you' (1.1.244–6). In a society the very fabric of whose authority structures are suffused with intelligencing, it may be expected that the otherwise seemingly irreproachable Antonio is also a watcher of a kind and, indeed, he asks Delio to 'observe' the Cardinal's 'inward character', since, as he says, the spring in his face is 'nothing but the engendering of toads' (1.1.156–8). As Antonio explains, the Cardinal is himself a part of the problem of illegitimate and immoral interpretation: 'where he is jealous of any man, he lays worse plots for them than ever was imposed on Hercules, for he strews in his way flatterers, panders, intelligencers, atheists, and a thousand such political monsters' (1.1.158–62). That the Cardinal gives birth to monsters fits perfectly with common imagery around the bestial nature of intelligencers and informers. They are often depicted as incontinently chattering or barking animals who are simultaneously voracious and obsequious. On the same score meanwhile, he observes that Ferdinand 'speaks with others' tongues, and hears men's suits / With others' ears . . . / Dooms men to death by information, / Rewards by hearsay' (1.1.173–4, 176–7), clearly signifying how the structures of social authority in Malfi have been compromised in their moral authority by reliance upon the word of intelligencers.

Bosola's own understanding of his position in this formulation requires some equivocation around the concept of 'intelligence'. In cursing the Officers who have been commenting variously on Antonio's character, Bosola says they were the kind of servants that would make their 'first-born intelligencers' and equates this on a moral level with them being happy to sell their daughters into prostitution (3.2.232–3). The indignation of this assertion is reminiscent of Nashe's use of the term in *Have with you to Saffron-Walden*, where he seems to feel the need to secure the reputation of an agent of the Queen, Thomas Bodley, who is clearly a spy, against what he terms the 'hellish detested *Judas* name of an Intelligencer'.[17] It is significant also here that the fundamental unreliability of 'an intelligencer's heart-string' (3.2.268) seems to be axiomatic even for one so enmeshed in the system of intelligencing for money as Bosola.

Tracking this motif throughout in the play's narrative, the vile Cardinal's advice to Ferdinand is to 'be sure you entertain that

Bosola for your intelligence' (1.1.224–5), and the first practical thing Ferdinand does is to offer him the reward of gold (1.1.246), not to cut a throat as Bosola expects, but simply 'to live i'th' court, here; and observe the duchess, / To note all the particulars of her 'haviour' (1.1.252–3). Additionally, in arranging for Bosola to inform upon the Duchess, the Cardinal is hoping to leave people unaware of his own involvement in the politicking of the court, and thus to leave Bosola to play the fall guy to the organising powers of his own existence.

In terms of his own motivations, Bosola has every right to 'haunt' (1.1.29) the Cardinal in expectation of a reward for his work, since the informer's reward is potentially substantial in this society which relies so heavily on the passage of information. Also in this vein, the Cardinal is known generally to 'bestow bribes . . . largely, and . . . impudently' for his own political purposes (1.1.164), so it is to be expected that he will stump up the cash for this relatively complex courtly intrigue and consequently quite egregious of him to renege on paying Bosola for, so to speak, legitimately contracted activities. But there seems also to be a contemporary sense in which theatre itself partakes of this accusation of illegitimate money-making and spurious imbursement of some kind. In his *Look on me London* (1613), which warns of all kinds of moral and financial dangers for the unsuspecting visitor to the capital, Richard Johnson speaks of gaming houses 'where the vulgar and inferiour sort of people resort', which, he says, never lack guests, and adds the logical inference, 'for where carion is, crowes will be plenty, and where mony is stirring, Theaters will not be idle'.[18] Johnson seems to express a contemporary adage here which links the propensity for theatres to generate money, presumably in what are also perceived to be illegitimate ways, with the immoral earnings of deceivers and opportunists. That he also uses the image of the crow and its carrion plays within the territory of imagery commonly associated with intelligencers.

In this play as in many others, gold is on offer for the suborning of otherwise seemingly moral beings. At first, although he is a notorious hitman for the Cardinal, Bosola is alert to the immorality of this situation and certainly does not jump at the chance, saying 'It seems you would create me / One of your familiars . . . / a very quaint invisible devil, in flesh: / An intelligencer' (1.1.257–8, 260–1). This resounds with implications of an evil, occult, insidious intent, and its unnecessary emphasis of the word 'intelligencer' suggests that the concept is under some scrutiny in this play. Ferdinand's response in detailing the nature of the job at hand is revealing of its connection to networks of patronage and favour: 'such a kind of thriving thing / I would wish thee', he says, and offers more, 'ere long, thou mayst arrive / At a higher place by't' (1.1.262–4). It seems worthy of notice then that Bosola is still reluctant to take the work, and tells Ferdinand in no uncertain terms:

> Take your devils
> Which hell calls angels: these curs'd gifts would make
> You a corrupter, me an impudent traitor,
> And I should take these they'd take me to hell.
>
> (1.1.263–6)

This is not a mere ruse, this is a forceful argument, and it should prove so in performance. However, Bosola's initial reluctance here is softened with a more concrete reward, and presumably a legitimate income in addition, after he is offered the Provisorship of the Horse. As he reluctantly concedes, 'for the good deed you have done me, I must do / All the ill man can invent' (1.1.274–5), and again he associates this work with the deceptions of Satan, saying that it is 'thus the devil / Candies all sins o'er' (1.1.275–6). The inherent sinfulness of these transactions is evident also later when Bosola is offered money by Ferdinand to procure the corruption of Delio's confessor and to find out the whereabouts of Antonio (5.2.133–5) in a gesture which further establishes the venality of the church's moral authority. But whatever Bosola's early objections suggest, Ferdinand basically ignores these with a breezy and modern-sounding 'be yourself' and sketches out the explicitly role-playing aspects of the intelligencing work he has in mind, recommending Bosola to 'keep your old garb of melancholy . . . / this will gain / Access to private lodgings', and describing him comically as 'a politic dormouse' (1.1.277–8, 280–2). Bosola immediately seizes on the implication that he must, dormouse-like, 'feed in a lord's dish, half asleep, not seeming / To listen to any talk' then be ready to 'cut his throat in a dream' (1.1.283–5). But, in comparison to other monstrous and bestial characterisations of the figure, the dormouse is a relatively gentle imaging of the informer, as is the creature that Antonio imagines Bosola to be in a metadramatic aside: 'this mole does undermine me' (2.3.14), although this is much less benign in the underground image which the Duchess develops, seeing him in this as a mine beneath her feet, probably with a military metaphor in mind involving explosives (3.2.156).

Bosola's phrase spoken as he laments his lack of information about why courtiers have been banished to their quarters, 'my intelligence will freeze else' (2.3.6), gives a sense of the normal expected fluidity of information as it passes along these social arteries. It also brings to mind the inner-play scene in Philip Massinger's later play *The Roman Actor*, where Aretinus, the characteristic informer figure, realises the crucial nature of Domitia's audience reaction to the actor in the inner play and aside to the offstage audience says collusively, 'there is something more / In this then passion, which I must find out, / Or my intelligence freezes' (3.2.293–5). Clearly intelligence is meant to flow freely. Bosola finds his answer to the question of the disappearing courtiers in the event of Antonio's dropped paper which turns out to be a horoscope on the Duchess's child's birth (2.3.55). As he says alone before the offstage audience, 'this is a parcel of intelligency' (2.3.67) and thus the course of information begins to flow again. It is after reassuring the Duchess that he is deaf to 'court calumny' (3.1.49) that Ferdinand asks, 'now Bosola, / How thrives our intelligence?' (3.1.57–8) as they muse on rumours about her children and lament the persistent anonymity of the father. These references clearly place these ostensibly domestic difficulties in the realm of high politics and the free play of information through its intelligence community.

Using imagery typically surrounding informers, Bosola describes his hardness and resilience to his circumstances by proposing that 'blackbirds fatten best in hard weather; why not I in these dog-days?' (1.1.37–8). When he complains of his 'miserable dependences' on people like the Cardinal, he claims that 'there are rewards for hawks and dogs, when they have done us service' (1.1.57–8), alluding to his own disappointment in these matters. These kinds of images of predatory or carrion birds and various types of canines draw upon the recurrent contemporary tropes of parasitic predation which are associated with the work of the informer. In describing Ferdinand and the Cardinal, Bosola says 'none but crows, pies, and caterpillars feed on them' (1.1.50–1) which recalls Johnson's axiomatic claim of the theatres that 'where carion is, crowes will be plenty'.[19] 'Pies' are the proverbially annoying chatty magpies and caterpillars are imaged here as voracious eaters of the leaves of their hosts. Bosola's 'could I be one of their flattering panders, I would hang on their ears like a horse-leech till I were full, and then drop off' (1.1.51–3) offers another, slightly more nauseating image that echoes Ben Jonson's *Poetaster* (1601), where Tucca conspires against Horace and declares to his accomplices that 'I'll be your intelligencer, we'll . . . hang upon him like so many horse-leeches'.[20] This is also apparent in Webster and Middleton's *Anything for a Quiet Life* (c.1621), when Franklin says of Knavesbee, the lawyer and pander to his own wife, that 'such caterpillars may hang at their lord's ears / When better men are neglected . . . / Hang him, hang him! / He's a scurvy informer' (1.1.201–2, 211–12).[21] These references to hanging at the ears of the authority point to contemporary perceptions of an extremely unhealthy connection between the function of the sycophantic flatterer or pander and that of the intelligencer who has the ear of reactionary authority and fattens itself on the lifeblood of the organ.

As part of her own plot to engineer the escape of Antonio, the Duchess also performs a metadramatic and intelligencing function when she deceives Bosola about Antonio's pretended mismanagement of funds. She then acts within her role, as the offstage audience is privy to, and has Bosola 'overhear' her and Antonio in dispute over the supposed anomalies as she sends him from the court. This is metadrama in combination with the *magnanima menzogna*, the Machiavellian manipulation of the 'noble lie' (3.2.180). Her mistake in this is to read Bosola's possibly genuine praise of Antonio as trustworthiness and she thus confides in him Antonio's fatherhood of her children. In this simple betrayal of not only his confessee but also of his own principles, Bosola is beating her at the game of the typical politicking intelligencer, characterised by poker-faced silence or whispered evil plotting, as he describes it: 'a politician is the devil's quilted anvil – / He fashions all sins on him, and the blows / Are never heard' (3.3.323–5). This is done throughout with the clear intent of the passing on of information, as he asks rhetorically, 'what rests, but I reveal / All to my lord?' (3.3.326–7). This lethal one-upmanship is immediately followed by the apt recognition of both the venality of the profession and its moral illegitimacy:

O, this base quality
Of intelligencer! Why, every quality I'th' world
Prefers but gain or commendation:
Now, for this act I am certain to be rais'd,
And men that paint weeds to the life are prais'd.
(3.3.327–31, italics original)

Bosola's particular social ambition, within the difficult circumstances which the play poses for him, contains the seed of its own destruction. His parallel with the other social riser, Antonio, flatters him to some extent, given that Antonio will attempt to reconcile with the brothers (5.1.1) and evinces an undesirable cowardice at times (3.5.91–2). Antonio is always a subject here, but for all Bosola's hopes to be 'raised', his outlook is of a leveling kind. His almost excessive encomium of Antonio both before and after the Duchess's confession that he is her husband and they have three children together suggests that, despite their rivalry, Bosola's sympathies lie that way. In answer to Antonio's accusation that he 'would look up to heaven' except that 'the devil, that rules i' th' air' stands in his light (2.1.94–5), he answers 'some would think the souls of princes were brought forth by some more weighty cause than those of meaner persons – they are deceived, there's the same hand to them: the like passions sway them' (2.1.101–4). Webster's own dedication to George Harding, Baron Berkeley, intimates a similar leaning in the dramatist himself, as he seems to express in declaring, 'I do not altogether look up at your title, the ancientest nobility being but a relic of time past' (Dedication 9–10). This indeed contrasts with other authors who 'typically strive to outdo one another in expressions of abject regard' for their patrons, as Michael Neill observes.[22] The disruptive self-sufficiency which arises from this tendency in Bosola – as he asserts, 'I will not imitate things glorious, / No more than base: I'll be mine own example' (5.4.81–2) – is a symptom of his ultimate self-determination which will finally result in the deaths of the authorities for whom he is working and whose very corruption he instances.

The beginning of his decision to turn against the machine of which he is a part can be located at the point of his great sympathy with the Duchess's confession of Antonio, despite the fact that he immediately colludes with the offstage audience about being raised. In this way his adoption of an independent agenda of redress and revenge is energised by his malcontentment and his rediscovered personal animus against social injustice.

Throughout the play, metadramatic devices and political intrigue are linked intrinsically with the depiction of personal manipulation. Even when the Duchess is speaking of her private desires and aims, she voices these through wordplay which cannot resist a narrative context of lying and plotting:

> I would have you lead your fortune by the hand,
> Unto your marriage bed: –
> ... We'll only lie, and talk together, and plot
> T'appease my humourous kindred ...
> O, let me shroud my blushes in your bosom,
> Since 'tis the treasury of all my secrets.
>   (1.1.495–6, 498–9, 502–3)

This sense of the violation of intimacy relates to the play's obsession with the keeping and discovering of secrets in the context of the toxic environment of Malfi. Bosola's almost entire function in the first half of the play is to make them known to his employers, the immorality of which is emphasised by Cariola acting as his antithesis in this practice. When the Duchess orders Cariola to hide behind the arras (1.1.361), she is set up to witness the Duchess's transaction with Antonio, for the Duchess's own security (1.1.350–1). Her particular purpose in this is to be a keeper of secrets and not a divulger, as would most often be the case with a metadramatic device of this kind. The effect of this on an offstage audience is to suggest an entirely benign sense of oversight: one which is trustworthy, faithful and sympathetic. Cariola's 'known secrecy' (1.1.350) therefore protects the Duchess's life and reputation, and is offered as a contrast to Bosola's venal willingness to betray secrets to his master with lethal intent.

In an intimate metonymy, intelligencing, and the political intrigue that results from it, are imaged poetically in the play as 'whispering'. As is often the case, reference to this arises concurrently with a metadramatic instance in the play. So, when the Duchess says 'I think this speech between you both was studied, / It came so roundly off', Ferdinand responds, 'I would have you to give o'er these chargeable revels; / A visor and a mask are whispering rooms / That were ne'er built for goodness' (1.1.329–35). As much as deception here is depicted as a form of theatre, so the very idea of theatre becomes a form of deception, as the disguises of play-acting are posited as almost inseparable from the false face of whispering plotters in a room set up to allow two people to exchange secret messages. The injustice of the necessity for this seems bemoaned by the Duchess herself, as she cries at her discovery by Ferdinand, 'O misery! methinks unjust actions / Should wear these masks and curtains, and not we' (3.2.158–9). Concern for the privacy of the intimate may be seen also in Antonio's breast pictured as 'a private whispering-room' (3.2.256).

Whispering moreover is associated with lethal dealings in the play when Ferdinand proposes strangling as 'a very quiet death' for killing the Duchess, and enjoins Bosola 'whisper, softly: do you agree to't?' (5.4.34, 36). Bosola's aside here, 'Nay then, I see I must stand upon my guard' (5.4.35) draws the offstage audience metadramatically into perceiving the mortal nature of his condition. When Bosola passes his information on the Duchess to Ferdinand, his paranoid vision imagines the outing of the intimate into a public arena, claiming that 'rogues do not whisper't now, but seek to publish't' (2.5.5). In contrast, as the Duchess discusses the manner of her death, she tells Bosola that she would be prepared to take it in 'any way . . . / So that I were out of your whispering' (4.2.203–4). The Duchess obviously perceives the fatal effects of such vicious vocalising in the context of the brothers' corrupt court, and here she surrenders her life to its inevitability, a martyr to the venal whispering Ferdinand deals in but fears.

In this lethal intelligencing context, Bosola's injunction to 'observe my meditation now' (2.1.44) cannot be read as merely neutral. I would suggest that it offers the possibility of another metadramatic moment, although the question of to whom this is addressed must be left to the mode of performance and the decisions of the director. It is noteworthy, however, that this metadramatic utterance is a precursor to the idea that the true nature of man is in some way bestial. Mankind, it is suggested, bears certain diseases 'which have their true names only ta'en from beasts, / As the most ulcerous wolf' (2.1.53–4); as Bosola proposes, within our 'rich tissue' (2.1.58) hides a lupine quintessence. This accords with many instances in which the hunger of the informer or intelligencer is represented as either canine or lupine, and universalises the function to accord with an idea of 'human nature'.[23] At this stage, however, Bosola is essentially confessing his own internal hunger and disease, which are typical tropes that mean to express the informer's inner corruption.

Antonio speaks soundly when he says that Bosola can 'libel well' (2.3.39), and Bosola is far from denying it when he responds 'copy it out / And I will set my hand to't' (2.3.40–1); at this stage he is very much the active informer whose language is in itself dangerous, as Antonio himself understands, saying 'this fellow will undo me' (2.3.29). Not only is Bosola clearly playing the informing intelligencer here, but it seems likely from the context that he has chosen his own variety of disguises in which to torment the Duchess, and it may be seen that these various roles, as played within the primary role, require a theatricality which is inevitably metadramatic in its nature. Antonio's own asides also include the audience in their subsequent discussion around the Duchess's secret pregnancy, attempting to enlist their sympathy quite as much as Bosola himself does in earlier asides which attempt to draw the audience into a collusive space, wherein the Duchess's pregnancy is made to seem shameful and illegitimate (2.1.117, 131, 147, 155). In this case it seems that the play foregrounds the battle for the sympathies of the audience as part of the theatrical experience.

In the pivotal hair brushing scene, when Ferdinand sneaks into the Duchess's bedchamber as Antonio and Cariola steal out for a joke while the Duchess is talking, the moment of overhearing and discovery is also engaging of the offstage audience in a deeply metadramatic way. Here, the Duchess's idle chat becomes an unwitting confession and the offstage audience ultimately perceive with horror the malintention of the spying onstage audience which Ferdinand forms. This aggravated self-informing resounds with what the offstage audience might experience as heart-stopping dramatic irony, but is not free from the pleasure of a voyeur watching a most intimate and joyful conversation trespassed upon by a stalking *malheur*. That it carries 'the howling of a wolf' (3.2.88) in its imagination is entirely appropriate to the shared inhumanity of the moment.

The wax tableau of the dead Antonio and their children operates as another instance of inhumanity linked with a metadramatic foregrounding of the theatricality of the exchange, which has its own author, presenting vice, and onstage audience (4.1.56ff.). This theatre of blood recalls that of Kyd's *Spanish Tragedy* (c.1587), Chettle's *Hoffman* (1602), even to some extent *Othello*, which draws on this motif for its own bloody bed scene, a tradition which de-animates the notion of theatre at the centre of a metadramatic exchange and fixes it in the instant of perception. It necessitates no interaction, but foregrounds the shared nature of the gaze of both offstage and onstage audiences. This may function as a moment of deep connection between the two perspectives of the theatrical artifice on display.

At this stage, Bosola's character is undergoing change and his reluctant sympathy for the Duchess seems to be exaggerated by the waxworks scene, as she is 'plagued in art', here primarily meaning 'artifice' – the device that the great wax worker employed by Ferdinand has wrought 'to bring her to despair' (4.1.113). When the Duchess tells Bosola, 'I account this world a tedious theatre, / For I do play a part in't 'gainst my will' (4.1.84–5), it is part of her own discourse of resistance, and she alludes to the bestial nature of the informer when she tells Bosola: 'go howl them this: and say I long to bleed' (4.1.109). Bosola must have found this attractive and, sickened at this point by her psychological torture, tells Ferdinand to 'end here: / And go no farther in your cruelty' (4.1.116–17). Since he never wants to see the Duchess again, when he is commanded to do so by Ferdinand, he demands that this must be 'never in mine own shape / That's forfeited by my intelligence / And this last cruel lie' (4.1.129–31). Here 'intelligence' is a simple and straightforward synonym for deception. But in this case, the deception is of a metadramatic kind and has destabilised his identity: his sense of an integrated self. This instability, derived from the personae he has been suborned to perform in various metadramatic roles, may paradoxically function as a point from which he is enabled to resist, and then to remake himself in an alternative mould of his own choosing. Ferdinand's claim that 'thy pity is nothing of kin to thee' (4.1.133) is not quite convincing, given what we know about Bosola's propensity to feel aggrieved at the injustice of his employment, almost to the point of feeling that has in some way been coerced into it, despite his apparent reputed willingness to commit murder for money at the Cardinal's request. Coming to the realisation at this point that 'ill offices are not the engines [he] desire[s] to rise by', like the reluctant informer in a later seventeenth-century play, Bosola is perhaps by now ripe for conversion from the dark side of the structures of power.[24] Although he does not quite get to the light, he at least acts as his own punishing nemesis and is the catalyst for structural change. Webster's own Calvinistic tendencies would surely have found this narrative combination of conversion and predestined doom attractive; as he says himself, *'black deeds must be cur'd with death'* (5.4.41, italics original).

The Duchess responds to her fate often with theatrical self-reference, and there seems to be some small metadramatic apology for theatre in her seeking comfort, or perhaps catharsis, of Cariola in her request that she would 'discourse to me some dismal tragedy' (4.2.8). She dips into another self-reflexive mode to bemoan the fact, as she puts it, that 'fortune seems only to have her eyesight / To behold my tragedy' (4.2.35–6). This simultaneously offers a view of her role as theatrical and her fate the result of a malign audience figure. Watson argues that the Duchess's stoicism in the face of death is not only an essential element in Renaissance tragic heroism, but also 'a commentary on tragic human destiny'.[25] As such, I would argue, it is necessarily constructed within the *theatrum mundi* tradition and defined by the parameters of the Machiavellian realpolitik expressed in contemporary metadramatic and intelligencing conventions. This is a tragic destiny indeed.

Meanwhile, as a contrasting example of a somewhat less stoical demise, Cariola dies protesting and pleading to no avail with her murderers. However, even she dies having 'kept her counsel' (4.2.288), as someone whose circumstances could easily have tempted her otherwise, in an honorable death which contrasts more with the wavering resolve of Bosola, the hypocrisy of the Cardinal and the increasingly incontinent and bestial madness of Ferdinand than with the somewhat hagiographical death of the Duchess.

In the post-Duchess world of the fifth act, the dominant power structures which have defined the action of the tragedy up to this point are now replicated in service of their undoing. When Bosola makes Julia his informer over the Cardinal, telling her that 'tomorrow I'll expect th' intelligence' (5.2.214), Julia takes control herself and insists on a more immediate metadramatic structure: 'tomorrow? get you into my cabinet, / . . . you shall see me wind my tongue about his heart, / Like a skein of silk' (5.2.215, 220–1). But as the Cardinal says to her ominously, 'think what danger 'tis / To receive a prince's secrets / . . . 'tis a secret / . . . like a ling'ring poison' (5.2.257–8, 262–3) as we have seen to be the case. Even if her bosom were a grave, as the Cardinal muses, the lupine forces of bestial injustice would claw them out of the ground like disembodied limbs. As the typical metadramatic informer of the early modern stage, and an instance of the natural interconnection between metadrama and informing that echoes throughout this play, Bosola watches as the hidden, and thus menacing, audience to the inner drama, placed there by one who is acting as his agent in an inner role of her own. It seems significant then that Bosola's occulted condition does not afford him the power to protect his metadramatic partner in this device, as he emerges too late to save Julia from the Cardinal's swift murdering ruse of kissing a poisoned Bible (5.2.267). But despite this, he has heard the Cardinal's confession of wishing to hide behind Bosola's guilt in the matter of the murders, or as he puts it again metadramatically, 'I'th' graves / Of those were actors in't' (5.2.299–300).

Besides its simple effectiveness, this churchman's killing device of the poisoned holy book perhaps also proposes a broader view of the corruption of social mores. It not only indicates a blasphemous betrayal of intimacy in the murder of his sexual partner, but also a general corruption of the idea of moral truth, as much as it does the specifically heretical doctrines of Catholicism that the Cardinal might seem to represent. At the time, a flagrant disregard for what is thought sacred, and this by authorities sanctified, goes hand in hand with treachery and murder in any doctrinal context. At the very outset of the play, Antonio describes just such a toxic court as a 'common fountain', of which he posits, 'if't chance / Some curs'd example poison't near the head, / *Death, and diseases through the whole land spread*' (1.1.13–15, italics original). In warning the Duchess against the exercise of her desire, Ferdinand himself calls the court a 'rank pasture' (1.1.306) and the word is used again when Antonio locates the pollution in Ferdinand's own 'rank gall' (3.2.154). These metaphors of poison emphasise the effect that a single person can have on a social formulation. If the fountainhead is poisoned then so are all the wells; but this also works conversely, that if the poison can be neutralised at source, then the society may survive.

There are also metadramatic moments in the Cardinal's asides to the offstage audience, which at this stage would be very unlikely to generate a sense of collusion, but do offer them a supervisory role which reminds them that, although the Cardinal is culpable too, yet he has not been punished by disease or debilitation for his role in the deaths of the innocents. Telling them he needs to 'feign somewhat' (5.2.87) in his explanation of Ferdinand's illness that appears to claim heredity rather than punishment does not endear him further. And his opening to the audience in the unhearing presence of Bosola that 'this fellow must not know / By any means I had intelligence / In our duchess' death' (5.2.103–5) suggests that he knows Bosola is on the lookout for an opportunity to avenge her death and perhaps to atone for his intelligencing part in it.

As the inevitable end approaches, with some irony for a character who is acting as an intelligencer, Bosola overhears his own demise being planned by the Cardinal (5.4.31) or, as he says in another metadramatic moment, 'My death is plotted' (5.4.39). This seems an unavoidable generic necessity. Despite Watson's argument that the Duchess's noble virtues 'redeem the genre of the play she inhabits from the satiric tragedy of decadence and horror envisioned by Bosola' and thus appeal to a Jacobean audience, it is Bosola himself who seems to determine otherwise, as he becomes the chief agent of change in the play.[26] His personal theatre is directed increasingly by his own desires and moral choices, not by a predetermined generic destiny that sweeps him before its omnipotent metanarrative. This murderous informer's moral conversion suggests a potential for a humanised vision of society in which even the conventionally predatory, wolfish and malcontent informer may evolve into a righteous avenger.

Simultaneous with this humanising conversion of the insidious intelligencer to the pursuit of justice, Ferdinand, the legitimating authority behind this intelligencing, moves in the opposite direction. The worsening of Ferdinand's lycanthropia is directly proportional to the gradual humanising of Bosola. As he descends into increasing wolfishness, losing his reason even to the point of attempting to disinter bodies from their graves, Bosola experiences a diminution of his own predatory voracity. In this same process, Ferdinand turns into the image of the bestial informer.

His lycanthropy is prefigured at the point he accuses Bosola of maliciously carrying out the orders he himself gave him, when he says 'the wolf shall find her grave, and scrape it up' (4.2.307). The etiology of Ferdinand's disease perhaps dates from his intemperate anger at the news of the Duchess's marriage, which, even the Cardinal protests, is 'so deform'd, so beastly' (2.5.57) that it speaks of a desperate imbalance of some kind. It is clear that Ferdinand has the lupine motif on his mind when Bosola has the children killed, and he replies to Bosola's appeal for pity by stating that 'the death / Of young wolves is never to be pitied' (4.2.256–7). Another scene sees Bosola arrive, metadramatically watching 'apart' (5.2.27 s.d.) from a distance as Ferdinand's lycanthropia manifests, and he chases his own shadow to 'throttle it' (5.2.38) until the doctor threatens to make him 'as tame as a dormouse' (5.2.74). This works as a parody of the kind of paranoia that may be generated by intelligencing. Wolf or dormouse, Ferdinand's metamorphosis from legitimate human authority to bestial groveller and grubber-up of graves is complete.

In contrast, even as Bosola interprets and defines Antonio's great qualities and elevated nature, he seems to develop a poetic quality and an increasing sense of humanity, a tendency towards authorship which perhaps results in his ability to author himself. His self-awareness grows as he reflects on taking 'revenge . . . / . . . for myself, / That was an actor in the main of all / Much 'gainst mine own good nature, yet i'th' end / Neglected' (5.5.81, 84–7). As C. G. Thayer was early in pointing out, Bosola 'has been, in effect, an actor playing a role. If he has been playing a role, then, necessarily, he has not been himself.'[27] As he becomes more authentically himself and less of an actor, so he also sheds his role as intelligencer, which is essentially the same thing. Bosola's ambiguity then is of the first order: that of reality and fiction, which he sits between, pointing out their overlapping nature and the dangers inherent in misapplying their legitimate roles within structures of authority. This may be seen in his killing of Antonio, where this 'wretched thing of blood' (5.5.92) has committed 'such a mistake as I have often seen / In a play' (5.5.96–7). His determination to be his own exemplar (5.4.80) is another sign that Bosola now wishes to eschew his social performance in favour of something more authentic. His ultimate frustration perhaps signals again a Calvinistic approach to the limits of self-transformation, as might accord with Webster's use of metadrama to interrogate identity and predestination, as Watson posits.[28] But to take a broader view, the fact that metadrama is the most apt aesthetic form with which to express this social complex speaks of a reflection that is more than simply structural and which has a bearing on the ethics of personal choices within that system.

Bosola's personal alteration is also energised by his continuing disaffection with the undervaluing of the work involved. After the murders, Ferdinand quibbles about the intelligencer's reward, offering merely a pardon for the murder committed under his own commanding authority. But worse perhaps, he questions why Bosola did not himself question the morality of the act and oppose it in some way, expressing this in a metadramatic mode which draws the audience's attention to the inner statement and thus makes the outer level of dramatic utterance in which he operates seem like reality: 'for thee, (as we observe in tragedies / That a good actor many times is curs'd / For playing a villain's part) I hate thee for't' (4.2.268–71). Bosola's response, 'I stand like one / That long hath ta'en a sweet and golden dream: / I am angry with myself, now that I wake' (4.2.321–3), speaks of just such a conversion-like experience from the somnolence of a past life. This awakening is initially evidenced by him administering a merciful lie to the Duchess of full reconciliation between Antonio and the brothers when she momentarily recovers before expiring.

Just as the most obvious form of its representation is metadrama, the most obvious outcome of the intelligencer's work is tragedy. When the Cardinal is about to be murdered by Bosola, he cries out 'Here's a plot upon me' (5.5.23) and again alludes to both the theatrical nature of his existence and the scheme of his demise as wrought by his intelligencer. The overhearing onstage audience of Pescara et al. have been primed to interpret cries for help as a mere attempt to distract the lupine Ferdinand in his fits of madness, and thus rescue is not forthcoming. The metadrama itself here reproduces the self-destruction of the corrupt system of authority and Ferdinand delivers the death-blow in the throes of his antic delusions of battle. As Bosola in his own extremity stabs Ferdinand, the transformation from human to beast is completed as Ferdinand asks 'give me some wet hay' and declaims 'I do account this world but a dog-kennel' (5.5.66–7). But this bloody transaction simply mirrors that which is established throughout the dramatic action of *The Duchess of Malfi*, and suggests that the mechanisms which maintain contemporary power structures are not merely sadistic but also deeply masochistic. As Ferdinand's death cry resoundingly asserts at the last, *'whether we fall by ambition, blood, or lust, / Like diamonds, we are cut with our own dust'* (5.5.73–4, italics original).

It is the questioning and ambiguous Delio who, at the end, is charged with reconstructing the legitimate order through the Duchess's son 'to establish this young, hopeful gentleman / In's mother's right' (5.5.112–13). But Delio is the remnant of the system which destroys itself, and his solution cannot be a hopeful one. In recognising the emptiness, brokenness and moral bankruptcy of 'these wretched eminent things' (5.5.113), his assertion that 'nature doth nothing so great, for great men, / As when she's pleased to make them lords of truth / Integrity of life is fame's best friend' (5.5.118–20) is a moral conclusion which deals inadequately with the issues the play raises with the structural basis of these social discontents and can only finally produce more of the same.

But some hope may be found in the deeply flawed and ambiguous figure of Bosola, that what seems to be an inescapable, self-defeating moral bankruptcy in the mechanisms of authority is in fact not entirely resistant to change. And perhaps it is even redeemable, despite the bars of what seems to be predestined, through the personal agency of its perpetrators.

Notes

1. John Webster, *The Duchess of Malfi*, ed. John Russell Brown (Manchester and New York: Manchester University Press, 2009). All references are to this edition unless stated otherwise.
2. Robert N. Watson, 'Tragedy', in A. R. Braunmuller and Michael Hattaway (eds), *The Cambridge Companion to English Renaissance Drama* (Cambridge: Cambridge University Press, 1990), p. 342.
3. Watson, p. 342.
4. Webster, *The Duchess of Malfi*, p. 65.
5. Webster, *The Duchess of Malfi*, p. 65.
6. Ralph Berry, *The Art of John Webster* (Oxford: Clarendon Press, 1972), p. 139.
7. Webster, *The Duchess of Malfi*, p. 65.
8. Lee Bliss, 'From *The Duchess of Malfi*', in John Webster, *The Duchess of Malfi*, ed. Michael Neill (New York: Norton Critical Editions, 2015), p. 295.
9. Bliss, p. 295.
10. Thomas Elyot, *Image of Governance* (1541), p. viii, quoted in Webster, *The Duchess of Malfi*, p. 82, n. 5–15.
11. Thomas Elyot, *The Governor* (1531), p. 48, quoted in Rocco Coronato, *Jonson Versus Bakhtin: Carnival and the Grotesque* (Amsterdam: Rodopi, 2003), p. 119.
12. This policing of the weights and measures style of informing is also in the public discourse at the time with the 'Act for the better Execution of Two other Statutes made against Alehouse-keepers, sithence the Beginning of his Majesty's most happy Reign'. Here Sir Edward Mountague 'moveth, that in all other Statutes where the Penalty goeth to the Poor, may Part of it be allotted to the Informer.' See *House of Commons Journal*, Volume 1: 31 May 1614 (London: His Majesty's Stationery Office, 1802), pp. 502–4, *British History Online*, <http://www.british-history.ac.uk/commons-jrnl/vol1/pp502-504> (last accessed 4 February 2018).
13. Webster, *The Duchess of Malfi*, p. 9.

14. For contemporary concern with 'misinformations' see *House of Commons Journal*, Volume 1: 27 May 1614 (London: His Majesty's Stationery Office, 1802), pp. 497–581, at pp. 499–500, *British History Online*, <http://www.british-history.ac.uk/commons-jrnl/vol1/pp499-500> (last accessed 12 February 2018).
15. M. H. Curtis, 'The Alienated Intellectuals of Early Stuart England', *Past and Present*, Vol. 23 (1962), pp. 25–43.
16. Webster, *The Duchess of Malfi*, ed. Michael Neill, p. xxi.
17. Nashe, *Haue with you to Saffron-Walden*, p. 106.
18. Richard Johnson, *Look on Me London, I am an honest Englishman, Ripping up the Bowels of Mischiefe lurking in thy sub-urbs and Precincts* (London: N.O., 1613), pp. 16–17.
19. Richard Johnson, pp. 16–17.
20. Jonson, *Poetaster* (4.3.126–8).
21. John Webster and Thomas Middleton, *Anything for a Quiet Life*, *The Works of John Webster*, Vol. 3, eds David Gunby, David Carnegie and MacDonald P. Jackson (Cambridge: Cambridge University Press, 2007).
22. Webster, *The Duchess of Malfi*, ed. Michael Neill, p. xv.
23. See Angus, pp. 15, 124ff.
24. Artesio, in James Shirley, *Andromana*, or *The Merchant's Wife* (1660) in Robert Dodsley and Isaac Reed (eds), *A Select Collection of Old Plays*, Vol. XI (London: J. Dodsley, 1780) (1.3.15).
25. Watson, pp. 342–3.
26. Watson, p. 343.
27. C. G. Thayer, 'The Ambiguity of Bosola', *Studies in Philology*, Vol. 54, No. 2 (April, 1957), pp. 162–71, at p. 168.
28. Watson, pp. 342–3.

Chapter 5

Metadrama and the Murderous Nature of Authority

In many ways the subject of this book is the nature of authority. Having slipped the grip of the Catholic Church through Elizabeth's excommunication by papal bull in 1570 as 'the pretended Queen of England and the servant of crime', and with her 'middle way' having morphed into a Church of England in the process of establishing itself, authority itself is in question.[1] This matter is not at all settled throughout the reigns of James and Charles Stuart, whose own personal connections with the threatening foreign power of the papacy, in combination with their own megalomaniacal insistence on the divine right, will eventually lead the country to discontent over the brink of civil war. Early modern debate around the legitimacy of theatre often concerned the question of the author's authority in relation to those of the licensing authorities and the religious factions which aimed to influence them. As we have seen, however, of greater concern to authors are the wildcard informers in the pay of these and the wider authorities, and especially those whose augmentative testimonies might land one in Newgate, Ludgate or the Clink.[2] The fear of misinterpretation by intelligencers who are perceived to be dishonest by their very nature thus expresses the ambiguity of authority in the dramatic structures of early modern theatre. It helps to generate a self-conscious metadrama which often aims to manipulate audiences' responses in a way most favourable to the author, for obvious defensive reasons. But since this metadrama is regularly concerned with the interchangeability of authority figures, informers and author-actors it also acknowledges the theatre's own potential for complicity in social control. In Philip Massinger's *The Roman Actor* (1626) these tensions and interconnections are embodied in the metadramatic representations of the dramatic productions in the tyrannous court of Domitian Caesar, which conflate the act of acting with the murderous nature of authority and its intelligencers, and finally reflect upon the nascent and highly theatrical court of Charles I itself.

Critical readings of this play have typically focused on the issue of theatrical constraints and artistic autonomy, and in this vein David A. Reinheimer cogently identifies here 'a condemnation of the practice and the politics of censorship from the practical concerns of the performer'.[3] I would suggest that any frustrations that may be felt over the specific issue of censorship are actually rooted in practical concerns and questions over legitimate social authority. Censorship, understood specifically as a means of controlling what is published, can be a fairly patchy affair at this time. What is of overriding concern, however, is the potential for various possible agents, including the Master of the Revels, to see in a play something so substantively offensive to the state or a person of power that the lives of the actors or the author might be placed in danger thereby. Reinheimer also sees the actor Paris' metadramatic oration in defence of the theatre as the 'point of departure for a greater project, Massinger's defence of Caroline performance'.[4] As with *Damon and Pithias*, however, questions may be asked of a defence of the stage delivered from the stage itself. As Charles Pastoor argues, *The Roman Actor* is not simply an 'angry critique of the way political power impedes art. It also reveals a fascination with the complex interplay between reality, political or otherwise, and art.'[5] This chapter deals with that interplay, which is negotiated through the various mechanisms of metadrama.

As we have established, a significant political reality with which authors had to deal was the disconcerting mediation of the authorities' ubiquitous intelligencers, whose extensive employment produced a hazardous environment that was by no means restricted to those at the centre of political life.[6] Contemporary legislation indicates that money was to be made from information relating not only to dramatic libel, political plotting, recusancy and murder, but also to the breaking of simple social rules about, for instance, the pannage of pigs or the stacking of timber.[7] In the context of a dramatic transaction, such activity effectively put a price on any potentially damaging interpretation that might have occurred to the alert viewer or listener. Understandably, this often produced tensions between the author, who was striving to dramatise without chastisement, and the authorities, who were concerned simultaneously to license and contain the disorderly artistic phenomenon taking place about them. Since the dread and loathing of informers was all but universal, the fact that the trace of these predatory and insidious characters figures especially in metadramatic texts is not surprising. However, it also suggests that an issue central to the production of metadrama is the moral status of authority as a whole in a system that is reliant upon the untrustworthy interpretations of a wholly reviled class.

This issue is not as simple as it may seem though, and this is not merely a case of the drama mirroring a reality it sees in society. In any case, a simplistic pseudo-Hamletian idea that drama's ideal is to hold a mirror up to nature is deeply problematic, since its original context is an Elsinore whose capacity for clear reflection is so far out of joint. Early modern theatre is often far from naive about its own potential for complicity in social interpretation and control; after all the aim of the ideal Horatian satire is to offer a social corrective that is intended ultimately to produce a more effective authority. In this way the roles of informer and author have the tendency to overlap, often causing much anxiety on the part of authors as they struggle with the 'narcissism of small differences'. It follows that early modern metadrama is far more concerned with the ambiguous connections, and even interchangeability, between authority figures, informers/intelligencers, and authors/actors as it is with staging protest about theatrical restrictions. These tensions and interconnections are regularly embodied in the explicit and implicit metadramatic devices of early modern drama as we have seen, and this is especially the case in representations of such tyrannous authorities as is found in the court of Massinger's powerful figure Domitian Caesar.

The Roman Actor is primarily concerned with the career of an actor, Paris, in relation to the rule of the tyrant, Domitian, who favours him. The continued success of the tyrant's regime depends upon the intelligencing network with which he surrounds himself, and this is focused in the play on the informer character Aretinus. The actor's relationship to this system is ambiguous. In service to the tyrant, Paris stages three inset plays, each of which has a distinct metadramatic flavour. The inner world of the first inset offers a corrective message to a miser of the outer play, whose misinterpretative audience response is instrumental to his fate at the hands of the tyrant in which he is aided by his obedient actor. The second has the ultimately fatal effect of causing Domitian's wife, who is operating both as author and audience, to confirm that she has fallen in love with Paris, as she confuses the inner play with her own reality. The third seals Paris' fate at the hands of the wronged Domitian who is playing an inner role of wronged husband and deliberately invading this dramatic world with the real effect of his own authority. There are also two other metadramatic episodes in *The Roman Actor* which reveal aspects of the interrelation of authority and the theatrical world: Paris' defence of drama before the Senate, and the public torture of the Stoics Rusticus and Sura. In each of these cases some of the roles of author, actor, audience, intelligencer and authority overlap or are combined or conflated in some way.

The danger of tyrannical violence necessitates the careful manipulation of discourses of power by those at risk and here representations of violence and death are mediated, and thus qualified, by the play's metadramatic structures. This allows connections to be subtly drawn between the potential corruption of audiences and the general authorities. It is inevitable that the disordered authority of Charles I's early reign should emerge in dramatic parallels, however out of joint they might be, and here the tyranny of Domitian entails the conflation of a corrupt and tyrannous monarch with the audience, the informer, the author and, of course, the actor. It is within the interrelationships between these that interpretative power is configured in this play and offered as models for its real, offstage audience.

As with any significantly metadramatic play, *The Roman Actor*'s exploration of interpretative authority requires actors and audiences to occupy continually shifting narrative spaces in relation to the metadramatic mode being employed at any given time. An audience's involvement in interpretative meaning-making is at any point dependent upon the metadramatic form being employed; audiences are a significant element in this interplay of authorities and are never merely passive or neutral.[8] In common with other metadramas, this play is very much concerned with the presence of informers in society generally and in audiences particularly. Further, Massinger's play pulls no punches in describing the potential for actors' involvement in this representative tyranny. Since the intelligencer's function is to interpret (and very possibly to augment) the words or actions of others to the authorities for profit, the shadowy boundaries of this role, in the hazardous and unstable contexts of both the theatre and the court, are something with which the author and actor find themselves uncomfortably familiar.

The Roman Actor engages its audience playfully in metadrama from the very outset, with the players entering and Aesopus asking Paris the tragedian and Latinus, also an actor, the question: 'What doe wee acte to day?' (1.1.1).[9] Here, as in *Hamlet*, actors are acting as actors and discussing the business of theatre. Within the play, however, these actors are not initially meant to be acting but rather they are off-duty; the offstage audience are therefore presented with a performance of pre-performance. This is immediately puzzling to the viewing perspective because at this stage the audience cannot place the opening statements in any authoritative interpretative framework.

This device generates an atmosphere of general self-reference, but it also suggests a metadramatic mode in which the audience is constructed as some other body, though they are not yet aware of what that is. When real actors, acting as actors, are performing in an inset play, the audience is to some extent presented with a clear view of what their interpretative position is to be, and this is often shaped or dictated by the reactions of the onstage audience of the inner play. Here, however, the implication is that there is no play yet being performed; this has the effect of suggesting that the 'actors' are not acting at all and therefore that the audience are not at a play. Thus this first diegetic stage of the play presents a kind of pseudo-reality which resists the normal dramatic pulsion but serves to suggest a shared level of experience between the offstage audience and the players onstage.

As is often the case where metadramatic structures are explicitly engaging the offstage audience as themselves, or constructing them as another body, much here depends on the actual manner of address of the actors. When Paris complains that 'our Amphitheater / ... Is quite forsaken' (1.1.8, 13) there is an opportunity, in either a packed or a relatively empty house, for a knowing glance at the audience. If this opportunity is taken then the audience gets to place itself explicitly in relation to the reason given for the actors' lack of audience – that those 'that raigne in euery noble familie / Declaime against vs' (1.1.7–8). If not, then this positioning remains implicit or allegorical and, in such a metadramatic scenario, may suggest that in relation to the onstage narrative the actual audience is invisible or hidden. And, in an atmosphere of self-interested informing, a hidden audience is always menacing.

In Shakespeare's equally metadramatic play, where Hamlet is instructing the newly arrived travelling players, pre-performance, on their inner presentation of *The Murder of Gonzago*, he is in a sense dictating the dramatic terms of the interchange between the onstage and offstage audiences. He makes explicit the manner in which he expects the players to perform, and takes time to define the dramatic content. But as a supposed non-actor, Hamlet also provides the offstage audience with an interpretative model which comes to serve as a dramatic fulcrum when he interprets the reactions of Claudius to the poisoning of the inner play's king. There, the audience is given a specific example of an empowered audience subject-position: that of the authoring interpreter.[10] In *The Roman Actor*, however, at this point where the players are acting as off-duty actors, the position of the audience remains undisclosed and therefore to that extent disordered.

In this context of anxieties over legitimate authority and interpretation, it is not surprising that the actor Paris has been having problems with his audience while his patron, the Emperor Domitian, has been away at the wars. Paris is disturbed to report that Aretinus, Domitian's intelligencer, has 'sayd at his Table, ere a moneth expir'd / (For being galld in our last Comedie) / He would silence vs foreuer' (1.1.36–8). The accusation is that Aretinus has been 'galld', that is traduced or insulted, and there is no intimation that this has involved a mere 'sinister interpretation' on the part of this audience member who is temporarily empowered by Domitian's absence. The actor thus longs for the return of the tyrant, whom, he says, the acting company 'oft haue cheer'd / In his most sullen moodes' (1.1.40–1). The re-establishment of even this tyrannous authority is required in order that he can 'repayre with ease the Consuls ruines' (1.1.42) and prevent Aretinus' revenge. Thus a power-play is being set up between the ultimate discursive authority of the Emperor and that of his intelligencer, in which the field of conflict is to be the play within the play.

When he is summoned by Aretinus, before Domitian's return, to answer to the court of the Senate for his dramatic misdemeanours, Paris declares assertively:

> We that haue personated in the Sceane
> The ancient Heroes and the falles of Princes
> With loude applause, being to act ourselues
> Must doe it with vndaunted confidence.
>
> (1.1.51–4)

As the primary onstage audience to this metadramatic statement, the First Lictor, responds "'tis spoken like your selfe' (1.1.58), and although the Lictor's words themselves are obviously also spoken by an actor, the statement expresses some level of ambiguity around whether Paris' speech is to be taken as 'acting' within his role as an actor or as the genuine words of the 'real' Paris. To adumbrate the metadramatic structure here is to quarry complex metadramatic strata touching on what is considered to be authentic or 'real' and what is considered to be merely acting or an inauthentic performance of the unreal. Within the metadramatic inner stage, which here is the authoritative body of the Senate, the actor playing Paris is asked to play a character who is either merely acting as himself, simulating the part of an orator or authentically speaking for himself. The Lictor here is also an actor, in this case acting as a member of an onstage audience, accusing an actor, acting as the actor Paris, who may be performing the authentic role of an orator in his own defence of merely acting. To this level of convoluted metatheatricality an audience's response can only be guessed, though the overriding impression is of the total performativity of the *theatrum mundi* and the universal vision of the real as performance. Lack of awareness of these structural and conceptual issues on the audience's part, however, does not preclude them from being situated by them as observers of a particular kind.

When the concerned nobles Lamia and Rusticus observe Paris being led away to appear before the Senate, Lamia asks with what may by now appear as familiar paranoia, 'may we being alone / Speake our thoughts freely of the Prince, and State, / And not feare the informer?' (1.1.67–9). Rusticus replies in the negative and develops the thought, stating that the informing has become so prevalent that 'sonnes accuse their Fathers, / Fathers their sonnes; and but to winne a smile / From one in grace in Court', and locating this malfunction in the unstable and self-oriented nature of the authority they serve, as he says 'they are onely safe / That know to sooth the Princes appetite, / And serue his lusts (1.1.75–7, 79–81). However, such noble lamentation over the state of affairs in general, occasioned as it is by the fate of Paris and the players, is studied irony. As mentioned, the Paris they are expending their pity upon actually pines for the tyrant's return in order to deal with the accusations of the informer Aretinus. His confidence in the favourable reaction of Domitian is based upon the safety he habitually enjoys as one who certainly 'know[s] to sooth the Princes appetite', and this is an appetite which is more often than not of a predatory nature. Paris the tragedian thus occupies a liminal ground between the celebrated authorial independence of the poet and the typically despised sycophancy of the flatterer and informer.[11]

In the theatre of the Senate, the initial scene of Paris' defence, a further coincidence of a metadramatic episode with troubled structures of authority emerges when Aretinus eulogises the Emperor, claiming somewhat unconvincingly:

> I am lost
> In th'Ocean of his vertues. In a word
> All excellencies of good men in him meet,
> But no part of their vices.
>
> (1.3.19–22)

When Rusticus responds with deep sarcasm, 'this is no flatterie!', Sura feels constrained to warn him 'take heed, you'l be obseru'd' (1.3.22–3). This possible threatening observation may be made by the speaker, by other audience members or both, again dependent upon the staging. Besides the good senators, the only parties not directly implicated in the threatening omnipresence of the intelligencer are the players. But Aretinus is persistent; he has a case to make, and his description of Paris and his company is damning:

> You are they
> That search into the secrets of the time,
> And vnder fain'd names on the Stage present
> Actions not to be toucht at; and traduce
> Persons of rancke, and qualitie of both Sexes,
> And with satiricall, and bitter iests
> Make euen the Senators ridiculous
> To the Plebeans.
>
> (1.3.36–43)

This accusation of deliberate misinterpretation and misrepresentation can obviously be levelled at both authors and intelligencers. As the author, Paris is accused of 'search[ing] into the secrets of the time', presenting 'actions not to be toucht at' and traducing 'persons of rancke, and qualitie'; as an informer, Aretinus does all of these himself. It appears then that Paris' real transgression here, quite predictably, is in making 'Senators ridiculous / To the Plebeans' under the cover of 'fain'd names'. In this case the consequences could be very serious.

As often noted, Paris' defence at this indictment is reminiscent of a conventional apologia for acting.[12] However, its setting is not: he defends his own authority at the heart of the Roman Senate – within the world of the play, the centre-stage of all 'worldly' authority. His response to Aretinus' question 'are you on the Stage, / You talke so boldly?' (1.3.49–50) is also framed within the concept of the *theatrum mundi*; as he puts it, 'the whole world being one, / This place is not exempted' (1.3.50–1). In this protective metadramatic context, Paris casts himself as the satirist, a kind of moral informant to society, offering theatrical correctives for the sins of the day. He defends his theatrical treatment of what he terms

> a man sould to his lusts,
> Wasting the treasure of his time and Fortunes
> In wanton dalliance, and to what sad end
> A wretch thats so giuen ouer does arriue at;
> Deterring carelesse youth, by his example,
> From such licentious courses; laying open
> The snares of baudes, and the consuming arts
> Of prodigall strumpets.
>
> (1.3.56–63)

Describing the 'wanton dalliance' and 'sad end' of 'a man sould to his lusts' may advertise itself as merely aiming to deter 'carelesse youth', purifying the author's intention, but recounting 'laying open / The snares of baudes, and the consuming arts / Of prodigall strumpets' casts him also in the familiar role of informing intelligencer, whose business is uncovering secrets in private places. These defences are strongly reminiscent of Nashe's informer, who 'could not live if (like the divell) hee did not from time to time enquire after the sinnes of the people.'[13] Under a tyranny, however, such enquiring after sins is rarely welcome, since it will be bound also to reflect upon the sins of the excessive authorities. Thomas Heywood's *Apology for Actors* (1612) describes such an author as scourge or informer to society of the sins of those in authority. Such authors, he says, 'held in awe the tyrants of the world, / And playde their liues in publicke Theaters, / Making them feare to sinne', since 'fearelesse' authors are prepared to 'wryte their liues in Crimson Inke, / And act their shames in eye of all the world'.[14] Paris' evocation of this apologetic convention founders, however, on his admitted dependency upon one of these very 'tyrants of the world', and despite what he has fearlessly written 'in Crimson Inke', his own life is one of a minion in thrall to a despot, however empowered a minion that might be.

Furthermore, Paris' authority to comment critically is also made questionable by a perceived lack of authenticity. The metadramatic strata here obscure the origins of this actor playing an actor who is being accused of further acting the part of an orator, as Latinus congratulates him: 'well pleaded on my life! I neuer saw him / Act an Orators part before' (1.3.143–4). Both onstage and off, the audiences see that Paris is defending himself in a serious legal context but at the same time the metadramatic self-reference draws the offstage audience's attention to the fact that that the actor playing Paris is merely acting. Thus his conventional moral defence is presented to an undoubtedly equivocal audience through a multi-layered diegetic haze. If they accept Paris' defence as serious it is within a context where roles and representations are fluid and where the framework of authentic authority is elusive. This perceptual layering cushions the author from the possible accusation, by either audience or authorities, of directly expressing controversial views. It also allows him freedom to represent both the audience and the authorities as potentially corrupt and to suggest a link between the two. After all, the Senate here is both audience and accuser. The Senate thus provides an example of an onstage audience of an inner performance, and its hostile character may be intended as a negative model against which the responses of the watching offstage audience may be persuasively shaped.

In further self-defence, Paris goes on to press responsibility for authoritative interpretation firmly into the hands of the onstage audience. He describes presenting the theatrical character of a murderous heir and declares, 'if there be / Among the auditors one whose conscience tells him / He is of the same mould, we cannot help it' (1.3.112–15), and reinforces his case with the example of 'bringing on the stage a loose adultresse', and asserting that:

> if a Matron,
> Howeuer great in fortune, birth or titles,
> Guilty of such a foule vnnaturall sinne,
> Crie out 'tis writ by me', we cannot helpe it.
>
> (1.3.119–22)

Evoking again the metadramatic *Hamlet* and referencing instances of personal conviction in early modern audiences, Paris here exonerates the players from the consequences of the reactions of their audiences. He then uses this powerful rhetoric to turn the accusation around and direct it back at Aretinus, subtly inviting him to recognise himself in an insulting vignette of a corrupt judge, condemning the innocent and declaring:

> If any of this reuerend assemblie,
> Nay e'ne your selfe my Lord, that are the image
> Of absent *Caesar*, feele something in your bosome
> That puts you in remembrance of things past
> Or things intended tis not in vs to helpe it.
>
> (1.3.136–40)

Paris then dismisses this authoritative audience with a couplet and an epilogue-like flourish: 'I haue said, my Lord, and now as you finde cause, / Or censure vs or free vs with applause' (1.3.141–2). This sequence of argument may not have gone well for him, but fortunately for Paris at this point Domitian arrives back from the wars, Aretinus declares 'breake vp the Court, we will reserue to him / The Censure of this cause' (1.3.149–50) and judgement in this case is suspended until the tyrant can offer a resolution.

Domitian's triumphant entry into Rome in this play, Martin Butler suggests, may be a reference to Charles I's coronation entry earlier that year, noting the Stuart monarchs' keen insistence on 'layering their imagery of kingship with imperial resonances'.[15] Like Domitian (and later his wife Domitia) in this play, Charles I and Henrietta-Maria were renowned for their continued practice and support of drama and the arts, and Butler notes further that, in his court entertainments, Charles I was wont to dance in the role of triumphant Emperor.[16] In Jean Howard's study of Shakespeare's second tetralogy, she posits 'the existence of audiences accustomed to judging, with various degrees of sophistication, such performances'.[17] In the case of *The Roman Actor*, the chaos of Charles's early reign would provide an appropriate backdrop to the portrayal of a tyrant and provide an audience sensitised to dramatical references about oppressive regimes.

Upon Domitian's return to Rome, very much contrary to his intelligencer's expectations, rather than censuring Paris he restores him to favour and the subject of Aretinus' objection to Paris' subversive playing is summarily dropped. Parthenius, Domitian's freeman, gives the audience a clue to the possible reason for Paris' easy transition from being accused of 'treason / As libellers against the state and *Caesar*' (1.3.33–4) to being favoured poet again when he addresses Paris about his relationship with the Emperor, saying

> his eare
> To you is euer open
> . . . many men owe you
> For Prouinces they nere hop'd for; and their liues,
> Forfeited to his anger. You being absent,
> I could say more.
>
> (2.1.70–1, 77–80)

The strength and depth of the ambiguity of this statement is dependent upon the actor's delivery, even upon his tone of voice. It is ambiguous nonetheless: the 'prouinces they nere hop'd for' which are owed to Paris by many men could mean either awards or banishment, and 'liues / Forfeited to his anger' could be either lives saved or lives lost. Parthenius' statement indicates that Paris is Domitian's beneficent adviser; its ambiguity implies that he is also acting as Domitian's malevolent intelligencer. This would further explain the rivalry between Paris and Aretinus, since both of them are in competition for preferment with Domitian and both are implicated in the oppressive machinery of authority, whether implicitly or explicitly.

In a favour to Parthenius, Paris stages the first inset play, *The Cure of Avarice*, as an intended corrective to his father Philargus' miserliness. Paris asks Parthenius to merely 'perswade the Emperour / . . . to command / Your Father to be a spectator of it' (2.1.100, 102–3). As payment for the staging of this dramatic snare Parthenius gives him money, saying 'there's your fee; / I ne're bought better counsaile' (2.1.108–9). Paris, aiming to manipulate a dramatic situation to elicit a certain response, is here a paid 'plotter' in the same dual sense as Antony Munday in Francis Meres's unsubtle pun.[18] The metadrama here focuses on the ambiguity, instability and potential for violence of the early modern audience.

At the performance, besides the miserly father, Domitian is also audience and the exercise of his authority exceeds the normal boundaries of interpretation. Here he is operating like Hamlet, reading and interpreting an audience reaction for his own ends, but his presence in the audience is also akin to that of the tyrannical audience member, the informer, whose accusations are so widely feared for their potentially debilitating results. In Domitian's case, the violent consequences of such an accusation are merely more immediate, as he casually intimates to Philargus, the main intended audience: 'sirrha sit still, / And giue attention; if you but nod / You sleepe for euer' (2.1.272–4). Domitian further dictates the terms of the performance which Paris has purposed for Philargus' instruction, saying 'let them spare the Prologue, / And all the Ceremonies proper to our selfe / And come to the last act' (2.1.274–6). Domitian's tyranny thus extends into the discourses of both playing and watching, as he switches freely between the roles of author, audience member and dangerous interpreter. Domitian here provides a tyrannous model of an onstage audience. It is significant that the text suggests that this amount of control over discourses of authority is necessitated by the presence of a notorious tyrant and the ever-present threat of excessive violence that he brings.

Unfortunately for him, the miser Philargus clearly mistakes the inner play for 'reality' and appeals to Domitian, 'as you are *Caesar* / Defend this honest, thriftie man' (2.1.337–8). But the Emperor is firm in pressing home the message of Paris' play as a corrective to his behaviour. When Philargus refuses the 'suddaine change of life' (2.1.432) that Domitian demands, he orders that he should be instantly hanged. Both Philargus and Domitian thus provide negative metadramatic representations of audiences. Domitian's capricious authority over words and representations is to be understood as absolute, leaving no room for unauthorised interpretations; in Philargus' case, his inattention and failure to correctly perceive the dramatic message is fatal. Moreover, despite the contrast which the text attempts to draw between the player Paris and the informer Aretinus, his defence of drama as a moral indicator shows that Paris is entirely complicit in this tyrannical judicial process of trial-by-theatre, and therefore in the execution of its intended audience.

Domitian next arranges a 'drama' of his own in the public torturing of two stoical senators, Rusticus and Sura, who have been 'condemn'd / At Aretinus his informer's suit' (3.1.37–8). Although not an inset play, this is the second distinct episode of metadrama outside of the play's conventionally embedded narrative structures. At this point the staging can include Aretinus' guards facing the offstage audience as he instructs them to observe the people 'with fix'd eyes' and commands that they 'charge vpon any man / That with sigh, or murmure does expresse / A seeming sorrow for these traytors deaths' (3.2.48–50). The offstage audience are now thus constructed by the metadramatic narrative as a crowd of spectators not of a play, but of an episode of public torment. This spectacle is, however, framed like a play; the onstage and offstage audiences are connected in their representation of a Roman crowd and where Domitian Caesar is the author of the drama the audience had better respond in a prescribed fashion. The effect of this prescription on the offstage audience is to set up an oppositional sympathy, if one were still lacking at this point, in which Domitian's violently excessive authority is revealed as both deeply immoral and potentially directed against them. The outcome, however, is to demonstrate the limits of his discursive authority over those with true integrity, as the torments his hangmen inflict are borne with philosophical fortitude, with the Senators' 'calme patience' perceived as 'treading / Vpon the necke of tyrannie' (3.2.95–6). Domitian, the disappointed author in this instance, orders them finally killed, but not before he is forced to become the subject and victim of his own metadramatic spectacle of total authority.

The second metadramatic inset, a play entitled *Iphis and Anaxarete*, has been co-authored by the ambitious Domitia; Hamlet-like, she has been instructing the players how to act and 'to cut off / All tedious impertinencie' (3.2.132–3). In this performance the metadramatic conjunction of author and courtly onstage audience disturbs the stability of what constitutes onstage 'reality' in terms of the inner narrative frame. After Paris' entrance in the inner play, Domitia interjects no fewer than fourteen times, speaking a total of thirty-one lines compared to Latinus' seven and the actress Domitilla's seventeen. Only Paris speaks more lines, with fifty-three in total. Domitia's interjections begin as commentary to Domitian. As she gets more involved, however, her commentary takes a more intrusive form and she constantly crosses the line which the metadrama is attempting to establish between onstage 'reality' and onstage 'fiction', the first and second dramatic strata. As a result the play never gets chance to settle into a definite fictional framework. For the offstage audience this means that there is a disruptive interruption in the play's diegetic gravity, the process of being drawn into the narrative as co-occupiers of a collective onstage viewpoint. Crossing the metadramatic frame in this way draws attention to Domitia as much as it does the fictionality of the whole and in this case it will not turn out well for her.

In Domitia we have an actor acting as the co-author, and now audience, of an inner play she has shaped herself. Hamlet-like she has shared the authorship of the inner play, but here it is she who is 'frighted with false fire' as she mistakes the acting in the inner play for the real thing and responds to Paris' threat to hang himself with 'Not for the world. / Restraine him as you loue your lives' (3.2.281–2). The multi-layered theatricality of the piece might render this a convincing mistake to make were it not for the fact that Domitia's interruptions constantly foreground the inner dramatic frame itself, thus giving the events of the inner play a continually fictional cast. Nevertheless her unwise interjections have undermined her tyrant-derived authority by opening her love for Paris to public scrutiny. Aretinus, the characteristic informer, makes the crucial negative interpretation of Domitia's audience participation and, in an aside to the offstage audience, tells them collusively, 'there is something more / In this then passion, which I must find out, / Or my intelligence freezes' (3.2.293–5). This has the incidental effect of including the offstage audience in acknowledging the efficacy of intelligencing as a means of gaining and maintaining social advantage.

But Aretinus is not the only spectator of Domitia's passion to want to turn it to some advantage. Both Julia, Domitian's niece, from the onstage audience, and Domitilla, his cousin, from the cast, wish to make capital of her excessive response to the play. Domitilla in particular is encouraged by Domitia's lack of restraint and she declares:

> By my hopes I thinke
> That she respects not though all heere saw, and mark'd it;
> Presuming she can mould the Emperours will
> Into what forme she likes, though we, and all
> Th'informers of the world conspir'd to crosse it.
>
> (4.1.8–12)

One slip in such a metadramatic context and suddenly everybody with an axe to grind is a potential informer: Domitilla's 'we, and all / Th'informers of the world' here carries the sense 'we, and all the *other* informers'. Consequently Julia and Domitilla pass their intelligence on this matter to Aretinus, who passes it on to an initially sceptical Domitian.

Meanwhile, since these informers are not wrong about Domitia, she is recklessly attempting to convince Paris of her sexual desire for him. In attempting her persuasion with belated caution, the first thing she does is to create an audience-free space, commanding her servants

> that none presume to dare
> On forfeit of our fauour, that is life,
> Out of a sawcie curiousnesse to stand
> Within the distance of their eyes, or eares.
>
> (4.2.1–4)

Within this informer-free performance space she feels at liberty to praise Paris, suggesting a connection between himself and the roles that he performs 'onstage', and, like a weird fan of some kind, framing their relationship in specifically fictional terms, 'thou art now my *Troyan Paris*, / And I thy *Helen*' (4.2.103–4).

Overlooking them here as a hidden audience, however, are Domitian and his intelligencers. In this, Domitian casts himself in his own words as 'Amphitrio' who, discovering the treachery of his wife and his friend, merely 'stands by, and drawes the curtaines' (4.2.113). Domitia's constant reference to the theatricality of the situation contributes to the diegetic gravity of the piece, drawing the attention of the offstage audience inwards to suggest a common view with the dangerous overlookers of their inner scene. Especially because she has attempted to make the space informer-free, this makes more explicit the offstage audience's empowered interpretative position.

The relative morality of the overlookers and the overlooked, often clearly defined in metadrama to provide an instructive contrast, is here rather more complex. Paris, for all of Domitia's praise, is a paid lackey of the tyrant; Domitia is ruthlessly ambitious and unfaithful; Domitian has all the traditional vices of the tyrant and Aretinus, Julia, Domitilla and Caenis are self-interested professional or amateur intelligencing informers. None of these viewpoints thus offers an entirely desirable subject-position. That of the overlookers, however, is at least explicitly empowered and provides the added attraction of voyeuristic pleasure. In this way the metadramatic structure here again suggests a oneness of the offstage audience with the tyrant and his spying entourage as he puts Domitia under house arrest pending his judgement on the subject. The authority of this viewpoint is, however, quickly dismantled. Aretinus declares in a collusive aside to the audience, 'now I step in, / While he is in this calm mood, for my reward – / Sir, if my service hath deserv'd –' (4.2.152–4). Aretinus' aside has the effect of shifting the audience into his subject-position, which is shown to be fatally unsafe when Domitian impulsively commands his guards to strangle him and lodge the others in the dungeons (4.2.159–60, 164–5).

In these ways Domitian's system of informing provides the means for the collapse of his world and he begins to crave blissful ignorance over the devastatingly excessive intelligence with which these informers have supplied him. It is interesting that at this point Domitian is the only one left standing as any kind of authoritative model or type of the audience; all the others are absent, in prison or dead.

Sparing Paris' life for the meantime, Domitian orders a command performance of a third inset play, *The False Servant*, one familiar to him. Domitian's motive for this becomes apparent when he determines to take the part of the 'iniur'd lord' (4.2.222) character himself and to act in the inner play opposite Paris, who is playing the 'false servant'. Ominously, he prefers his own sword to the theatrical foil offered to him and announces that, though he is a new actor to the tragedy, 'when I come to execution you shall find / No cause to laugh at me' (4.2.237–9).

The play now becomes highly metadramatically charged as the words of the 'wife' character of the inner play echo those of Domitia to Paris in the outer play. Domitia has said to Paris, 'you are coy, / Expecting I should court you ... That holds command o're *Caesar*, and the world' (4.2.73–4, 8). The 'wife' in *The False Servant* is made to ventriloquise the same conventional sentiments, asking 'must we intreate, / That were borne to command, or court a seruant ... / For that, which thou ambitiouslie shouldst kneele for?' (4.2.247–50). This inner play works as an indictment of Domitia's actual crime, but it goes even further, suggesting that, had Paris refused her advances, she would 'swear vnto my Lord at his returne / ... That brutishly thou wouldst have forc'd from me / What I make suit for' (4.2.268–71). Paris thus loses hope for his survival, declaring aside to the audience (both offstage and onstage) that 'this he will beleeue / Vpon her information. 'Tis apparent. / And then I am nothing' (4.2.274–6). This is again very much a case of the conflation of the onstage and offstage audiences, with a similar set of modalities to the torture scene.

Contrary to his hopes, when Domitian receives his prompt to enter the stage play he makes a ridiculous figure, blundering into the action and forgetting his lines: 'O villaine! thanklesse villaine! – I should talke now; / But I haue forgot my part. But I can doe, / Thus, thus, and thus' (4.2.281–3). But it is with this halting performance that he executes Paris, arguing that this form of punishment is a mercy killing in comparison with the types of death he could have ordered. Paris' final words are 'Oh, I am slaine in earnest' (4.2.283) as Domitian's sword cuts across their respective performative modes. In the hands of the tyrant, death knows no theatrical boundaries.

As the only viable model of the audience in his discovery of the central crisis of the play – the betrayal of Paris and Domitia's assignation – Domitian has opted to instigate, and act in, a further play within the play and to use its theatrical parameters to both instruct his audience and to mitigate and execute a 'just' punishment. That he must descend into Paris' theatrical world to do this speaks of an authority which is extreme in its moral ambiguity and arbitrariness. He is at once the tyrant on a hair trigger, punishing the smallest misdemeanours with death, and at the same time the merciful friend, magnanimously allowing the betrayer to 'dye in action, and to crowne it, dye / With an applause induring to all times, / By our imperiall hand' (4.2.298–300). Further, when Domitian enters the frame-narrative as an actor it thus becomes open-ended in that his own 'real' fate is bound up in its staging. He has moved from being an onstage audience of Paris and Domitia's tryst to being an inner-stage representation of an audience turned executioner. This is an elaboration of metadrama in which the audience is overtly represented to itself and the subject held up for their interpretation is authoritative interpretation itself. Domitian here models an authoring, commanding, producing, acting, interpreting and finally murderous audience, and will eventually pay the price himself for this. The effect of this exemplum on the offstage audience would be complex to say the least; their reaction to it, however, need not be. As this excessive interpreter enters the action, the viewpoint of the offstage audience will only shift with him to the extent that they sympathise with his predicament. What causes the scopic pulsion in this case is the realisation that Domitian is carrying an unbated sword into the inner play. There is nothing quite so compelling as the inevitable.

With his poignant interjection, Domitian makes sure that the actor, here as is often the case in this period, bears the brunt of the violence which is kindled by the interaction of drama and corrupt authority. But there are other repercussions also. When he offers the compromised Domitia mercy, the very basis of Domitian's authority is questioned. Domitia replies that she

> (When circl'd with thy Guards, thy rods, thy axes
> And all the ensignes of thy boasted power)
> Will say *Domitian*, nay adde to it *Caesar*,
> Is a weake feeble man, a bondman to
> His violent passions, and in that my slaue.
>   (5.1.39–42, 44–9)

The argument she offers here is that because Domitian cannot rule his passions he is not only unfit to interpret Domitia's actions as immoral, but also implicitly unfit to rule the Empire. And this is borne out further in the circumstances of his own demise as it turns out that Domitian's own murderers have all been victims of his fickle and theatrically excessive appetite. But, despite this, his murder is ultimately made possible because he loses his authority to one who plays her role of tyrannical audience more convincingly than Caesar. Domitia sticks to her interpretations of Domitian's actions as much as to her love for Paris and the outcome of this is as obvious as a knife blade. Paris dies because Domitia's passionate audience response reveals her excessive tendencies which have been prohibited by Domitian's authority, and Domitian dies because Domitia exposes the dramatic and interpretative limits of that authority.

As both excessive author and audience, then, Domitian ultimately fails: in the first place by attempting to regulate the deaths of people as if they were mere characters in a play, to be written off; and in the second to fully control the results of his own interpretations. His only success is as an authoritative actor-executioner, though even here his performance merely adds to the case against him.

After all of these connections have been drawn between metadrama and troubled authority it is significant that the collective killing of the tyrant is played entirely without recourse to metadramatic framing. When Domitian dies in the 'outer' play, with a 'real' audience occupying their default viewpoint as paying customers of the Red Bull or the Blackfriars and subjects of King Charles, he does so not within a metadramatically layered frame-narrative but as a simple representation of a bad king. Though *The Roman Actor* begins by presenting an ambiguous metadramatic state of non-play and progresses through various configurations of the dramatic relationship between author, actor and interpretative audience, it arrives at a fairly plain message:

> Good Kings are mourn'd for after life, but ill
> And such as gouern'd onely by their will
> And not their reason, vnlamented fall;
> No Goodmans teare shed at their Funerall.
> (5.2.90–3)

When it was printed in 1629, these words in support of those who govern by 'reason' must have resonated, for any who knew both texts, with the 'Petition of Right' of 1628, which Charles was forced to accept in order to placate an enraged Parliament and in hope of receiving subsidies. But even when it was first played by the King's Men in 1626, the arrogant actions of the king which would lead to this petition were already making him deeply unpopular, including the enforcing of loans on pain of imprisonment without trial, the billeting of military personnel on ordinary citizens and the imposition of martial law resulting in various injustices.

These considerations, allied to the king's propensity to dance about triumphantly in the dress of a Roman Emperor, suggest that a contemporary audience of *The Roman Actor* could not help but ponder to whom the play's title refers. Its ambiguity, like that generated by the metadrama it contains, affords both Massinger and his audience the luxury of social criticism free from the misinterpretation of the intelligencer and the accusation of libel 'against the state and *Caesar*' (1.3.34).

Notes

1. Patrick McGrath, *Papists and Puritans under Elizabeth I* (Poole: Blandford Press, 1967), p. 69.
2. Ludgate might be the prison most favoured for such misdemeanours. The Fleet prison, being in such poor shape at the time, seems to have

been reserved for particularly egregious offenders. As John Taylor, the 'water poet', puts it:

> By Lud was Ludgate founded from the earth;
> No Iayle for theeues, though fome perhaps as bad,
> That breake in policie, may there be had.

John Taylor, 'The Praise and Vertue of a Jayle and Jaylers', *All the Workes of Iohn Taylor the Water Poet* (Menston, Yorks: Scholar Press, 1973).

3. David A. Reinheimer, '*The Roman Actor*, Censorship, and Dramatic Autonomy', *Studies in English Literature, 1500–1900*, Vol. 38, No. 2 (Spring 1998), pp. 317–32, at p. 317.
4. Reinheimer, p. 320.
5. Charles Pastoor, 'Metadramatic Performances in *Hamlet* and *The Roman Actor*', *Philological Review*, Vol. 32, No. 1 (Spring 2006), pp. 1–20, at p. 16.
6. For more information on the connection between authority and the collection of information, see Breight, p. 101.
7. In 1542 the king commanded the Earl of Southampton to investigate pannage for swine on Enfielde Chase from Michaelmas to Martinmas, commanding that 'hogs on the chase [are] to be ringed or pegged under a pain of 12d., half to go to the king and half to the informer.' William Page (ed.), *Forestry. A History of the County of Middlesex*, Volume II (1911); *British History Online*, <http://www.british-history.ac.uk/report.asp?compid=22179&strquery=informer#p17> (last accessed 16 February 2018). For issues pertaining to the early modern woodmonger versus the informer, see *House of Commons Journal*, Volume 9, p. 12 (London: His Majesty's Stationery Office, 1802); *British History Online*, <http://www.british-history.ac.uk/report.asp?compid=27052&strquery=informer#p12> (last accessed 29 January 2018).
8. Audiences are often represented by authors as bestially inadequate in their powers of interpretation, and even potentially dangerous to the health of both the theatre and the state. See, for instance, Thomas Carew's commendatory poem on William Davenant's *The Just Italian* (1630) where Carew blames the play's lack of commercial success on the audience's comedically inadequate analytical powers, adding, with a possible reference to the assassination of Buckingham in 1628, that

> this churlish fate
> Rules not the stage alone; perhaps the State
> Hath felt that rancour, where men great and good,
> Have by the Rabble beeene [sic] misunderstood.

Sir William D'Avenant, *The Just Italian* (London: Thomas Harper, 1630), <http://gateway.proquest.com/openurl?ctx_ver=Z39.88-2003&res_id=xri:eebo&rft_id=xri:eebo:citation:99844957> (last accessed 4 February 2018).
9. Philip Massinger, *The Roman Actor*, in Philip Edwards and Colin Gibson (eds), *The Plays and Poems of Philip Massinger*, Volume III (London: Oxford University Press, 1976).
10. William Shakespeare, *Hamlet* (1601), ed. Harold Jenkins (London: Arden Shakespeare, 2000) (3.2.1–45).
11. This is of a kind which recollects Ben Jonson's anxious distinction between satyr and faun. See Jonson, *Poetaster* (4.7.9–10).
12. See, for example, Douglas Howard, 'Massinger's Political Tragedies', in Douglas Howard (ed.), *Philip Massinger: A Critical Reassessment* (Cambridge: Cambridge University Press, 1985), pp. 117–37, at p. 123.
13. Nashe also suffers for his writing. See Breight, p. 49.
14. Thomas Heywood, *An apology for actors* (London: Nicholas Okes, 1612), <http://gateway.proquest.com/openurl?ctx_ver=Z39.88-2003&res_id=xri:eebo&rft_id=xri:eebo:citation:99841838> (last accessed 10 January 2018).
15. Martin Butler, 'Introduction', in Philip Massinger, *The Roman Actor* (London: Nick Hern, 2002), p. xi.
16. Butler, p. xi.
17. Jean E. Howard, *The Stage and Social Struggle in Early Modern England* (London and New York: Routledge, 1994), p. 140.
18. Francis Meres, 'Poetrie; Poets; and A Comparatiue discourse of our English Poets, with the Greeke, Latine, and Italian Poets', in *Palladis Tamia Wits Treasury* (London: P. Short, 1598), <http://gateway.proquest.com/openurl?ctx_ver=Z39.88-2003&res_id=xri:eebo&rft_id=xri:eebo:citation:99845635> (last accessed 27 February 2018).

Chapter 6

The Burning Issue: Metadrama and Contested Authority in Chettle's *Hoffman*

In Henry Chettle's only extant solo-authored play, *The Tragedy of Hoffman* (*c*.1602, pub. 1631), the metonymic device of the burning crown, used to execute usurpers, suggests an authority uneasy with its constituent elements. The play posits an authority, like many others depicted in the early modern theatre, whose very apparatus of power puts its own legitimacy in question. In *Hoffman*'s contemplation of authority, however, metadramatic devices, though clearly linked to the exercise of advantageous oversight, have alternately destabilising and restorative functions. This may provide a useful comparative, but it also simply testifies to the flexibility of the form in representing various degrees and types of menacing oversight. In the context of a country seemingly awash with recreational intelligencers, revealing these can only be subversive to the mechanisms of control.

Throughout the narrative, whether they are pretenders dealing with the problematic anomaly of misused authority or established and dealing with misappropriated authority, the play's usurping and informing metadramatic actors seem to be punished in one way or another by hidden audiences. The limited nature of Chettle's success as a writer may have inflected his attitude to authority and the arbiters of power, and, as John Jowett argues, may have fashioned in Chettle a voice which is 'contingent on circumstance, and mediated through personae', so much so that 'his authority to speak is compromised'.[1] It is compelling to read *Hoffman* in this respect as something of an exploration of frustrated authority and this chapter will argue that Chettle's vision of the nature of authority here is as a performative construct that is deeply troubled by its own contingent control mechanisms.

The play has a very direct opening, as the eponymous protagonist is discovered in a coastal cave accompanied by the remains of his revered father, whose body appears to be displayed somehow. We discover that one Duke of Luningberg has put the father to death for piracy by crowning him with a red-hot iron crown. Somewhat conveniently for the narrative, Hoffman finds Luningberg's son, Otho, shipwrecked nearby and kills him in the same blistering way. He then goes on to steal Otho's identity to aid his project of revenge on the rest of the family. This seems to be working out until he shows the weakness of falling for Otho's mother, and he is thereby himself ensnared through metadramatic means. Hoffman is then condemned finally also to die by the device of the flaming crown for his murderous revenges, the sin of usurpation and his daring encroachment on the positions of power.

Although the play's metadramatic structures initially facilitate the active power of the vengeful protagonist and serve to draw the off-stage audience into his confidence, they are also used by the play's antagonists, the Luningbergs and their associates. In their case they set onstage audiences up to redress what they see as an ill rather than primarily to provoke one, and thus cause the downfall of the plotters. The fact that these are used to exert vengeance on the revenger suggests a society dependent on the mechanisms of the intelligencer for the exercise of social power and one to an extent destabilised by cycles of violent repression and confrontation.

Chettle himself apparently led a relatively unstable life, continually struggling with money, as various references in the diary of theatrical impresario Philip Henslowe indicate, and found himself in detention for debt on a number of occasions, including spending a spell in the Marshalsea.[2] Mark Eccles demonstrates the critical condition of Chettle's funds in 1600 that saw him carrying the considerable liability of £40.[3] Henslowe's diary gives a general sense of the vagaries of playwrights' wages, and in Chettle's case it records that in 1598–9, he earned something over £18, but that in the previous theatrical season this was less than £3, a no doubt distressing fluctuation.[4] Chettle was certainly one of the 'needy band of poets who were dependent upon Henslowe for loans and were occasionally rescued from prison by his help', as A. W. Ward and A. R. Waller attest, and this in itself makes him vulnerable to the mechanisms of social authority.[5] Such pecuniary unease alone, besides the general company of theatrical types, will very likely have brought him personally into the purview of informers feeding into the broader intelligencing community. In this respect it is tempting to read in Henslowe's reference to Chettle's arrest by one 'Ingrome' a shady association with Ingram Frizer, the intelligencer who killed Christopher Marlowe and was subsequently peremptorily and suspiciously pardoned by Elizabeth herself. In his diary, Henslowe writes, 'lent Thomas Dickers and harey chettell, the 2 of maye 1599, to discharge harey chettell of his areste from Ingrome, the somme of twenty shellyngs in Redy money.'[6] It would have been most likely that the person so named in Henslowe would be the creditor of the transaction, not the arresting officer, but in fact, besides being a known informer, Frizer was a notorious money-lender and guller of duller financial brains.[7] His associations with Walsingham might also place him there in either capacity.[8] Since Frizer retired to Eltham in later life, and the 'Mrs. Ingeram' who was buried there on 25 August 1616 may well have been his wife, it is at least circumstantially suggestive that he may have been commonly known by his first name Ingram/Ingrome, as this reading of Henslowe suggests.[9] The possibility of Thomas Dekker's involvement in this also adds a circumstantial implication in that one who writes so forcefully of the demonic nature of the intelligencer would have experience of such figures in the hard reality of daily life.

But even without this possible connection with the Elizabethan underworld, Chettle's pecuniary difficulties would certainly have attracted the attention of contemporary cony-catching predators. The conventions of the world Chettle inhabited were comprehensively corrupting in this respect, and in fact he may himself have arrested someone for debts owed, as again Henslowe seems to suggest.[10] Financial difficulty goes in tandem with the attractions of selling information at this time, and the fact that Chettle calls his writing collaborator Anthony Munday a 'chattring Py' suggests that he is living in that world. Although this might seem to be an obscure jibe, it is entirely in accord with Munday's contemporary reputation as an informer, even one associated with the infamous intelligencer and torturer Richard Topcliffe.[11] Chettle also seems to have been no stranger to accusations of false reporting on his own part: in February 1601 he was a co-defendant in a Star Chamber examination where he was accused of 'conspiring to libel Alderman Paul Baynin', as Eccles notes.[12] When Chettle signs himself as 'your old Compositor' in a prefatory epistle to Thomas Nashe's *Have with you to Saffron-Walden*, this primarily refers to his involvement in setting up Nashe's *Martin Marprelate* tracts for printing in 1589–90.[13] It may, however, also contain a possible mischievous play on the word 'compositor' to imply that he was in a sense a 'collaborator'. This work places him, at least at the beginning of his career, within a secretive subculture involving an illicit press that had to continually relocate to evade the authorities, and in connection with which John Penry, the ostensible author of the Marprelate tracts, was hanged. His statement in this same epistle that his setting out of the text 'shall page and lackey [Harvey's] infamie after him' alludes to the fawning and sycophancy associated with the informer figure who might do just that kind of insidious work.[14]

Chettle's intermittent association from 1591 with the printers William Hoskins and John Danter apparently provided work, perhaps including in the writing of ballads.[15] But this in itself was hardly reputable employment and Danter has been indicted for his 'record of piracy and secret printing', as W. W. Greg noted.[16] Danter's press was eventually closed down in 1597 for an unauthorised printing of *Jesu's Psalter*.[17] In this respect, Jowett describes Chettle's 'liminal status' in the twilight world of 'stationer's agent, editor, and ghost-writer'.[18] This marginal position also perhaps offers him a convenient deniability during the controversy surrounding Greene's *Groatsworth of Wit*.[19] The epigram in Chettle's *Kind-Hart's Dreame* contains the device which reads, 'il vostro malignare non giova nvlla' or 'your enmity / ill-speaking will not prevail', a choice which can hardly be read as neutral in the contexts we are describing. This is borrowed from John Wolfe's printing of Machiavelli, and he may reproduce it here as 'a banner under which to advance surreptitious dealing', as Jowett argues.[20] In his *Kind-harts Dreame* (1592), Chettle, employing the ironic voice of the actor Tarleton to imitate anti-theatrical writers, exclaims:

> Fie upon following plaies, the expence is wondrous; upon players speeches, their wordes are full of wyles; upon their gestures, that are altogether wanton. Is it not lamentable, that a man should spende his two pence on them in an after-noone, heare covetousnes

amongst them daily quipt at, being one of the commonest occupations in the countrey; and in lively gesture see treacherie set out, with which every man now adaies useth to intrap his brother. Byr lady, this would be lookt into: if these be the fruites of playing, tis time the practiser were expeld.[21]

Being couched in this way in the tones of the famous actor, this passage may be intended to mock conventional Christian attacks on the perceived dishonesty of playing at a fundamental level but it nonetheless suggests that a recognisable element of the discourse around theatre-going is the idea that players' words are tricky and 'full of wyles'. To advance further the ironic attack, the argument that the effect of seeing 'treacherie set out' in 'lively gesture' in an early modern playhouse is that 'every man now adaies useth [it] to intrap his brother' is replete with sarcastic hyperbole. The devices commonly used in plays are thus mapped here onto the perceived deceptions and politicking of wider society and their inherent similarity is presented as part of a familiar argument in which plays are perceived as subversive to truth and legitimate authority. In Tarleton's voice, however, this cannot be a lament for the ways in which life imitates art, but rather must be an ironic assertion of the opposite: that the devices of plays merely reflect the forms and practices common to society. In fact neither would be the case in an absolute sense but rather each might feed the other in an example of Greenblatt's 'circulation of social energy'.[22] Chettle's awareness of this equivalence, however, taken together with all of the above associations and material connections, fitted him into a world where the mechanisms and conventions of informing, intelligencing and the metadramatic devices of early modern theatre may be seen to overlap to a significant degree.

At the play's commencement we are presented with a displaced and disturbing authority structure which is intrinsically linked with a kind of self-conscious performance. When Hoffman is in his cave at the play's outset and he reveals 'the dead remembrance of my living father' (1.1.6), as the stage directions determine he *strikes ope a curtain where appears a body*, accompanied highly theatrically by strikes of thunder and lightning.[23] By the time he is named to the audience as 'Hans Hoffman's son that stole down his father's anatomy from the gallows at Luningberg' (1.1.98–100), we have begun to perceive the grisly theatricality of the main protagonist's persona. The melodramatic and metadramatic revelation of the body sets at the centre of the drama the dead audience of the authorising father, the locus of the dead hand which animates the revenge to be acted. From the very beginning, then, the drama is to be acted in front of this dead authority figure, who bears the evidence of his own arrogation of authority – as we see, 'upon the dead skull there's the iron crown that burnt his brains out' (1.1.100–1). When Hoffman invokes the pathetic fallacy of the very winds and sea, commanding them to roar 'with celestial fires', he links these elements to his ambitious plotting when he says, 'quicken high projects, with your highest desires' (1.1.26–7). There is a kind of covert authorising in this, as the natural sympathies of the weather are supposed to mirror the disturbances below, and the word 'projects' here is far from a neutral usage but rather one linked with the idea of ambitious commercial or political dealings, including the intrigues and manoeuvres of the intelligencer.

When Otho's servant Lorrique enters after being shipwrecked on Hoffman's coast, he is quick to identify the shifting nature of authority in the place. Here, as he says, he need 'fear no sergeants' and adds the jest that it seems that the locals 'keep not a constable at sea'; yet he admits to the disturbing aspect of this situation, where, as he says, 'a man's overwhelmed without order' (1.1.31–4). In the play's first small metadramatic overhearing, Hoffman, who has been observing Lorrique, now enters and replies, 'thou liest: there lives upon the earth more beasts / With wide-devouring throats than can be found / Of ravenous fishes in the ocean' (1.1.37–9). The fact that this responds to Lorrique's musing on sergeants and constables suggests that this is not merely a general assertion that man is a wolf to man, but a statement directly attributed to the felt nature of authority in the place. That he has been a hidden audience of Lorrique's musings is also suggestive of Hoffman's own bestial and ravenous nature: a hidden audience is always a source of potential danger on the early modern stage. His accusation that Lorrique is lying rather than merely mistaken also seems a pretty aggressive conversational opening, especially in the contemporary contexts we have been sketching, and, besides serving to build a picture of Hoffman's angry nature, is prophetic. The reference here to the devouring throats of 'cormorants' (1.1.44) recalls images of the intelligencers and informers of the day as rapacious birds of one kind or another. The anonymous tract, *The Character of an informer wherein his mischeivous nature, and leud practises are detected*, describes the predatory intelligencer as 'a half-starved Cormorant' whose presence people dread 'more than a Partridge does a Hawke'.[24] Perhaps not surprisingly, this reminder of his helplessness in the face of predatory structures of authority helps to effect the instantaneous change of Lorrique's allegiance. Principally of course it is their embodiment in the dangerously immediate figure of Hoffman which founds his sudden willingness to bargain for his life by turning traitor to his master and assisting Hoffman in his plan of revenge, as his assistant plotter, metadramatic actor and intelligencer.

When, soon after this, Hoffman takes his swift revenge against the unluckily shipwrecked Otho by having Lorrique kill his own master, he does this in the same way as Hoffman's father was killed, with the burning crown. In this act of seeming equivalence, Otho cries out in his distress, 'I feel an Etna burn / Within my brains' (1.1.218–19). Boiling the brain in this manner was a mode of execution thought fitting at times of rebellious upheavals of authority, somehow perhaps signifying the upwards ambition of headship, distinction or even majesty. Otho of course is innocent of such aspiration and is merely being punished for the sins of the father. Hoffman, however, in his own context, actually carries the guilt of this ambition to be elevated, as Saxony says of him later in the play: 'he seeks dignity, / Reason he should receive his desperate hire, / And wear his crown made flaming hot with fire' (5.3.141–2).[25] Various precedent sources are possible for the use of this gruesome device. In Shakespeare's *Richard III* (c.1592), Anne, protesting her coming marriage with Richard, cries 'O, would to God, that the inclusive verge / Of golden metal, that must round my brow, / Were red-hot steel, to sear me to the brain!' (4.1.59–61). In the anonymous play *Look about You* (1600), Henry the Elder threatens Gloster thus:

> By heauen put on thy Coronet, or that heauen
> Which now with a clear, lends vs this light,
> Shall not be courtain'd with the vaile of night,
> Eare on thy head I clap a burning Crowne,
> Of red hot Yron that shall seare thy braines.
>
> (2853–8)

Chettle may also have had a hand in this play, as might Anthony Munday and Thomas Dekker, his known associates in various artistic and financial scrapes, as also may Antony Wadeson, Stephen Knight suggests.[26] For his rebellion against James I of Scotland, the Earl of Atholl was tortured to death in 1437 by being 'crowned with a diadem of burning iron'.[27] These punishments seem to be related to the classical myth of Medea giving a poisoned or burning crown to her rival Creusa thus incinerating her and others.[28] All of these examples speak of the troubled nature of authority and its bloody and spectacularly theatrical mechanisms of self-protection and self-perpetuation. In this case, the killing of Otho with the burning crown is played out before Hoffman's onstage audience: the tableau of the accusing bones of the dead parent. Hoffman then says, with a direct reference to the metadramatic nature of the unfolding drama of plotting and revenge, 'come, Lorrique: / This but the prologue to the ensuing play, / The first step to revenge. This scene is done / Father, I offer thee thy murderer's son' (1.1.228–31). With this self-conscious reference to prologue and scene, Hoffman orients our progress to the ensuing revenge play via a metadramatic awareness of the onstage audience of the dead father, whose body is acting as both material accusation and motivating evidence. The suggestion here that the offstage audience share the point of view of a murdered cadaver offers perhaps a macabre model of interpretation, but it must be admitted that its perspective is hard to argue with.

Like most authors of the time, Chettle seems very much concerned with the processes and dangerous implications of self-interested interpretation. The use of the dead as onstage audience in this way suggests both the presence and absence of the authority of the father, a disconcerting embodiment of a legitimating interpretative context, and a dead, quiescent and passive audience, yet one primed to justify the scene of revenge. If it also provides an interpretative lacuna that is to be filled by the living audience offstage, it is one predicated on the unjust and extremely violent death of a beloved. This may be persuasive. In his *Kind-hart's Dreame* (1592), Chettle expresses such concern over interpretation, stating that 'if envious misconsterers arme themselves against my simple meaning, and wrest every iest to a wrong sense. I thinke it policy to fly at the first fight, till I gather fresh forces to repress their folly.'[29] This sense of 'wresting' is very much a source of paranoia in the writing community throughout the early modern period, as may be seen from Jonson's linking of 'wresting' with spy-like suggestions' and 'promoting sleights'.[30] This is what Thomas Carew's character Momus, the 'Arch-Informer' of his 1640 masque *Coelum Brittanicum*, describes as the intelligencer's 'præogative of wresting . . . to any whatsoever interpretation'.[31] As may be perceived from these examples, the anxiety is that a meaning may be wrested by 'misconsterers' to the writer's great undoing, rather than merely to cause damage to his reputation. Chettle's stated policy on this being 'to fly at the first fight' might be the best expedient, either metaphorically or in physical reality.

This pacey dramatic opening leads to the entry of Ferdinand Duke of Prussia, Lodowick, Rodorick, Mathias, Ferdinand's foolish son Jerome, his companion Stilt and the beautiful and eligible Lucibel. To this crowd Rodorick announces his intelligence of the forthcoming further arrival of the Dukes of Austria and Saxony, which he has acquired 'by true report of pilgrims at my cell' (1.2.18). This is a small indication of the nature of the necessary upward flow of information, which follows the paths of patronage, favour and money in the direction of authority. Here we also find that Ferdinand is ashamed of his witless son Jerome, whose aim to fight at a tournament given in honour of Lucibel is ridiculed, and as we will see, this will have consequences that the plotters can exploit for their own nefarious ends.

After Lorrique fools Ferdinand into thinking that the favoured Otho is still alive, Hoffman simply steals Otho's identity in a metadramatic move which will see him impersonating the dead character and playing the role within his role for much of the remaining play. When he enters alone and speaks directly to the offstage audience, it is unclear whether he has been standing aside and watching the previous scene with its crucial information unfold. This should be made apparent in the staging of any given production. Either way, he hangs Otho's body up alongside his 'long-injured father's naked bones', and explains to the offstage audience in a chorus-like manner that Otho's fate, authored by himself and acted at his servant's hands,

> was the prologue to a tragedy,
> That, if my destinies deny me not,
> Shall pass those of Thyestes, Tereus,
> Jocasta, or duke Jason's jealous wife.
>
> (1.3.18–21)

This works as a relatively typical metatheatrical reference to 'tragedy' as a model for other onstage acts of 'real life'; the allusion to Medea, Jason's jealous wife, is also somewhat conventional in as much as her excessive revenge is proverbial. As a mode of metadramatic reference, it can have the effect of suggesting that the 'real' is to be found somehow in the form of address from actor to audience, rather than entirely offstage. This draws the offstage audience into a kind of implicit collusion in an agreed 'real' which the drama will present for them. Hoffman then reinforces this with an explicit connection of acting in the real world with stage acting, saying 'shut our stage up: there is one act done / Ended in Otho's death; 'twas somewhat single. / I'll fill the other fuller' (1.3.22–3). Here, he shows himself as both malcontent vice, crossing the boundaries of fictional worlds, and Machiavellian protagonist with intelligencing tendencies. The fact that these character types dovetail with the self-conscious metadrama of the piece will be no surprise in the contexts which we have been examining throughout this present study.

It is with a metatheatrical flourish that Hoffman, role playing within his role and disguised as Otho, is crowned by Ferdinand at the very chair of state (2.1.48 s.d.) and in a gesture which is filled with the imagery of transferred or borrowed authority. This is surely the intelligencer's dream fulfilled. As a fantasy of elevation based on the skills of acting and plotting, it is at once authorly and informerly. The situation seems to get even better when Ferdinand decides to disinherit the ridiculous Jerome in favour of Otho/Hoffman, although Jerome responds belatedly, and somewhat lamely, that he will seek out his 'notes of Machiavel', adding that 'they say he's an odd politician'; his servant Stilt emphasises this but again in a seemingly obvious manner, saying 'he's so odd, that he hath driven even honesty from all men's hearts' (2.1.69–72). This would-be Machiavellian is soon showing himself also to be a poetaster, and there is a possible connection between the self-making and ambitious functions of these roles which Jonson makes much of in *Poetaster* (1603).[32] In this aspirational role, Jerome self-consciously attempts to dramatise his own demise, choosing awkward words stumblingly, as he poetises pathetically to Stilt, 'we will tread on stilts / Through the purple pavement of the court, / Which shall be – let me see, what shall it be? / No court, but even a cave of misery' (2.1.77–80). This turns out to be an example of entirely metadramatic self-reference as Jerome interprets his own words, saying 'there's an excellent speech Stilt' (2.1.81). Further, when Jerome entreats Stilt to serve him in restoring his princedom, Stilt replies again metadramatically, 'O, Stilt will stalk, and make the earth a stage, / But he will have thee lord in spite of rage' (2.1.83–4). One of the implications of this is perhaps that the offstage audience are not at a play, but rather sharing a common referential field with the actors in which plays may be referenced. Thus here too, the metadrama provides an offset for the truly Machiavellian vice, Hoffman, where revenge is linked with both poor acting and inadequate authorship. The extent to which Hoffman himself is more successful in this is yet to be seen, but Jerome's abortively performative attempt at producing authority is suggestive of a construct that undermines its own credibility.

To some extent the 'trusty Lorrique' (5.2.9) competes with Hoffman in this play for the title of vice in his dual role as actor and intelligencer. Speaking to the audience alone, he confesses his nature, claiming 'I am half a monarch, half a fiend. / Blood I begun in and in blood must end' (2.3.17–18), and telling them 'this Clois [Hoffman] is an honest villain [who] . . . kills none but his father's enemies', but adding that this is 'meritorious: where? in heaven? no, hell' (2.3.20–2). The audience are thus invited to share the interpretative perspective of one self-interested parasite on another, the eponymous revenge villain. Hoffman's excessively vengeful bloodthirst might qualify an offstage audience's sympathy with him by this point, so they may be tempted by this other deceiver's viewpoint, although the fact that Lorrique is entirely complicit in the play's violent action may also be incentive enough to suggest a critical interpretation of either. As depictions of the mechanisms of control on which authority is contingent, neither is attractive.

Lorrique's next act, along with Hoffman again playing a role within a role in disguise as the hermit, is to misinform Lodowick and Lucibel about a supposed plot on Lodowick's life by Ferdinand, who they say intends to abduct Lucibel. Lodowick of course pays Lorrique for this false information (2.3.74). The acting within the act here is both metadramatic and Machiavellian, a doubled instance of plotting, with the figure of the informer prominent in its outworking. When they leave and Hoffman elaborates on his plan to kill the princess and the princes, he offers Lorrique authority, even to the extent of a dukedom, when his plots are fulfilled. Lorrique for his part responds enthusiastically, as well he might, and like Puck in *A Midsummer Night's Dream* declares, 'I am nimble as your thought, devise, I'll execute what you command' (2.3.97). This very willing accessory then exits, only for Hoffman now to address the offstage audience about Lorrique, confessing his own double-dealing and asserting that if Lorrique will 'honey me in my death-stinging thoughts – / I will prefer him', but adding, ominously, that 'he shall be prefered to hanging, peradventure' (2.3.101–2). The direct address engages the audience in the cross-biting of these plotters' mutual utility and disregard to the extent that neither perspective seems sound. As the play progresses, more deception, plotting and promises of preferment hang in the air as the two conspirators play another metadramatic role within the role, this time for Mathias. Hoffman asks for his theatrical accoutrements, saying 'my cloak, a chair. I must turn melancholy' (2.3.112) in order to misinform Mathias with the lie that Lucibel has 'fled with a Grecian' (2.3.140). Throughout all of this deception of other characters, the audience is aware of what is going on and get to share the predatory perspective of the devices being employed. This gives a pleasurable sense of dramatic irony of course, but also offers a perspective that sees these devices for what they are. The outcome of the theatrical deception is that Mathias determines to kill the 'Grecian' and, in such a predacious atmosphere, it is therefore quite appropriate that Lucibel is watching out 'for fear / Of venomous worms, or wolves, or wolvish thieves' (3.1.39–40). But despite her caution Mathias kills him by mistake, and when Lucibel is attacked herself and she cries out that 'some savage beast hath fixed his ruthless fang / In my soft body' (3.1.67–8), we can only think of the savage beast Hoffman. He it is who twists the knife by 'confessing' that this was the result of what he saw as a hidden audience of the narrative he is spinning, saying 'I lay within an arbour, whence I saw / The princess, and yourself in this disguise / Departing secretly my uncle's court' (3.1.101–3). Meanwhile Hoffman's plotting and misinformation ensures that the hermit Roderick is soundly framed for the fatal lie, his 'double tongue' (3.1.166), according to the dying Lodowick, having caused the error. When they find that the hermit has an alibi, Hoffman concludes deceptively that 'then there is villainy, practice, and villainy' (3.1.181), and Mathias merely echoes this, also attributing the deception to 'practice and base villainy' (3.1.185), which, along with its perpetrators, the offstage audience of course knows to be the case. The fact that they are sharing the perspective of Hoffman here generates considerable dramatic irony and opens the possibility, however remote, of some sympathy for the Machiavellian schemer, despite his excessive revenging. After more stabbings occur in the ensuing confusion, Lorrique is then sent to 'run with the news; away' (3.1.279) to Ferdinand to further proliferate the misinformation by which Hoffman's schemes prosper.

In this scenario of troubled authority, Jerome's feeble attempt at rebellion against the rightful ruler is painted in gaudy colours and hampered by much linguistic confusion, with his soldiers depicted as being 'dissembled together' (3.2.31). To some extent this mystification of language follows the expected pattern of any assault on legitimate authority. Hoffman's dramatic stand between the two armies to 'plead their pardons with a peaceful tongue' (3.2.75) is another act designed to portray his tongue as benign, when the audience knows it to be anything but so. Discord is his business and he is uniquely unfitted to be a peacemaker here.

Just after the battle scene, metadramatic self-reference and dangerous plotting again go hand in hand when Hoffman approaches Lorrique, who is somewhat bizarrely playing the part of a French Doctor, saying, aside, 'now or never play thy part: / This act is even our tragedy's best heart' (3.2.195–6).[33] Lorrique replies, 'let me alone for plots and villany / Only commend me to this fool the Prince' (3.2.197–8), suddenly exhibiting his own agency in both metadramatic role playing and politic plotting. The continued attempt to draw in the offstage audience to collusion in his deceptive and highly authorial tragic plotting may be made explicit when Hoffman, again aside, invokes a bloody red deity as an approving audience, invocating 'now scarlet mistress from thick sable clouds / Thrust forth thy blood-stained hands, applaud my plot, / That giddy wonderers may amazed stand, / While death smites down suspectless Ferdinand' (3.2.210–14). This bloody red audience may refer to Nemesis or contain a reference to the biblical Whore of Babylon which the book of Revelations also describes in lurid and sanguinary scarlet in St John's psychedelic apocalypse: 'I saw a woman sit upon a scarlet coloured beast, full of names of blasphemy ... And the woman was arrayed in purple and scarlet ... And I saw the woman drunken with the blood of Saints, and with the blood of the Martyrs'.[34] The fact that Hoffman does this in speaking alone to the offstage audience may be intended to position them interpretatively in contrast to such a demonic deity, whose very plaudits offer to drip blood into the dramatic scene.

After arranging for Jerome and Stilt to poison Ferdinand, Lorrique lays off his disguise, personifying it with 'Doctor, lie there' (3.2.257), and exposes the connection between his metadramatic nature and his Machiavellian plotting plainly to the offstage audience. In this he shares with them his own poisonous perspective as he exits, saying self-consciously, 'Lorrique, like thyself appear. / So now I'll post unto the hermitage, and smile / While silly fools act treason through my guile' (3.2.257–9). This may be a means by which to draw attention to the kinds of interpretative perspective which lead to false accusations of treasonous challenges to authority.

In the next metadramatic inset, behind a curtain is revealed the 'blacke dormitory / Where Austria and Prince Lodowick are laid' dead (4.1.1–2) and this revelation of murdered authorities seems ominously to presage the falling apart of the revengers' plots and schemes. When Hoffman jokes darkly at Mathias 'yourself to kill yourself were such a sin / As most divines hold deadly' (4.1.54–5), Lucibel, who has now been driven mad as another consequence of Hoffman's plotting and is exercising her fool's licence to speak the truth, pipes up: 'Ay but a knave may kill one by a trick / Or lay a plot, or foe, or cog, or prate / Make strife' (4.1.56–8), and this is the beginning of the revelation of Hoffman's true nature. Also, after Ferdinand is poisoned, Otho's newly arrived mother Martha recognises that Lorrique is a 'base two-tongued hypocrite' (4.2.134), an idea which persists until Hoffman and Lorrique convince her that she should play along with their presentation of Hoffman as Otho, somewhat implausibly. After warning off Lorrique from going to the extent of raping Martha, Hoffman then declares his own lust for her, telling the audience at the end of the scene that he will rape her himself if she does not submit to his desires (4.2.224–5). Hoffman now is at the zenith of his confidence in his own politicking using the language of intelligencing in daring the fates, asking 'what can fortune do / That may divert my strain of policy?' (just after the death of Ferdinand). Tempting fortune thus is nothing short of foolish, and a contemporary offstage audience of tragedy could be in no doubt that this was the case.

Though without designation as such, these end-of-scene revelations, occurring after the other characters are gone from the stage, are like confessional asides delivered to the audience, showing the workings of the collaborators' deceptions and devices in operation and in planning. Their metadramatic quality is understated and this has the potential effect of drawing the audience into the narrative in a way that occludes their own independent existence. In other words they work as a more illusionary form of audience engagement, though this is always bound to be dependent on the style of delivery and the actor involved in their presentation. Although these soliloquies speak to the characters in question, perhaps more so they speak also to the depth of the immorality of the politicking functions of both. And although this is how onstage plotters and intelligencers are expected to behave, these revelations surely have the effect of realising a diminution in the plausible level of an audience's sympathy with these excessive revengers.

As Lorrique and Martha return to the hermit's cell, the metadramatic tables are fully turned when Saxony, Roderick, Mathias and Lucibel form a hidden audience to overhear their conference, as Roderick requests, asking, 'stand close, I pray: my heart divines / Some strange and horrid act will be revealed' (5.1.69–70). In addition, the two anatomies of old Hoffmann and Otho now hang in the vicinity, overseeing the whole play with their own outraged corpses. Taken together, their audienceship might offer a conflicted perspective, in as much as the dead can be said to have such a thing. This metadramatic situation represents the first time the dramatis personae on this side of the narrative adopt this self-consciously advantageous dramatic position, and it empowers them, as Lucibel tells Saxony: 'nay tarry, you shall hear all the knavery anon' (5.1.99). As the audience offstage watch along with this hidden audience onstage, standing 'close', Lorrique is observed still to be operating in deceiving mode, even as he seems to be confessing to Martha. At this point, the mad Lucibel interprets truthfully again, saying 'I thinke he lies. / Now by my troth, that gentleman smells knave' (5.1.118–19), and then carries her innocent antidote to plotting and deception with her as she steps into the inner metadramatic scene when Martha asks Lorrique 'whether young Hoffman did the most he might / To save my son' (5.1.121–2), and Lorrique answers pitilessly, 'it seems he did, but all was vain / The flinty rocks had cut his tender skull, / And the rough water washed away his brain' (5.1.122–4). Lucibel, having overheard him as onstage audience, crosses over the dramatic boundary, which also denotes the parameter and boundary of plotting, and interjects with simply 'liar, liar lick dish' (5.1.126). It is telling at this stage of the narrative that the perspective of a madwoman is the most compellingly authoritative.

In this respect, Lucibel seems to have come by some information through her passionate wanderings, as she has somehow also come by the clothes of Otho, untainted by sea water. The metadramatic scene thus provides the structure for the girl driven mad by murder to gain some justice over the agent of her misery, as Lorrique is thereby caused to confess fully his role in the murders before promising the resolution of killing himself. Even this is framed metadramatically, as Lorrique says, 'I'll tell you. Having ended, act my fall' (5.1.173) and accuses Hoffmann of being the lying dissimulator who 'gilded o'er his envy with fair shows'(5.1.188), as he claims, 'bitter deceit useth the sweetest speech' (5.1.191). But even as he offers this forced confession, Lorrique still continues to lie, claiming that it was Hoffman who 'taught the foolish prince, in the disguise / Of a French Doctor, to prepare a poison, / Which was the death of Princely Ferdinand' (5.1.234–6), and elaborating on the authorial nature of proceedings by alleging that in his 'next plot, he purposed your grace's death, / And had he opposed my strength of my tears, / You had been murdered as you lay asleep' (5.1.237–9). As Martha purposes her own revenge, this always metadramatic turncoat parasite then requests, 'let me be prologue to your scene of wrath' (5.1.252), offering his own blood sacrifice in his despair: 'as you hope to thrive in your revenge, smite me, / That have been pander to this injury' (5.1.260–1). Here he uses the imagery of the informer and intelligencer, the 'pander' to the wishes of the authorities in an apt description of himself. No mechanism of authority escapes this critique of its theatrical and intelligencing nature.

When Mathias hears this, he begins to think like the plotting intelligencer himself and he asks that, in order for Hoffman, who 'by sly deceit . . . acted every wrong' (5.1.280), to suffer the same kind of acted deceit as he has practised on others, Martha should 'pardon Lorrique / Upon condition, that he lay some plot / To intercept the other' (5.1.286–8). Lorrique of course agrees, his plot being for Martha to be the bait to lure Hoffman to his cave where he might try to rape her, and there to set an ambush to 'change his pleasures into wretched / And redeemless misery' (5.1.312–13). Lucibel sees clearly enough the mad anomaly of hiring a paid loyalist and issues a warning thought about this telltale, asking them 'what if / This knave that has been, play the knave still, / And tells tales out of school, how then?' (5.1.316–18). Lorrique's reply, that in this case 'by all the gods that shall give ill men life, / I am resolved chief agent in his end' (5.1.322–3), alludes to both his agency and his job as an 'agent'. When, in the working out of this device, Martha asks Hoffman to take her to the cave, as she exits with her retinue, he exclaims, again as an aside, 'tricks and devices! Longings! Well, 'tis good: / I'll swim to my desires through seas of blood' (5.2.31–2). After he exits, Lorrique returns, with reference to the bestial imagery associated with the intelligencer, saying 'fox, you'll be taken; hunter, you are fallen / Into the pit you digged' (5.2.34–5), and betrays his own continued duplicity with his confession that he has 'wealth hoard up which I'll bear / To some strange place: rich men live anywhere' (5.2.42–3). Hoffman, however, returns on to the stage and overhears this last in a final metadramatic flourish. Lorrique of course denies any such intention, and Hoffman's reply to him is replete with imagery associated with intelligencing:

> You are a villain damned as low as hell!
> An hypocrite, a fawning hypocrite:
> I know thy heart. Come, spaniel, up, arise:
> And think not with your antics and your lies
> To go beyond me. You have played the slave,
> Betrayed me unto the duchess, told her all,
> Disappointing all my hopes with your base tongue.
>
> (5.2.56–62)

Lorrique, however, manages to convince him otherwise by metadramatically inviting him to consider 'how shallow such an act would seem / In me, chief agent in so many ills' (5.2.76–7). Hoffman, with a general reference to the conventions of the false informer, again replies:

> Thou hast a tongue as glib and smooth to lies,
> As full of false inventions and base fraud,
> As prone to circumvent believing souls,
> As ever heretic or traitor used.
>
> (5.2.78–81)

He is apparently convinced again by Lorrique's eloquent protestations and the plan to entrap Martha at the cave, saying 'Oh my good villain! how I hug thy plots' (5.2.142), though his justifiable paranoia about Lorrique is shown when he asks 'Thou wilt not talk of this?' (5.2.147). Lorrique replies asking 'will I be hanged? / Ne'er take me for a blab, you'll find me none', and the offstage audience are fully aware of the ironies here. But Hoffman is not so naive to the machinations of intelligencing, and offering 'another secret' he delivers a knife blow to Lorrique in its place (5.2.159), the fatal nature of the secret. He ends the scene with a profane burial in a ditch, the proper place for the interment of a fawning spaniel, and again exits with a metadramatic signal that the 'next plot' is for 'Mathias and old Saxony, / Their ends shall finish our blacke tragedy' (5.2.170–1). When Lorrique finally dies by his master and controller's hand, Lucibel declares the moral outcome of the intelligencing informer character's plotting: 'thou art now paid home / For all thy counselling in knavery' (5.3.26–7). The performative authority that this intelligencer has attempted to produce has been defeated by the very nature of its control mechanisms.

In the attempted restoration of authority to its rightful place, there is then some confusion in the soldiery about whether their plot should carry on or whether they should attack Hoffman openly in the field. But the Duchess has matters in hand herself, and it seems that 'with him alone her plot is' (5.3.54). As she appears conversing with Hoffman, Saxony commands the others onstage to set Lorrique's body up like a scarecrow, another accusing dead audience, here being also employed in mocking reference to the proverbially rapacious crow-like parasitism of the intelligencer (5.3.58 s.d.). Saxony arranges further the hidden audience, now literally and immediately dangerous, for an ambush of the inner drama: 'this bush shroud you, this you, / Stand close, true soldiers, for revenge'. Lucibel replies 'Ay: do, do, do, I pray you heartily do; stand close' (5.3.61) as they watch the inner drama of this 'black tragedy' play out until they strike. It is Mathias this time who interjects, calling him a 'smooth-tongued hypocrite' (5.3.138) as they rush upon Hoffman and finally arrange to boil his brains with the red-hot crown, just as they did to his father. Hoffman dies unrepentant, cursing them with hell, as 'despairing men, / That wring the poor, and eat the people up / As greedy beasts the harvest of their spring' (5.3.172–4), turning the accusation of bestial appetite back upon his attackers.

As is often the case, the metadramatic structure here allows for the empowerment of the audience, in this case ostensibly to redress an ill rather than to cause one, though this to some extent depends on the sympathy one has for the wronged protagonist. The hidden audience is either way a frightening prospect. It may be attributed to early modern dramatic convention by this time or the simple fact that it sits so well with plotting, informing and deception that metadrama recurs naturally, so to speak, wherever there is a structure or device depicting the activities of such lethally deceptive practices. Here it also provides the downfall of the plotters against the murderous structures of authority.

In terms of the application of these issues to Chettle himself, it may be impossible to decide whether *The Tragedy of Hoffman* is 'truly representative of the large dramatic output of Henry Chettle ... [since] what we have of it may not be in any sense characteristic', as Jowett says.[35] However, assuming that it is so, this play clearly functions as 'a means for negotiating authority for the author ... [as a] legitimizing but barely legitimate presence', as Jowett claims, for Chettle's prefatory epistles.[36] In its metonymic capacity, the burning crown certainly seems to bespeak an authority troubled by its own mechanisms of control and punishment. Ultimately, the revenger's deceptive usurping of authority is punished by the burning crown that boils the brains of the subject, and this perhaps seems a fitting punishment for the thought-crime of assuming or impersonating authority, either as pirate, pretender or plotter. Chettle's *Hoffman* may well be read as a meditation on the nature of authority then, and if so it seems to be an authority which is always borrowed, like a representative cadaver, usurped like a title, or craved like a crown, the object of burning ambition and aspiration frustrated to death.

Notes

1. See John Jowett, 'Henry Chettle: "Your Old Compositor"', *Text*, Vol. 15 (2003), pp. 141–61, at p. 151.
2. Henry Chettle, *Hoffman, or a Revenge for a Father* (London: Thomas Hailes Lacy, 1852), p. viii, <https://babel.hathitrust.org/cgi/pt?id=mdp.39015009206064;view=1up;seq=14> (last accessed 27 January 2018).
3. Mark Eccles, 'Brief Lives: Tudor and Stuart Authors', supplement to *Studies in Philology*, Vol. 79 (1982), pp. 22–3.

4. Neil Carson, *A Companion to Henslowe's Diary* (Cambridge: Cambridge University Press, 1988), p. 62.
5. A. W. Ward and A. R. Waller (eds), *The Cambridge History of English Literature*, Vol. V (Cambridge: Cambridge University Press, 1910), p. 365.
6. Philip Henslowe, *The Diary Of Philip Henslowe*, ed. J. Payne Collier (London: Skeffington, 1853), p. 151
7. Nicholl, p. 25.
8. Park Honan, *Christopher Marlowe: Poet and Spy* (Oxford: Oxford University Press, 2005), p. 325.
9. Frederick S. Boas, *Christopher Marlowe: A Biographical and Critical Study* (Oxford: Oxford University Press, 1940), p. 327.
10. Henry Chettle, *Hoffman, or a Revenge for a Father* (London: Thomas Hailes Lacy, 1852), p. ix.
11. Jowett, 'Henry Chettle: "Your Old Compositor"', pp. 141–61, 158. See also E. K. Chambers, *The Elizabethan Stage*, Vol. 3 (Oxford: Clarendon, 1923), p. 445.
12. Eccles, pp. 22–3.
13. Ward and Waller, p. 359; also Jowett, p. 156.
14. Jowett, p. 156.
15. See Jowett, p. 145.
16. W. W. Greg, '"Bad" Quartos Outside Shakespeare: Alcazar and Orlando', *The Library*, 3rd series, 10 (1919), p. 197.
17. Ward and Waller, p. 359.
18. Jowett, p. 147.
19. See John Jowett, 'Credulous to False Prints: Shakespeare, Chettle, Harvey, Wolfe', in John Batchelor, Tom Cain and Claire Lamont (eds), *Shakespearean Continuities: Essays in Honour of E. A. J. Honigmann* (Basingstoke: Palgrave Macmillan, 1997), pp. 93–107.
20. Jowett, 'Henry Chettle: "Your Old Compositor"', pp. 154–5.
21. Chettle, *Kind-harts Dreame*, p. 32.
22. Stephen Greenblatt, *Shakespearean Negotiations: The Circulation of Social Energy in Renaissance England* (Berkeley, CA: University of California Press, 1988).
23. Henry Chettle, *Tragedy of Hoffman*, in Emma Smith (ed.), *Five Revenge Tragedies* (London: Penguin, 2012), pp. 244–324.
24. *The Character of an informer wherein his mischeivous nature, and leud practises are detected* (London: T. P., 1675), pp. 4–5, <http://gateway.proquest.com/openurl?ctx_ver=Z39.88-2003&res_id=xri:eebo&rft_id=xri:eebo:citation:15564016> (last accessed 22 December 2017).
25. There may be an echo of Christ's crown of thorns here too, as Sarah Redmond has suggested (conversation, 3 September 2017).

26. Stephen Knight, *Robin Hood: A Complete Study of the English Outlaw* (Oxford: Blackwell, 1994), pp. 116, 131–2.
27. Bruce A. McAndrew, *Scotland's Historic Heraldry* (Woodbridge: Boydell Press, 2006), p. 121.
28. Gaius Julius Hyginus, *Fabulae 25*, <http://www.theoi.com/Text/HyginusFabulae1.html#25> (last accessed 14 February 2018); see also Katherine Heavey, *The Early Modern Medea: Medea in English Literature, 1558–1688* (Basingstoke: Palgrave Macmillan, 2015).
29. Chettle, *Kind-harts Dreame*, p. 6.
30. See Jonson, *Poetaster* (Ind. 23–6).
31. Thomas Carew, *Coelum Brittanicum* (Thomas Walkley, 1640), <http://gateway.proquest.com/openurl?ctx_ver=Z39.88-2003&res_id=xri:eebo&rft_id=xri:eebo:image:7793:106> (last accessed 27 February 2018).
32. Angus, pp. 115–35.
33. Hoffman is now ascribed 'Sarlois' in the text. For an exploration of this see John Jowett, 'Notes on Henry Chettle', *Review of English Studies*, Vol. 45, No. 180 (November, 1994), pp. 517–22, at p. 520.
34. Geneva Bible (1599), Revelations 17: 3–4, 6. Amelia McGill suggested that there may be an element of Hoffman's absent mother in this figure, which is an intriguing possibility (conversation, 22 September 2017). Something of this is reflected in Hoffman's description of Lucibel too, as in her grief 'her tender hands smiting the stone / Beweep their mistress' rage in tears of blood' (4.1.43–4).
35. Ward and Waller, p. 345.
36. Jowett, 'Henry Chettle: "Your Old Compositor"', p. 159.

Conclusion: No One Is There – Ubiquity and Invisibility

In early modern society, the figure of the intelligencer is perceived to be everywhere and yet felt to be appearing nowhere. This often demonic figure may be said to express a culturally significant pathology that is also simultaneously universal and indeterminate and which affects the concept of authority at its deepest level. In daily life, the actual intelligencer would most often by necessity be anonymous, except to the authorities to which they fed their information and in the case that they were required to appear in court to support their assertions. Their nature, within the contested space of early modern authority, is to be occulted via a social mode that allows for this anonymity and invisibility. Their widely supposed ubiquity, however, was a necessary and facilitating function of their role as pervasive projections of the influence of the powerful over the communities they wished to supervise. Although resistant to clear definition, the intelligencer/informer nevertheless finds its place on the early modern stage and, as should be plain by now, the metadrama of early modern theatre was the cultural form most appropriate to the embodiment of this social phenomenon. There are various reasons why this is the case, and the nature of how this dramatic mode accords with the figure of the intelligencer has been the subject of this book, which maps the common practices, forms and structures of each onto the other and posits explanations for why this symmetry might exist.

There is a further possible connection, however, and this is related to metadrama's structural concern with conventions of both absence and presence in the workings of its self-reference and especially in its depiction of audiences. In the many modes of metadrama, offstage audiences are imagined within the structures of inner plays, posited as characters in the drama, referred to in their extra-dramatic actuality, mirrored, parodied, marginalised, recast as other bodies, defined onstage or simply ignored in favour of another imagined audience. In these various ways, the audiences of early modern drama should be very well used to the regular alternation of being perceived as absent or present at any given time. There is also the possibility that they experience the logic of both of these states in simultaneity, wherever their absence is conventionally required for the author to present a coherent illusion, but where their presence is always assumed by the dramatic action of the Sartrean 'look', which is defined by its reciprocality. Such a simultaneous experience of presence and absence may be seen to mirror that of the intelligencer in the very core of his social function.

Further, in being involved in the interactions of metadramatic structures, as much as to some extent in the very act of coming to the theatre, the audience is also theatricalised into the roleplaying processes of drama. It can also be posited that in leaving the theatrical space they take something of the duality of that interaction of the real and the role away with them. Having this kind of affective impact upon the audience is of course one of the aims of the dramatist. But in this way, even without the disruptive influence of the intelligencer and informer, the watching function of the audience of drama and metadrama is projected into the real world beyond the theatre. In accordance with the *theatrum mundi* convention, these states are interpermeable. As we have seen, however, the extra-dramatic is a world whose own narratives are unencroachable and whose authors and protagonists tolerate only minimal incursions into their conceptual territory. Here, their account of authority brooks little resistance to their self-serving mechanisms, as the very many mutilated victims of Elizabethan and Stuart justice might attest.

In general terms, surveillance has to be perceived as all-pervasive to be effective and therefore needs to be to some extent reflexive and immediate. These readings of the era's dramatic output suggest that ambiguity around the figure of the informer and intelligencer both feeds this sense and therefore helps to generate its efficiency. Both the ambiguity and the pervasiveness have a symbiotic and self-perpetuating relationship and produce the crucial effect of not knowing when or if one is being watched, but knowing that that is always a possibility. In *1984*, George Orwell's Winston is not only drilled to believe that 'surveillance is ubiquitous and there is no escaping it', as Michael Yeo says, but crucially 'in this belief, he censors himself'.[1] This is the desired effect of such projection of power, and the central authority depends on it. As much as a religion that wishes the believer to keep to a required moral code at all times requires a belief in a God who is omnipresent, an authority that wants a populace to police themselves requires that any given human eye or ear might at any given time function as a hidden proxy for the organs of state, which thereby become all-pervading.

These omnipresent intelligencers and informers of early modern perception have rarely emerged into the record as named individuals, and where they have, they have been duly made notorious and therefore to that extent they become avoidable and their influence is compromised. The shadowy nature of the function therefore requires their anonymity, and the awareness of this is also contemporary, as the writer T. G. laments sarcastically in 1616: 'No-body telleth strange newes, inuenteth lyes, disperceth libels, setteth friendes at varience, and abuseth many millions: for when a priuie search is made for the authors, no-body is found to auoch the actions.'[2] The figure that T. G. paints telling 'strange newes' is both interestingly authorial and indefinite to the point of forming a hauntingly absent presence which we may recognise from many of the dramatis personae found in the texts of the period. It is echoed in the relative reluctance of dramatic texts to entitle informers as such in the character lists, and instead to rely on understood conventions of character and imagery to depict them and their actions. This is aided also by the fact that the job of informer is often an ad hoc arrangement or a function of other jobs, and often closely linked to networks of patronage. The anonymity and ambiguity of the function is further protected by the fact that to criticise the intelligencing system is to potentially draw fire on yourself. Not only is this the case, but some are constrained to acknowledge the necessity for informers, as may be seen in Robert Pricket's 1607 report on the corruption endemic in the role, which laments that 'it seldome happeneth, that an honest man is imployed therein', but reluctantly nevertheless concedes 'their Office, I confesse, is necessarie.'[3] This sense of social necessity complicates the explicit dramatic depiction of such figures considerably, especially from a self-defensive point of view, results in the couching of the job within other roles, as courtier, master of horse or manservant, and thus reduces its visibility and therefore the effect of its satirical critique.

Neither does the contemporary equation of the intelligencer with the very Devil offer much comfort in this respect. Although popular Christian theology suggests that the Devil is invisible and inhabits ethereal realms as well as the earth, he exists as the 'prince of the power of the air', as the 1611 Bible puts it, and may appear disguised in many forms, but the conception of the Devil as intelligencer to God obviously invites the suggestion of guilt by association on the part of the deity.[4] But more disturbingly to an early modern moral mindset, this tends towards the thought that these spiritual beings are to some extent dependent on, and indeed necessary to, each other, corresponding within religious discourse in such logical pairs as tempter/saviour and spoiler/restorer. Both God and the Devil share an absent presence built on invisibility and pervasiveness and in this model of the passing of information would also share the moral taint of underhand informing and betrayal. They might also suffer their own version of the 'narcissism of small differences'.

These issues of occulted and yet pervasive sites of authority have now taken on a menacingly geopolitical effect as the anonymous producers of 'strange newes' have exerted a pervasive influence on globally important political programmes through the dissemination of bogus viral stories from extremely dubious sources and even from 'newspapers' that lack any of the normally accepted credentials of objective existence.[5] The new presidential strategy of turning the accusation of fake news back on itself is a playground tactic, the ability to perform which depends upon the clouding of sources. This has now reached the extent that many American universities have been driven to issue guides for students addressing the problem of how to tell real news from fake news and true scholarship or reliable journalism from 'those who inuenteth lyes, disperceth libels [and] setteth friendes at varience'. A study by Stanford University was shocked to discover the extent to which this was necessary among university undergraduates at some of the nation's top institutions.[6] This dire situation is reminiscent of the informer in John Day's *Isle of Guls* whose 'informations growing stale' became a writer who 'could fashion the bodie, of [his] discourse fit to the eare of my auditorie.'[7] Here information is merely a performative utterance and 'facts' invent themselves in the speaking of them. This dangerous revisionist presentism plays upon the absence and presence of conventions in interpretative authority, to the obvious detriment of all concerned.

It has been curious to find that the aspects of dramatic context with which this book has been dealing around intelligencers and informers have also been largely absent from the critical record on metadrama over the years. The question may be posed, has this interpretative absence been because informers are so rarely explicitly named in the texts, or is there something more insidiously political going on, if perhaps this has been unconscious in its intent? If traditional readings of metadrama as pertaining only to artistic experimentation and addressing dangers only to one's satiric reputation spring from the desire to perpetuate a notion of Shakespeare's time as some kind of seminal golden age, then this may be balanced by the fact that it was also the golden age of the Machiavel in many ways, and was thus with an intensity to rival any modern political intrigue or even some of the purges of the twentieth century. Without wishing to overstate the case, many of the pressures and contradictions inherent to authority, to which these dramatic case studies constantly refer, will, in the relatively brief course of time, emerge in a more militarised form in the civil conflicts of the seventeenth century and thus reveal themselves in their true form. The centres and sites of early modern authority clashing over the imposition of unjust taxes; wildcard royal authority, overstepping the mark in terms of its own political scheming; the strong desire to purge society of religious disaffection, either by affirming or resisting a new orthodoxy; the emergence of a middle class with sufficient economic power and interpretative independence to resist the immediate unreasoned desires of an absolutist monarch – these are issues which have been in play throughout the period that produces both the mechanisms and networks of control that intelligencers inhabit and the pointed metadrama which mirrors it. The English Revolution, as it may be termed, directly or indirectly caused the deaths of around 2.5 per cent of the population, or one in forty people in one decade. For comparison, although estimates vary, in the decade 1966–76, China's notoriously bloody Cultural Revolution killed up to three million people, representing around 0.37 per cent of the median population of the country over that time.[8] This surely represents the outpouring of tensions felt in the decades immediately previous to its ripping apart of the social fabric: the decades in which the English theatre both flourishes and sparks with all kinds of social tensions and pressures. The tendency to see Shakespeare's age as an earlier version of the Edwardian summer, preceding the brutality and atavism of the First World War, suffers from the same misguided prelapsarian nostalgia of those whose personal disaffection with the political world tends to produce a naively depoliticised vision of history. This example of E. P. Thompson's 'enormous condescension of posterity' may represent a genuflection to some fantasy of gentlemen players and aristocratic patrons or, more so, a costume drama which serves only a morally inert and ultimately reactionary worldview: an early modern *Downton Abbey*. But rather than see the era as a simplistic dystopia of insidious betrayers and dark control networks, this book simply offers to redress the balance of scholarship which has tended to wish to minimise the role of the shady side of the era's politics in the production of drama by some of the most active minds in dramatic history. The extent to which these writers themselves ran a gauntlet of physical risk and wrote bravely despite this is as yet not fully understood. There are, however, many indications of the casual violence of the authorities which subjected them, and of the anonymously present 'no-body' that at this time sustains such an abusive system. In that respect, this book has attempted to give credit to the valour and creative intellect of the penmen who wrote under such an inhuman political state of affairs, and to thereby open a context which might be pursued by other authors and honourable critics of those tainted by complicity with vicious authority of the kind which now, without any dramatic hyperbole, certainly 'abuseth many millions'. It is our sincere hope that creative intellects will emerge to avert the development of our current tensions around absent and present authority into far more destructive theatres.

Notes

1. Michael Yeo, 'Propaganda and Surveillance in George Orwell's *Nineteen Eighty-Four*: Two Sides of the Same Coin', *Global Media Journal*, Vol. 3, No. 2 (2010), pp. 49–66.
2. T. G., *The rich cabinet furnished with varietie of excellent discriptions, exquisite charracters, witty discourses, and delightfull histories, deuine and morrall* (London: I[ohn] B[eale] for Roger Iackson, 1616), p. 99.

3. Robert Pricket, *The Lord Coke his speech and charge VVith a discoeurie of the abuses and corruption of officers* (1607), <http://gateway.proquest.com/openurl?ctx_ver=Z39.88-2003&res_id=xri:eebo&rft_id=xri:eebo:citation:99840729> (last accessed 16 February 2018).
4. Bible, Authorised Version (1611), Ephesians 2:2.
5. Zeynep Tufekci, 'Mark Zuckerberg Is in Denial', *New York Times*, 15 November 2016, <https://www.nytimes.com/2016/11/15/opinion/mark-zuckerberg-is-in-denial.html> (last accessed 15 December 2017).
6. Brooke Donald, 'Stanford Researchers Find Students Have Trouble Judging the Credibility of Information Online', 22 November 2016, <https://ed.stanford.edu/news/stanford-researchers-find-students-have-trouble-judging-credibility-information-online> (last accessed 15 December 2017).
7. Donald, n.p.
8. 'English Civil Wars', <https://www.britannica.com/event/English-Civil-Wars> (last accessed 15 December 2017); Maurice Meisner, *Mao's China and After: A History of the People's Republic*, 3rd edn (New York: Free Press, 1999), p. 354; Jung Chang and Jon Halliday, *Mao: The Unknown Story* (London: Jonathan Cape, 2005), p. 569.

Index

Abbot, George, *Exposition upon the Prophet Jonah*, 68
amity, 27, 39–40, 42–4, 54, 58–60
Anything for a Quiet Life, 119
authority, 27–9, 39, 41, 46–9, 51–3, 58–62, 64–5n, 73, 82–3, 85–6, 94–5, 103–5, 106–7, 108n, 127–30, 132–5, 143–5, 154–6, 159–1, 172, 175, 177, 179–80
   actors and, 20, 94, 97, 132–7, 141, 149–51, 154
   audiences and, 46–8, 53, 94–9, 106–7, 141–5, 148–51
   authors and, 3, 10, 19–20, 27–9, 41, 44–7, 54–5, 57–62, 64–5n, 82, 94–8, 103–7, 132–6, 141, 144–5, 149–50, 164, 172, 176, 180
   dramatic, 45–6, 94, 106
   informers and, 1, 3, 5, 13–20, 27–8, 55, 71–2, 75–6, 81–2, 87–8, 94, 96–7, 106–7, 115, 119, 163, 169
   interpretation and, 25, 28, 41, 92, 94, 107, 135–7, 141, 143–4, 149, 167
   morality and, 27, 28, 59, 71, 73, 85, 111, 117, 130, 134, 145, 149
   as performative construct, 29, 155, 158, 164, 171

Baines, Richard, 72
Banu, Georges, 5, 34n
Bawcutt, N. W., 70
Beaumont, Francis, 28, 94, 107
Berry, Ralph, 112
Bevington, David, 68, 71, 73

the Bible, 3, 9, 19–20, 125, 166, 178
the Blackfriars, 150–1
Bliss, Lee, 112
Borot, Luc, 70
Brown, John Russell, 112
burning crown *see* punishment

Calvinism, 111, 124, 128
Carew, Thomas, 152n
   Coelum Brittanicum, 162
Catholicism, 43, 126, 132
Chapel Royal, 42
Chapman, George, 20, 93
The Character of an informer wherein his mischeivous nature, and leud practises are detected, 160
Charles I, 73, 132–3, 135, 142, 151
Chettle, Henry, 15–16, 42, 154–7
   Kind-Hart's Dreame, 5, 22, 157–8, 161
China's Cultural Revolution, 179
Church of England, 132
Cicero, *De Amicitia*, 39
Clark, Sandra, 6
Compass, 21
Court of the Arches, 105, 107
crown of thorns, 173
Cure for a Cuckold, 21
Curtis, M. H., 114

Damon and Pithias, 27, 39, 42–3, 46–7
   Aristippus, 48–9, 51–2, 54–6, 58–9, 61
   Carisophus, 40, 48–9, 51–7, 61–2
   Damon, 43–4, 47–62

Dionysius, 43–4, 46, 48, 52, 54, 56–61
Eubulus, 56, 58, 62
Pithias, 43–4, 48–62
Stephano, 49–53, 55–8
Will, 55
Danter, John, 157
Darcy, Francis, 19–20
Dasent, J. R., 43
Davenant, William, *The Just Italian*, 152n
Day, John, *Isle of Guls*, 21–2, 178
Dekker, Thomas, 10, 156, 161
  The Bellman's Second Walk, 6–10, 22–3
  The Gull's Hornbook, 97–8, 108n
  Lantern and Candlelight, 6
demons *see* the Devil
Derrida, Jacques, 37n
the Devil
  informers and, 1, 4–10, 54, 69, 116, 119, 140, 156, 175, 178
  politics and, 68
  theology and, 6, 9, 67, 117, 120, 178
diegetic gravity, 26, 53, 145, 147
Downton Abbey, 180
The Duchess of Malfi
  Antonio, 112–15, 117–23, 126, 128–9
  Bosola, 28, 40, 70, 110–30
  the Cardinal, 115–16, 118, 124–7, 129
  Cariola, 121, 123–5
  Delio, 114–15, 117, 129
  the Duchess, 28, 110–12, 116–27, 129
  Ferdinand, 111, 113–18, 121–9
  Julia, 125
Dutton, Richard, 19, 42, 44–5
Dymock, Edward, 20

Earl of Atholl, 161
Eastward Ho, 20, 93
Eccles, Mark, 155, 157
Edwards, Richard, 43, 62
Elizabeth, 8, 10, 17, 19–20, 132
Elyot, Thomas
  The Governor, 39, 113
  Image of Governance, 113

English Civil War, 114
English Revolution, 179

Fischer, Gerhard, 3
Ford, John, 111
Fox, George, 4
France, 14, 64–5, 112, 113

the Globe, 150–1
Greenblatt, Stephen, 158
Greene, Robert, 17
  Groatsworth of Wit, 157
Greg, W. W., 157
Greiner, Bernhard, 3
Guilpin, Everard, 'Skialetheia', 68–9
Gyles, Edward, 19

Hall, Joseph, 5, 39
Hamlet *see* Shakespeare, William
Hammond, Antony, 67
Harding, George, 120
Harington, John, *Orlando Furioso*, 10
Hayward, John, 20
Henslowe, Philip, 155–6
Heywood, Thomas, *Apology for Actors*, 63–4n, 140–1
hidden audience, 23, 85–6, 125, 136, 147, 154, 159, 165, 168
Hopkins, Lisa, 71
Horace, 36n, 45–6, 113, 134
Horace (character) *see* Jonson, Ben
Horsey, J., 20
Hoskins, William, 157
Howard, Jean, 142
Hunter, G. K., 42, 75
Hutson, Lorna, 24, 33n, 41
Hutton, Luke, *The Black Dog of Newgate*, 7–8

Iago *see* Shakespeare, William
informers
  actors and, 19–20, 22, 28, 47, 50, 62, 68, 70, 76, 101, 110–11, 118, 128, 132–6, 160, 164
  authors and, 2–3, 8–9, 15, 20, 22–4, 52–7, 60, 68, 80, 93, 105–7, 132–6, 139–40, 144, 163, 177
  Bacon, Anthony, 24
  Bacon, Francis, 24
  Bowes, Robert, 11

informers (cont.)
 Cecil, Robert, 10–11, 40, 82
 Cecil, William, 11–13, 15, 18, 40, 41
 Chambers, 13
 de Montaigne, Michel, 24
 Drury, Thomas, 24
 employment of, 7, 10–18, 22, 55–6, 72, 93, 110, 133
 Flood, Griffin, 21
 Floyde, Richard, 19
 Frizer, Ingram, 156
 Gascgoine, George, 24
 Guildenstern, 40, 98
 imagery and, 4, 6, 72: avian, 71–2, 79–80, 118, 160; canine, 4, 7–8, 48–9, 72, 74, 78–80, 118, 122, 129; lupine, 4, 122, 125, 127, 129, 165; vulpine, 10, 170
 interpretation and, 28–9, 41, 52, 74, 93, 95, 105, 107, 115, 132–4, 139, 143–4, 161–2
 Justice Overdo see Jonson, Ben
 Kyd, Thomas, 18, 20, 101
 the law and, 15–17, 55, 65–6n, 93, 133
 morality and, 1, 6, 28, 68, 71, 74, 77, 83–5, 88, 111, 115–16, 119, 127, 140, 171, 178
 Patricke, James, 41
 payment of, 16, 18, 66, 93, 111, 116, 143, 164
 as predators, 6–8, 42, 53–4, 79, 118–19, 127, 134, 138–9, 159–60, 165
 reliability of, 1, 12–16, 22, 113, 115, 134
 religion and, 3–9, 27, 71, 80, 88, 177–8
 Rosencrantz, 40, 98
 Sejanus, 40
 spying and, 9–10
 surveillance and, 5, 10, 113, 176–7
 Topcliffe, Richard, 10–11, 156
the Inns of Court, 43
intelligencer see informers
The Isle of Dogs, 20
Italy, 36, 112, 113, 142

James VI/I, 11–12, 16–17, 70, 73–4, 94, 132, 161
The Jew of Malta, 27, 67, 69–70
 Abigail, 72
 Barabas, 73
 Calymath, 72
 Ithamore, 72
 Machiavel, 68–73
 Pilia-Borza, 72
Johnson, Richard, *Look on me London*, 116
Jones-Davies, M. T., 99
Jonson, Ben, 15, 20, 24, 93, 119, 162
 Bartholomew Fair, 75, 92–3, 113
 Poetaster, 14, 23, 66n, 78, 119, 163
Journal of the House of Commons, 13
Jowett, John, 154, 157, 172
Judas, 3–6, 67, 115

Kinsayder, W. see Marston, John
The Knight of the Burning Pestle, 28, 42, 92–4, 96, 99, 106–7
 the Boy, 106
 the Citizen, 92, 94, 96–107
 Jasper, 100, 102–3
 Luce, 100
 Mistress Merrythought, 103, 105
 Nell, 92, 96–7, 100–7
 Rafe, 96–7, 100–6
Kramer, J. E., 42
Kyd, Thomas, *Spanish Tragedy*, 88, 123

Lacan, Jacques, 26–7
lawyers, 16, 43, 65n, 119
 Pettifog, 21
Lenton, Francis, 5, 41
The Life and Death of Griffin Flood, 21
Lodge, Thomas, 101
Look about You, 160
Lowin, John, 76
Lukács, György, 5
Lyly, John, 24, 95
 Campaspe, 65n
 Sappho and Phao, 95

Machiavelli, Niccolò, 68, 70–1, 75
 The Prince, 68
Machiavellianism, 5, 7, 27–8, 67–88, 157

The Malcontent, 27, 67, 74, 88
   Aurelia, 78–80
   Bilioso, 80
   Celso, 77, 79–80
   Ferneze, 78–9
   Giovanni Altofronto *see* Malevole
   Malevole, 70, 73, 75, 77–81, 113
   Mendoza, 78–81
   Pietro, 77–80
Marlowe, Christopher, 20, 24, 71–2, 77, 156
Marston, John, 74, 75, 78, 81
   2 Return from Parnassus, 74
   The Scourge of Villainy, 74
Martin Marprelate controversy, 101
Mary I (of England), 43
Massinger, Philip, 151
Master of the Revels, 19, 47, 133; *see also* Tilney, Edmund
Mearns, Adam, 65n
The Merchant's Wife, 131n
metalepsis, 26
Middleton, Thomas, 82
Mulcaster, Richard, 101
Munday, Anthony, 24, 65, 101, 156, 161

Nabb, Thomas, *Covent-Garden*, 23–4, 41
Nashe, Thomas, 3, 140
   Have with you to Saffron-Walden, 3, 115, 157
   Martin Marprelate tracts, 157
Neill, Michael, 120
Nicholl, Charles, 10, 14

offstage audience, 26–7, 41, 45–8, 51, 54, 56–8, 61–2, 67, 77, 79–80, 86–8, 93–5, 98–106, 108n, 112, 120–3, 132, 135–7, 148–51, 155, 163–8, 175–6
   construction of, 24–5, 57, 77
   empowerment of, 2, 28, 45, 58, 93, 99, 103, 141–4, 147–51, 172
   informers and, 2, 21–2, 28, 45, 47, 53–4, 87, 92, 94–5, 100, 105–7, 135
   relationship with onstage audience, 24–6, 50, 86, 92, 96, 99, 123, 136–7, 161

onstage audience, 28, 76, 80, 82, 86–99, 106, 129, 136–8, 141, 144–6, 149, 155, 161, 168–9
   dead, 159, 161, 171
   informers and, 85–6, 95, 106
Orwell, George, *1984*, 177

Pastoor, Charles, 133
Penry, John, 157
policy, 72
Pricket, Robert, 177
prologues, 21–2, 44–7, 50–2, 57, 69, 70, 94, 96–7, 144, 161, 162
Protestantism, 68, 71
Prynne, William, *Histriomastix*, 20
Puck *see* Shakespeare, William
punishment, 7, 15–16, 19–20, 149, 154
   execution, 19–21, 41, 44, 72–3, 86, 149, 160–1, 172
   fines, 15, 19–20, 66n
   imprisonment, 13, 19–20, 40–1, 93, 132, 148, 151–2n, 155–6
   mutilation, 19–20, 41, 176
   torture, 11, 20, 135, 156, 161

Raymond Williams, 1–2
Reinheimer, David A., 133
The Revenger's Tragedy, 27, 67, 82
   Castiza, 83–4
   the Duchess, 84, 86
   the Duke, 83–4, 86–8
   Gratiana, 84
   Hippolito, 83, 85–8
   Lussurioso, 83–8
   Spurio, 84–7
   Supervacuo, 87–8
   Vindice, 70, 82–8
Ribner, Irving, 70
Rid, Samuel, *Martin Markall, Beadle of Bridewell*, 10
The Roman Actor, 28, 42, 88, 132–7, 142, 151
   Aretinus, 118, 134, 137–40, 142–8
   The Cure of Avarice, 143
   Domitia, 118, 142, 145–50
   Domitian Caesar, 133–5, 137–8, 142–51
   Domitilla, 145–7
   The False Servant, 148–50

The Roman Actor (cont.)
  Iphis and Anaxarete, 145
  Julia, 146–7
  Lamia, 138
  Latinus, 136, 141, 145
  Paris, 133–50
  Parthenius, 143
  Philargus, 143–4
  Rusticus, 135, 138–9
  Sura, 135, 139, 144
Row, Thomas, 19

Saint Paul, 9
Sartre, Jean-Paul, 26
  Sartrean 'look', 26–7, 38n, 50, 176
Satan *see* the Devil
satire, 9, 22, 25, 74, 76, 82, 134
Scott, Margaret, 70
Severus, Alexander, 113
Seymor, Francis, 19
Shaa, Robert, 20
Shakespeare, William, 29, 142, 160
  Hamlet, 42, 83, 136, 142, 143–6
  Henry IV Part One, 72
  A Midsummer Night's Dream, 42, 165
  Othello, 66, 68, 110, 123
  Richard III, 68, 160
  Troilus and Cressida, 113
Shannon, Laurie, 42, 43, 59, 61
Sheldon, R., *Sermon at St. Martin's*, 108n
Shirley, James, *Andromana*, 131n
Skinner, Quentin, 40
Sly, Will, 76
Spenser, Edmund, 101
Spenser, Gabriel, 20
spies, 3, 5, 9, 14–15, 162
stage-sitting, 99
Stanford University, 178

Stephens, John, *Essays and Characters*, 5
Stubbs, John, *The Discovery of a Gaping Gulf whereinto England is like to be Swallowed*, 20

T. G., 22, 177
taverns, 41
  Mermaid Tavern, 93
  tavern-talk, 98
Taylor, John, 152n
theatrum mundi, 25, 47, 125, 138, 176
Thompson, E. P., 180
Tilney, Edmund, 19
The Tragedy of Hoffman, 29, 123, 154–72
  Duke of Luningberg, 155
  Ferdinand, 113–18, 166–7, 169
  Hoffman, 155, 158–74
  Jerome, 162–4, 166–7
  Lodowick, 162, 164–5, 167
  Lorrique, 159–62, 164–71
  Lucibel, 162, 164–5, 167–71, 174n
  Mathias, 162, 165, 167–9, 171
  Otho, 155, 159–63, 167–9
Tuvill, Daniel, *The Dove and the Serpent*, 41

Volkstheater movement, 29n

Walsingham, Francis, 14, 18–19, 40, 156
Ward, Edward, 21
Watson, Robert N., 110, 125, 127–8
Watson, Thomas, informers and, 24
Webster, John, 21, 114, 120, 124, 128
Weyneman, Thomas, 20
Whitehead, George, 4

Zoilus, 108n

EU representative:
Easy Access System Europe
Mustamäe tee 50, 10621 Tallinn, Estonia
Gpsr.requests@easproject.com

www.ingramcontent.com/pod-product-compliance
Lightning Source LLC
Chambersburg PA
CBHW070825250426
43671CB00036B/2077